AF480692

STOP AVOIDING YOUR NUMBERS

STOP AVOIDING YOUR NUMBERS

The Guide to Financial Confidence
for Small Business Owners

By Andy Weins and Lynn Corazzi

ENDORSEMENTS

"We started working with Andy last year after 18 years in business, and we had never truly understood the power of our numbers until then. Andy came in and helped us fix the chaos in our backend, bringing clarity and structure to our operations. His straightforward, no-nonsense approach was refreshing and challenged us to make changes that, while sometimes uncomfortable, ultimately propelled us forward.

Together, we faced things head-on and grew throughout the process. Andy's energy is infectious, his drive is unmatched, and his deep knowledge of how numbers fuel a business is impressive.

He's a true leader and visionary, and the type of person who will roll up his sleeves and do the work alongside you.

We are grateful for Andy—he has genuinely changed our business."

Jennifer & Rick Dempsey
Owners
CHUCK-IT Removal Services

"Andy and Lynn don't just talk the talk—they live it. I've worked with over 100 businesses, and Andy is the only one who reviews his numbers every single month without fail. This book gives you the exact systems successful owners use to stop avoiding their finances and take full control. Read it, apply it, and watch your business transform."

Michael J. Reisel
Founder/Advisor
Redwood Financial Strategies

"Working with Andy completely changed how I look at my business. He built me a simple Excel dashboard (on the fly) that tracked my clients, sales, hours, and billing and then broke it all down with charts and formulas that showed me exactly where I was making money and where I was wasting time. For the first time, I could actually see how small adjustments could lead to big financial changes, including letting go of clients who drained more energy than they were worth. Letting those clients go helped me well beyond the financial impact.

As a freelance graphic designer, I was never taught to think about my business this way. Andy listened closely, spotted the gaps, and gave me practical tools that shifted my entire perspective. I'm honestly so grateful for his guidance and the impact it's had on my work."

Stephanie Kern
Fractional Creative Director
VanderBloemen Creative

"I've been working with Andy for several months in a strategic capacity to elevate my team, clean up our processes, and pull myself out of the day-to-day operations while maintaining oversight of our performance and goals. Andy has a refreshingly direct approach, calling out what isn't working with a no-nonsense honesty that is both rare and invaluable. His work getting me organized has elevated our company's mission and helped us achieve our goals."

Courtney Eaton
CTO/CIO
Elsey Enterprises

"I've had the pleasure of witnessing Andy Weins and Lynn Corazzi share their business acumen on many occasions, and I have worked with both Andy and Lynn personally. Together, they've created a powerhouse resource for small business owners who want to stop guessing and start leading with clarity. Andy brings his trademark straight talk and entrepreneurial lessons, while Lynn adds the kind of financial brilliance that makes everything click.

As someone who fully admits I don't look at my numbers enough, this book spoke directly to me. It's approachable, relatable, and genuinely empowering. *Stop Avoiding Your Numbers* helps you see that understanding your finances isn't about spreadsheets; it's about building the business and life you want.

The best part is that it's written by two pros who will not let you play small."

Susie Moon
Owner
Susie Moon Consulting

"I've had the opportunity to see Andy's work firsthand over the past several years, and he has an incredible ability to help business owners truly understand their numbers. I've watched him guide entrepreneurs to focus on what really matters—not just the top line but also the numbers that drive success. His approach is clear, practical, and grounded in real-world experience. *Stop Avoiding Your Numbers* captures that same straightforward, results-driven style. Any business owner who's ever felt overwhelmed by their finances will find Andy's insights both eye-opening and empowering."

Alan M. Fischer, RICP, AAMS
Senior Wealth Manager
Great Lakes Wealth Advisors

"This book is a wolf in sheep's clothing. Lynn and Andy clarify your business vision and purpose and then quickly shift to a clear, easy-to-understand explanation of how numbers function in day-to-day operations. If financial conversations make your eyes glaze over, this one will change how you think about money's role in making your business dreams come true."

Pat Miller
Founder
Small Business Owners Community

"As a small business owner in the junk removal and dumpster rental industry, I've always been confident in my hard work, but not necessarily in my numbers. Working with Andy completely changed that. His guidance has helped me understand the financial story behind my business and make confident, data-driven decisions that have led to a more profitable and sustainable model. What I appreciate most is how he breaks down complex financial concepts into clear, actionable insights that matter day to day. He's not just a CFO—he's a partner who genuinely cares about helping business owners build something lasting. This book captures the same mindset and clarity that he brings to every conversation: practical, empowering, and transformative. Working with him has been one of the best investments I've ever made in my business."

Brooke Dearwester
Owner
Trash Queen

"This book made my numbers finally make sense. Lynn and Andy take you inside the mind of a small business owner and guide you step by step toward clarity and confidence. It's practical, uplifting, and written in plain English—no jargon, only results you can see and feel. I now understand what really drives my business and how to make decisions that align with my goals."

Deb Yelvington
Owner
Dynamic Permits

"Lynn Corazzi and Andy Weins have written the kind of book every small business owner needs: straightforward, practical, and surprisingly engaging. *Stop Avoiding Your Numbers* takes the stress out of financials and turns them into something you can use to lead your business with confidence. It's not about accounting. It's about understanding your story through data. This is the kind of book that earns a permanent spot on your shelf and gets passed around to every business owner you know."

Amy Wall
Founder
The Innovation Hub for Entrepreneurs & Innovation Hub TV

"Approachable, practical, and surprisingly reassuring, *Stop Avoiding Your Numbers* helped me feel confident taking charge of my nonprofit's finances. The authors explain everything in a way that feels human and accessible, with just the right touch of humor to keep it enjoyable."

Melissa Songco
Executive Director
Habitat for Humanity Waukesha–Jefferson–Rock

DEDICATIONS

For my wife, Jenna, whose growth mindset and curiosity led us from the volleyball court to becoming best friends—and, ultimately, an entrepreneurial couple. She has encouraged me to become the man I was destined to be.

For my parents, in-laws, grandparents, and great-grandparents, who forged ahead through uncertainty—owning, growing, and building their individual businesses and paving the way for me to follow. Their shared knowledge, experience, and stories continue to guide me in my journey.

—Andy

For my wife and best friend, Tina, whose belief and confidence gave me the courage to leave corporate America and who has shared every step of my journey. And to my father, who always thought I belonged in a college classroom—I'm teaching now. Thanks, Pop.

—Lynn

TABLE OF CONTENTS

PREFACE

We didn't initially plan to write this book together. We met at a business conference and kept bumping into each other at networking events. After Andy published his first book, *Words Fucking Matter*, the joke began. "You know, numbers matter too. When are we going to write that book?"

We talked about our common experiences working with people and their numbers. Although there had been different clients, different industries, and different challenges involved, every story led down the same path: business owners were working hard, doing everything they thought they "should" be doing, yet still flying blind when it came to their numbers.

We have seen it over and over. Confident people who could sell, lead, and create would freeze the moment a financial statement hit their desk. It wasn't because they weren't smart; it was because no one had ever shown them how to listen to the stories their numbers were telling them. And we figured out why. Business owners know a lot about a couple areas of their business. Other parts? Well, not so much.

Here's what we typically see when it comes to owners and money management:

- Owners are taught that when you have a bookkeeper and pay taxes, you're "covered," despite inherently knowing every big business has someone called a Chief Financial Officer (CFO) leading their accounting and finance teams.

- Owners are not told that accounting and finance are two completely different disciplines, they add value in very different ways, and neither is particularly difficult to understand once they know the basics.

◆ The gap between what owners are told they need to learn and what they really must know is costing them money, and causing them stress.

That's what connected the two of us. We both understood that when owners know their numbers, it not only changes their business—it also changes their lives. Once their numbers stop causing anxiety and start becoming a source of power, they gain clarity, confidence, and control.

We wrote *Stop Avoiding Your Numbers* on this premise to help business owners move from being victims of their circumstances to victors of their own story. When we first started talking about the book, what struck us most was how two people could end up doing the same fractional (part-time) CFO work, seeing the same problems and believing the same thing, even though we come from completely different backgrounds.

Andy's Story

Every Tuesday night, without fail, the yelling would start. I was only a kid, and I still knew the routine. Mom would sit at her desk downstairs, surrounded by a pile of receipts from their home-improvement business Dad had handed her, trying to make sense of those small, smudgy numbers. Within minutes, voices would rise about money collected that week, hours worked, and why there was never enough money to pay for everything: drywall, fuel, credit-card bills, groceries, Catholic education, hunting land—you name it.

My mom is a second-generation entrepreneur, my dad is a third-generation entrepreneur, and I'm fourth. You'd think by then someone would have figured out how to handle the damn numbers without a weekly war breaking out!

Funny enough, the person who did have it figured out did so long before those battles. My grandmother ran a farm with my grandfather for over 50 years and tracked every penny by hand. When she passed on Christmas Eve 2014, she still had

50 years of handwritten ledgers in spiral notebooks. She even managed to still have $6,000 under her mattress 20 years after the last cow had left the farm. That's knowing your numbers. Still, somewhere between her generation and mine, that wisdom got lost, with my parents drowning in receipts and arguments.

When I was 10, my dad tasked me with helping him create invoices for his business. By then, Mom had stopped doing it, so someone else had to step up. There I was, a kid with a typewriter and carbon-copy paper, cranking out bills. Something clicked during those long nights that would end up changing my life. I got curious, asking why the numbers were what they were. I started asking questions. "Why are we charging this much?" "How much does this cost?" "Is it cheaper to buy in bulk?" I figured out that 25 sheets of drywall installed, taped, mudded, and sanded at $40 a sheet was a $1,000 job and started asking, "Is that good?" "How long does that take?" "Are you even making money?"

By 12, equipped with a computer, I was copying and pasting my way through quotes, change orders, and invoices. I was able to see the progression. I had data to back up my dad's gut feelings and memory of past projects. From there, I could build quotes and challenge his assumptions. I was doing back-of-the-envelope math, using curiosity to boost my instinct. The seeds for what I call "Hillbilly Math" were planted.

When I started my own business, I was determined to do it differently than my parents had. My brother was involved, and I didn't want to repeat those Tuesday-night fights with him. I borrowed money from my parents and maxed out all my credit cards at 0% APR. Within a year, I was able to pay my parents back with 10% interest and clear all my credit-card debt. I knew exactly what I could afford and when because I understood my numbers before I'd even fully learned my business. That made all the difference.

Numbers are in my DNA. Maybe it skipped a generation— it never disappeared, though. And for a long time, I assumed most business owners were the same way.

I was wrong. Dead wrong.

Most business owners don't know their numbers at all. They're flying blind, like my parents used to, making decisions on gut and hope, wondering why they're working so hard for so little.

Lynn's Story

I've always believed that numbers tell stories—when you know how to listen.

That belief started long before I became a fractional CFO. My first "business" was a paper route, which ended up paying for my first trip to Paris at age 17. I didn't realize it then, but I was already learning one of life's biggest lessons: effort turns into earnings, and choices turn into opportunity.

After studying finance at the University of Cincinnati, I joined Procter & Gamble (P&G). My dad thought I belonged in a college classroom; I knew I belonged in the "real world." At P&G, numbers spoke loudly. They weren't just reports and spreadsheets. They provided information that guided million-dollar decisions. Over 14 years, I worked across the full Profit & Loss (P&L) Statement, learning how to project profits, manage costs, and transform data into insight that helped leaders achieve goals.

While at P&G, I also earned my MBA from Duke University. I still recall the day I shared a remarkable document with my marketing professor. It was a hand-written accounting ledger that recorded one P&G brand's advertising from 1908 to 1953. I was fascinated at how you could see, once a year for 45 years, someone updated annual marketing spending by type, company sales, and US population, all in neat, handwritten rows. My professor showed me how those numbers traced the rise of modern marketing, US history, and society. Long before spreadsheets, someone understood what many today still don't: when you track what matters over time, numbers stop being math and start becoming meaning.

Eventually, I decided I wanted to make a bigger difference within a smaller company. Grande Cheese gave me that chance. Seven plants. Seven accounting systems. No consistency. But I helped change that, and then went further. I championed the creation of a proprietary system that aligned marketing and sales strategy, sales bonuses, and distributor programs around a few key numbers. The impact? Sales growth rate doubled for three straight years.

That success created the opportunity for my next chapter: founding Data2Profit, with a mission to redefine CFO as "confident financial outcomes" for my clients. Over the years, I'd seen the same pattern again and again: smart people surrounded by data yet starving for insight. They had plenty of numbers but little direction.

That truth has guided my work ever since. Accounting is about precision and the past. Finance is about decisions and the future. And small business owners deserve and need both: the accuracy that grounds them and the clarity that guides them.

This book is your bridge between the two. Because once you understand the story your numbers are trying to tell, you'll never run your business the same way again.

INTRODUCTION

You're avoiding your numbers. You know it's true—or else you wouldn't be reading this book. Sure, you check your bank balance every now and then or open the reports your accountant sends you. Chances are, however, you're only skimming them.

We get it. You started a business because you wanted to do what you love, to build something only you could imagine, or to create freedom for yourself and your family (probably all the above). That fire is what got you to where you are today.

Your passion is also what has kept you from the numbers. You've been so focused on building, creating, and serving customers that sitting down with spreadsheets feels like a distraction from the "real work." We've heard it before: "Numbers aren't my thing."

There's another reality, though. The day you started your business, something else happened. You became the CFO. Sorry to break it to you. It's not your bookkeeper, your accountant, or your business partner. It's you. And because you're the CFO and you're avoiding your numbers, your business isn't performing the way it could.

The stress is all yours. We've seen this play out hundreds of times—business owners too embarrassed to admit they don't understand their financials. In meetings, they nod along and hope no one asks questions. Others can't explain their financial performance even after years of operation. All of them have passion and hustle; none of them have a clear picture of their money or control over their future. The next move is usually the same. They hand their numbers to a friend, a spouse, a book-keeper, an accountant—anyone—and hope they do the right thing. Maybe they will; maybe they won't.

When you completely hand over the financial keys to your business without knowing your numbers, there are two truths you and the 34.7 million other small business owners in the United States[1] will encounter:

1. You have no way of knowing what's really going on or the questions you ought to be asking.

2. No one will ever care about your money as much as you do.

This is why so many businesses fail. Even when they are profitable, too many run out of cash. It doesn't happen overnight; it happens slowly—one avoidance and/or bad decision at a time. All that passion, all that hard work, and all those years of building gone because no one was watching the money.

With so much at stake, why do smart, capable people avoid their numbers? It usually comes down to one or more of these excuses they keep telling themselves:

- "I'm not a numbers person."

- "Accounting is too complicated."

- "I've been successful so far without understanding all this."

- "I have no idea where to even start."

- "My accountant handles that, so I'm good."

- "I trust my gut."

- "I know I should know, but the other parts of my business are doing great."

What they really mean is, "I don't understand my numbers, so I put them off, hope they'll sort themselves out, and tell myself I'll deal with them 'later.'"

Sound familiar? Know this: You're not alone. You're not broken. You're definitely not the only person who feels this way. The good news is that when you strip away the title, a "CFO" is simply the person who understands how to manage money and make confident financial decisions. And you already know how to be responsible with money; you manage it every day in your personal life. Your business numbers work the same way. They're telling you stories you haven't learned to listen to yet.

Numbers Are Stories

"Where'd all the money go?"

"How do I get more sales?"

These are the first two questions we get when we tell people we work with numbers. The answers to these questions and all others about your business can be found within your numbers. It's time you started listening to the story they're telling you.

A lot of business owners will say they hate numbers. At the same time, they love a good story—everyone does. Have you ever binge-watched an entire Netflix series in a weekend or read a mystery novel in a day because you couldn't put it down? Ever listened to a friend talk about the crazy thing that happened on their vacation for 45 minutes without checking your phone once? You were hooked. Yet when it's time to look at your P&L, you suddenly need to reorganize your entire desk drawer.

The problem isn't that you don't like numbers; it's that no one taught you how to understand the language of numbers. Your P&L isn't a spreadsheet; it's the story of where your energy went last month and whether it paid off. Your Balance Sheet isn't algebra; it's the story of whether you're building something sustainable or slowly bleeding out. Your Cash Flow Statement isn't merely rows of data; it's a history of where your money went as you built this hobby into a sustainable business.

Think about it: When you hear a good story, you lean in. You get curious and ask, "What happens next?" That's exactly how you can feel about your numbers. They're not random, and they're definitely not only for accountants. They're the story of your business—and whether that story ends in your fortune or failure depends entirely on whether you're paying attention. We're here to make sure you know what to pay attention to.

Who We Are

We're the guys who have sat with business owners whose hands were shaking when they finally said out loud, "I have no idea what these numbers mean." We're the ones who have watched owners find out—sometimes in time, sometimes too late—that no one was really watching the money. And we're also the ones who have seen the relief on their faces when the fog lifts and it all finally makes sense.

We're not here to turn you into a finance or numbers geek. Our job is to make you aware. We want you to know enough so you can ask good questions and get the information you need to make confident decisions. Finally, we want you to understand how numbers can create accountability within your team so your business can run without you.

We work for you. Between the two of us, we have a formal accounting and finance education, CFO experience, and years of real-world practice working directly with small business owners who were drowning in reports they couldn't understand. One of us came up through corporate finance. The other built businesses in the trenches, figuring out what matters and what's noise.

In our fractional CFO work, we each kept seeing the same pattern over and over again: owners struggling across multiple areas of their business. When we would assess these areas, one bucket consistently stood out as the weakest—you guessed it: finance. Not a single business owner we consulted with had solid financial confidence. Not one.

That's why this book exists. We're not here to do your bookkeeping or prepare your taxes. We're not here to impress you with credentials or accounting jargon. We're here because we've spent our careers translating financials into plain English to bridge the gap between what accountants know and what owners need to understand.

We have seen what happens when owners avoid their numbers. We have also seen what is possible when they finally face them. This book is everything we wish we had told those business owners sooner—and everything you need to hear right now.

How to Use This Book

This isn't a textbook. And you don't have to read it cover to cover or take notes like you're studying for an exam. Consider it a field guide to smart money management for your business.

Although it will likely make the most sense when you read it in order, feel free to look ahead when you have a specific problem and want immediate guidance. After you've read it, come back to it when you're making a big decision and need clarity on what your numbers are telling you to do.

As you work through it, keep the following in mind:

- It's okay to not understand everything at first. No one does. That's the point.

- It's okay to not be tracking everything you need to yet. You'll get there.

- It's okay to not have the right financial people on your team (or any financial people at all). We'll help you figure out who you need and when.

- Read it without your financials to start. Then use it as a reference when you're looking at your numbers.

- When you have financial people on your team, loop them in. Share chapters. Ask questions. Make them part of the journey instead of handing things off.

You'll move through these three phases:

1. **Awareness**—recognizing what you don't know

2. **Understanding**—learning what the numbers mean

3. **Execution**—using numbers to make better decisions

Learning and acting take time. Expect it to take 12 to 18 months to fully implement everything in this book. That's because understanding your numbers doesn't happen in one big transformation. It's through consistent, simple steps that compound over time. That's why every chapter ends with a "Quick Win"—one small action you can take immediately to build clarity, confidence, and momentum. No matter where you are in your life or business, or how confused you are about your numbers, this book will teach you what changes you can make today to change your trajectory.

What's Inside

In the chapters that follow, we'll start by getting clear on your vision. Why are you really in business? We do this because your business needs to serve your life, not the other way around.

From there, we'll follow the money—where it comes from, where it goes, and what it means. We'll guide you in deciding who you need on your financial team versus who you think you "should" hire. Then we'll cut through the noise. You'll learn which data matters for making decisions and which numbers are distractions, wasting your time.

And of course, we'll tackle the "big three" financial statements: Income Statement, Balance Sheet, and Cash Flow Statement. We'll show you how to read the stories they're telling you so they stop being scary and start being useful.

Finally, we'll show you how to put it all to work: how to assign dollar values to your decisions so you can see the real trade-offs in business and in your personal life. When you choose to do one thing, you're choosing not to do something else, and every one of those choices creates ripple effects. Every decision also has a cost—in money, time, energy, and opportunity. Jeff Bezos famously chose to drive a Honda Accord for years, even after becoming a multi-millionaire, because he understood what mattered to him and made intentional choices about where his money went. You'll learn to do the same.

Playing Again Tomorrow

Like a sport, your business isn't about one big win—it's about staying in the game. The real goal isn't to win today; it's to put yourself in a position to play again tomorrow. When you run out of cash, you can't do that. Game over. No second chances.

This book is here to make sure that doesn't happen to you. By the end, you won't be able to claim ignorance. Such ignorance is expensive—and it's over now.

We're going to put you in control of your numbers. You'll see how the money flows through your business and how to make decisions with clarity instead of merely hope. You'll create systems that keep you moving forward, not firefighting what's in front of you. When crisis hits, when opportunities arise, and when hard decisions land on your desk, you'll know what to do. Ultimately, you'll make choices that align with the vision you have for your business, and for your life.

It's time to stop avoiding your numbers and start building your future.

LET'S FUCKING GO!

PART I

CREATE YOUR VISION

You're a business owner. You're excited, energetic, and optimistic. At the same time, you're also feeling overwhelmed, frustrated, and out of control. We get it.

You took Sunday off for the first time in forever and then came in Monday. Your inbox is exploding, inventory is still a mess, and your team needs you for the same problem you solved last week. By mid-afternoon, customers are demanding to talk to you, and the bank is calling about your late payments. And you're thinking, *Do I need some foo-foo business vision? Really? I can barely see the end of today!*

The chaos you're living in is exactly why you need a vision. Honestly, you don't have time not to have one.

What do we mean by "vision"? It's not some fluffy corporate nonsense. It's a picture of where you want your business to be at some point in your future and why this is important to you. You're telling yourself clearly, "This is where I want to go." Now every decision has purpose. With a clear vision, every move will be evaluated with "Is this getting me closer?" to your goal or your objective. And you begin to plot how you will get there. You are in control.

Without it, you will continue to drive blindly, taking whatever chance looks good in the moment. Your destination today?

Fatigue. Burnout. Hoping and praying you'll like where you end up.

Now, you're probably thinking, *But what if I pick the wrong destination? What if the market changes? What if something better comes along?*

Stop. Please stop. A "what if?" scarcity mindset didn't get you to where you are today!

You know what's worse than picking the "wrong" direction? Not picking any direction at all. At least with a vision, when things change (and they will), you can adjust with purpose instead of panicking like a deer in headlights.

Here's what we want you to do right now: stop thinking about this week's problems for five minutes. Only five minutes. And think about this instead: *Where do you want to be in three years? Five years? What will your life look like when your business actually works for you instead of the other way around?*

Your answers to these questions are creating your vision. And here's what happens when you get crystal clear on where you want to go:

♦ Decisions become simpler (does this move me toward my goal or away from it?).

♦ You stop chasing every shiny opportunity that comes along.

♦ Your team actually knows what they're working toward (and so do you).

♦ You can say no to the wrong clients and "Hell yes!" to the right ones.

Think of it like planning a vacation. You don't simply show up at the airport and see what happens, right? You pick where you want to go, figure out what it costs, and start making it happen. Your business can work the same way.

What's Next

Before we dive into the tactical parts—scaling, finances, all that good stuff—we need to get your head right and your destination locked in. For PART I of this book:

- Chapter 1 is about guiding you to a mindset and systems that work. Having a big vision means nothing when you don't have the mindset and foundation to execute it.

- Chapter 2 is where you get real about what you actually want. Not what you think you want. Not what worked for your buddy's cousin's business. What **you** want. Maybe that's building a $3 million company. Maybe it's grooming a successor. Maybe it's positioning for a big exit. We'll guide you to figure out what success looks like for **you**, then reverse-engineer the path to get there.

Get these things right and everything else becomes possible. Skip them and you'll keep spinning your wheels forever. Your choice. Your work begins now.

As much as you want to read on, put the book down, get a piece of paper, and write down where you want to go, when, and why. Go!

YOU CAN DO THIS

You did it. You actually did it.

You took the leap, started a business, and joined the ranks of people who don't simply talk about their ideas. You make them happen. That alone puts you ahead of the 99% of people who are still sitting on the sidelines, making excuses.

And now that you're here, you're probably wondering, *What the hell comes next?* Maybe you're riding high on the excitement. Maybe you're lying awake at 3:00 AM wondering whether you've made a huge misstep. Most likely both. And maybe you're still thinking this way 20 years into your business.

We want you to know that feeling is totally normal. Starting a business takes guts. Now, building one that lasts? That takes something different entirely. It takes clarity, focus, and the discipline to work on the right things instead of merely working harder.

You've probably already heard all the scary stats. Half of all businesses tank within five years. Two-thirds don't make it to 10.[2] What those statistics don't tell you, though, is that it's not because those owners aren't hustling. Most of them are grinding 70-plus-hour weeks, pouring their hearts into it.

The problem is they are still working in the dark. They don't understand their numbers, so they ignore them. They made decisions based on gut feelings instead of real information, or "data" (dare we say "data" this early in the book?). They threw money at problems without knowing whether it would solve anything. They got stuck in survival mode and never learned to build the processes and systems needed to establish control.

The businesses that make it (the ones that grow, scale, and eventually give their owners real freedom) aren't necessarily the ones with the best products or the biggest bank accounts. They're the ones with the right mindset and the right systems. And that's exactly what this chapter is about. We're going to show you how to think like a business owner who builds both business value and personal wealth, not an owner who merely stays "busy" being the owner.

The truth is in the chapter title itself: You can absolutely do this. You've already proven you've got what it takes to start. Now let's make sure you've got what it takes to win.

The Mindset Shift

We're both pretty direct, so we're going to cut to the chase here: your relationship with numbers is probably screwing you over. That's because most business owners treat their financials like that pile of mail they don't want to open. They know it's important, and every time they think about diving in, their brain starts screaming, "Not today!" and they find something else to do. Sound familiar?

The reason is when you feel overwhelmed or freaked out about numbers, your brain literally goes into fight-or-flight mode. The same response mechanism that kept your ancestors alive when facing down a saber-tooth tiger now kicks in whenever you see an Income Statement. The emotional part of your brain (the amygdala) hijacks the rational part that actually knows how to solve problems.[3] The result? You can't think straight, you can't learn, and you definitely can't make smart decisions. You ignore your numbers.

"But I'm Not a Numbers Person"

If we had a dime for every time we heard that…

This isn't about being "bad at math" or "not a numbers person." That's a story you've been telling yourself since high school algebra kicked your ass. The truth is that most successful business owners aren't math geniuses. They learned to stop being afraid of the numbers that matter.

Take this one guy we worked with. Smart dude, successful business, and yet he'd been running from his financials for decades. He was the kind of guy who could sell ice in a snowstorm—great instincts, incredible energy, and a knack for growth. And when it came to his numbers? Total avoidance. He assumed money would always keep flowing. He poured cash into house renovations, luxury vacations, and new toys, and he never stopped to ask himself, "Am I actually building wealth or only spending it?"

At age 50, the cracks started to show. His kids were headed to college, his body was tired, and suddenly, the question hit him like a freight train: *How the hell am I going to retire?*

The scariest part? His business was still doing fine. There wasn't a looming crisis or major debt. The real issue wasn't in his bank account—it was in his mindset. He had spent years equating "busy" with "secure" and "income" with "intelligence." But he never stopped to understand his financial picture beyond what was in his checking account that month.

Once he stopped panicking and started getting curious, everything changed. He realized that he wasn't behind—he was uninformed. With our guidance, he established a solid financial plan and got excited about his numbers because he'd come to realize that they tell him a story about where he's going, not merely where he's been. Feeling safe, supported, and capable made his brain more open to learning what he needed to learn.

Like him, you don't need to be a spreadsheet wizard or an accounting expert. You only need to release the fear around your numbers. And as we were with him, we're here to guide you to rewrite the narrative.

Here's what we want you to do right now: stop and think about your stories around numbers. When someone mentions cash flow or profit margins, what's your first reaction? Do you tense up? Change the subject? Blame your high school math teacher?

Whatever it is, notice it. Don't judge it; see it.

Then ask yourself, "Could this be different? Can numbers actually be my friend instead of my enemy?"

That's it. That's all we want you to do right now.

You don't have to be good at math to follow the advice in this book. You can hire people for the complicated stuff. You only need to release your fear and any preconceived notions that you're not cut out for this. Because whether you believe it or not, your numbers are trying to guide you to win. They're not the enemy; they're your early warning system, your growth tracker, and your road map to freedom all rolled into one.

Once you make this shift—once you start seeing your financials as tools instead of torture devices—everything else becomes possible. It won't happen overnight; it will happen eventually, especially when you have the structure to support it.

Here's Some Good News: It's Not All on You

Throughout this book, we are going to tell you things that nobody else will. As much as you're avoiding your numbers, you've probably never heard, in plain English, compelling reasons why you need to look at them. You don't know what you don't know.

We want to start changing your ideas about numbers with three things that don't get a lot of attention:

1. There's a huge awareness gap between what you are taught you "should" do to manage your business money and what you really **must** do. The general message is, "You have a

bookkeeper and pay taxes; you're covered." This is way, way wrong!

2. Accounting is **not** designed to guide you to grow your business. In fact, we believe the most important numbers you need to know are not even in your financial statements.

3. Accounting and finance are two very different things. We'll cover this in more detail later. For now, remember that accounting is about your past. Finance is about the future and your potential failure or fortune.

The journey we're guiding you on will bring clarity to how to take control of your operations and guide you to proactively, confidently lead your business. Along the way, you'll develop both structure and discipline. Ready to start?

Why Structure Matters

Think about your personal finances for a second. You probably know your mortgage/rent payment, your car payment, maybe even your average monthly grocery bill. You are likely to have one checking and one savings account and a couple credit cards. Spending is relatively consistent, except when the washer dies or the car breaks down. Hopefully, you have set aside a little savings for those events—and perhaps a vacation. We hope you also have started some long-term saving. We understand that managing personal money is not very difficult.

Now think about your business. It can be stress on steroids! For a lot of the clients we work with, everything is a mess. They've got expenses on three different credit cards and payments scattered across Venmo, Zelle, and whatever other apps seemed convenient at the time. They're making decisions based on whatever their bank balance looks like today. Honestly? They're flying down a curvy road in dense fog. They have no idea what's coming. They've been winging it, hoping good intentions and hard work will somehow keep everything together.

Spoiler alert: they won't.

Maybe you're thinking, *Wait, I became a business owner to get away from structure. I don't want someone to tell me what to do.* We get it. Freedom, flexibility, being your own boss—that's the whole point, right?

The truth is structure doesn't mean restriction; it means support. It's what lets you take bigger risks because you know exactly where you stand. It's what prevents you from making decisions based on panic instead of facts. It's what turns your business from a chaotic mess into a moneymaking machine. Think of it like scaffolding. You wouldn't build a skyscraper without it, and once the building's up, you take the scaffolding down and admire what you've built. Structure in your business works the same way: it supports your biggest dreams without limiting them.

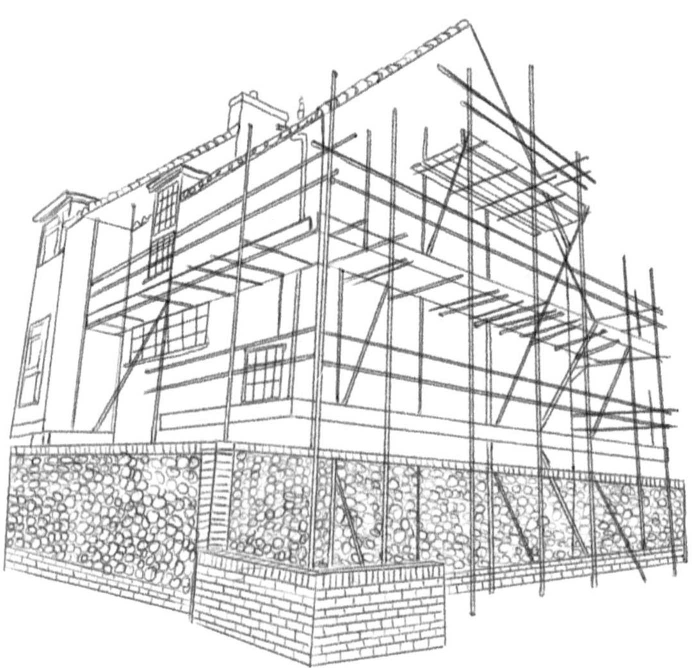

Take, for example, a restaurant owner we worked with in Milwaukee who made the best chicken wings in town. Seriously, people drove from other cities to eat there. And still, they had zero financial structure. Every month sales tax came due, they scrambled. No money set aside, so they'd panic and throw everything on personal credit cards at 28% interest. Year after year, it was the same cycle: great food, loyal customers, and financial chaos. After 13 years in business, they were still living paycheck to paycheck, still owned by their business instead of them owning it.

This wasn't a product problem—it was a structure problem. We dove in and started very simple. We set up a system where a percentage of every sale automatically went into a tax savings account. We created clear categories for tracking expenses. We established a weekly 15-minute money meeting where they'd review their numbers. That's it. Nothing fancy, nothing complicated.

Within three months, the structure allowed us to make tax payments with money already put aside, not taken from Peter to pay Paul. No panic, no credit cards, no sleepless nights. The structure shifted the owner's entire mindset about their numbers.

The same thing can happen for you. You don't need to overhaul everything overnight. You need to start building the structure that will support everything else you want to accomplish. Because without structure, you're not running a business—your business is running you.

Go at Your Own Pace

We're about to throw a lot at you in the coming chapters. Strategies, tools, systems—the whole nine yards. You don't have to do it all at once.

You may be ready to tear everything down and rebuild it properly. Or you need to take baby steps because, frankly, you're already drowning and can't handle much more on your plate.

Both approaches work. The only approach that doesn't work is doing nothing, ignoring your numbers.

The great thing is that even simple changes create massive ripple effects. We're talking about fixes that take 10 minutes and save you hours of confusion every month. Case in point: We worked with a nonprofit that was spending money like water and had no idea where it was going. Turns out they had one vendor showing up in four different expense categories: software, vendor services, operations, and marketing. Four different places for the same company.

Nobody could answer the simple question: "How much are we spending with this vendor?" They were making budget decisions based on complete guesswork.

The fix? Twenty minutes of cleanup. Yes, 20 minutes.

We consolidated those expenses into one category, set up simple rules for where things will go, and boom—instant visibility and consistency. Suddenly, they could see exactly where their money was going and make smart decisions instead of panicking every time a bill came in.

That's the power of all this. Simple fixes, big results.

We've watched this transformation happen over and over. Business owners who were completely overwhelmed by their numbers suddenly become confident decision-makers. People who used to avoid their financials now check them weekly because they actually make sense.

You don't need an MBA to figure this out. You don't need to be a math whiz. What you need is to get curious instead of being scared. Start asking questions instead of avoiding them. Where's your money actually going? What are your real profit margins? Which parts of your business make money, and which parts keep you busy?

This can be as simple as blocking 30 minutes every week to review your numbers from the previous week, creating clearer categories in your bookkeeping, asking your accountant one good question instead of simply nodding along, and reading the next chapter of this book.

The point is you get to choose your pace. Fast or slow, big changes or small ones—it all counts as progress. Remember: You don't have to fix everything right now. You get to take the next step that's right for you.

Quick Win: Take One Hour a Week to Rewire Your Mindset

Block one hour on your calendar each week—for you and your business. Use it to read this book, reflect, and take one simple action to improve your financial clarity. During that hour, repeat this affirmation: "I understand my numbers."

When you catch yourself thinking, *I'm not a numbers person*, pause. Acknowledge the thought—and replace it. Your brain listens to your patterns. The more you shift your mindset, the more confident you'll become. One hour a week is all it takes to start making a real change.

I USED TO ______________(limiting belief)

AND NOW ____________ (truthful adjustment)

SO THAT______________(result)

Example:

Limiting belief: I used to avoid my numbers…

Truthful adjustment: and now I make my numbers a priority…

Result: …so that I make informed decisions consistent with my goals.

I used to avoid my numbers, and now I make my numbers a priority so that I make informed decisions consistent with my goals.

Mindset + Structure = Momentum

When you combine the right mindset with solid structure, something powerful happens: You stop reacting and start creating. You stop hoping and start knowing. You stop surviving and start building. That's momentum. And once it kicks in, everything changes. Your numbers start making sense instead of making you sweat. Your decisions become clear instead of confusing. Your business starts working for you instead of owning you.

It all starts right here, right now. Not when you have more time. Not when things slow down. Not when you feel "ready."

Today.

The question isn't whether you're capable—you've already proven that by starting your business.

The question is are you ready to stop playing small and start building something that lasts?

Your future self is counting on the answer being yes.

CHAPTER 2

START WITH THE END IN MIND

What do you want? Where are you going? What are your life goals? What does retirement look like for you? Future-focused questions like these set your direction for your life and business. You're working toward something, not merely reacting to things that come your way.

How often do you start your car with no idea where you're going? Almost never, right? Now think about the built-in navigation system. You don't start driving and hope you end up in the right place. You punch in your destination and it maps out the best route to get there. Along the way, it also tells you when you may want, or need, to change routes.

This is exactly why you need to start with the end in mind with your vision. It's what helps you align your business with the life you want to live. Consider it your BS detector cutting through all the noise and separating opportunities that could help you build your dream from the ones that will fatten your wallet temporarily. The vision you create now becomes your destination.

The bottom line is that owning a business isn't about working yourself to death—it's about building a life worth living. When you start making choices with your big picture in mind, you'll see how much simpler it becomes to line up your business with what you really want. Don't stress about making it perfect or figuring out every detail. You need to start somewhere. We'll tackle the "how" later in the book. Right now, only focus on the "what"—what do you want your business and life to look like?

We're going to guide you to answer that question in this chapter. Like that navigation system we talked about, once you know where you're trying to go, the path there becomes a whole lot clearer.

Personal vs. Business Vision

It's important to think about your personal and business visions separately. They are distinct and also interconnected pieces of your larger puzzle. Your business vision answers the questions "What do I love to do?" and "Whom do I want to serve?" This is about your mission, your impact, the problems you're solving, and the legacy you're building through your work. It's the engine that drives everything else.

Andy

My wife and I live a life of the four freedoms:

- Freedom of time
- Freedom of money
- Freedom of relationships
- Freedom of purpose[4]

When faced with decisions, we look at them with this mindset. Which choice gets us closer to living a life of freedom? The answer becomes abundantly clear once we put this lens in place.

Your personal vision is different. It's focused on the lifestyle you want to live outside work—how you want to spend your time, where you want to live, what experiences matter to you, and how much money you need to make that life possible. This is about freedom, fulfillment, and the life you're working so hard to create.

Your business is the vehicle that will get you to your personal goals. When your professional and personal lives align, your business becomes more than a way to make money—it becomes the bridge between where you are today and where you want to be tomorrow. The clearer you are on both, the better decisions you'll make about everything from pricing to hiring to which opportunities to pursue.

> **Your business is the vehicle that will get you to your personal goals.**

Without this clarity, you might build a successful business that traps you in a life you never wanted. Or worse, you might chase a lifestyle that your business model can never actually support.

Creating Your Vision

As the title of this chapter suggests, when we talk about vision, we want to begin with the end in mind, like Steve Covey has suggested.[5] Start big: think about what you want your life to look like 10 or 20 years from now. We know that sounds pretty abstract and maybe impossible to put real numbers to. Go there anyway, and let yourself get excited about it. This is about getting as clear as possible. What does success look like for you personally?

Once you have that bigger picture brewing, pull it back to a three-year vision. Three years is close enough that you can almost taste it, yet far enough out that you can think bigger than "survive next quarter." That's where you can start adding real details. What would your business need to look like in three years to get you closer to that 10- or 20-year dream? We're talking about something you can plan for and make proactive decisions on. You're no longer going to be reactive and wait to respond to something. You are going to actively seek out opportunities that are consistent with your vision.

When you get to that place, write it down. Put it where you can see it every day. Studies show you're 42% more likely to achieve goals you can see every day.[6] Make it specific. The clearer your vision, the easier it becomes to spot opportunities that align with it. Make it inspire you—something you'd be proud to share with others, not some generic "I'm going to live my best life"—a real picture of what success looks like for you.

It's Not About the Numbers—at First

This might sound a little backward right now: your numbers and finances start with your vision, not with a bunch of complicated spreadsheets. You get to picture the life you want first, then figure out how to pay for it later. It feels weird to start with dreams instead of dollars. Trust us; it's the only way that works.

Before you crunch a single number, you need to get crystal clear on what you're working toward. That's why we start with the fun stuff. Think about what your ideal life looks like. Is it travel? A cabin in the mountains? Sailing? Endless spending on grandchildren? A legacy of wealth for your kids? Or even your own foundation? There are no right or wrong answers.

Different dreams cost different amounts of money. Broadway shows and business-class flights cost more than walks in the park and backyard barbecues. Neither lifestyle is better than the other, and you absolutely need to know what you want and roughly when you want it. Once you're clear on your personal vision, you can figure out what your business needs to look like to make that life possible.

Prioritization and the Danger of Debt

Let us be very clear: painting this picture doesn't mean you get it all right from the start, or that it's ever finished. We once worked with a dentist who had big dreams of acquiring multiple new practices. Ambitious, right? She also wanted to keep taking multiple $50,000 vacations every year. Those two goals were pulling in opposite directions. Something had to give. After working with us, she chose to hit pause on the luxury trips to free up the financial capacity to pursue her expansion. Within three years, she'd purchased the practices she wanted—and with the growth that followed, she now takes even better vacations while the businesses generate wealth in her stead.

Her story shows the gap between dreaming big and paying for it. You can have the clearest vision in the world, and when your bank account is working against you, you won't have much luck getting there. That's because the biggest dream killer for most business owners isn't thinking too small; it's being buried alive in debt.

When you're stuck in financial chaos with revenue that barely covers expenses, unpaid loans or taxes, and maxed credit cards, it doesn't only mess with your business; it messes with your head. When you're trapped in survival mode like this, you're reacting to disasters instead of creating opportunities. Every decision you make is about putting out fires, not building something bigger. No one wants this, and we don't want it for you. Your debt might be part of your story; it doesn't get to write the ending, though.

Now, don't get us wrong; survival mode can teach you a thing or two that comfort never could. It strips away everything that doesn't matter and shows you what you're made of. Those firefighting skills are really crisis management and quick decision-making abilities. They will come in handy later as you respond to opportunities. The pressure you feel today is preparing you to handle success tomorrow. You can't stay stuck in survival mode forever.

Getting unstuck means making moves now that will help you in the future. Maybe that's finally building a budget or cash-flow forecast that works. Maybe it's facing the truth about where your money goes. Maybe it's saying no to stuff that feels amazing right now yet doesn't get you closer to where you want to be. Whatever it is, choose to make the move because it aligns with your vision.

To do so, use the OODA (observe, orient, decide, act) loop, a rapid decision-making process that emphasizes speed and adaptability. Originally developed for fighter pilots, it's now widely used in business to stay ahead of competitors by making faster, more informed decisions:

- **Observe**—Take note of your current circumstances. Gather information. Intake stimuli.

- **Orient**—Determine your position relative to stimuli, as well as your desired outcome.

- **Decide**—Based on observations and orientation, decide what move to make.

- **Act**—Put your decision into motion.

The OODA loop is shaped like a circle because it's a continuous process. It's always ongoing. Steps in the cycle can be revisited at any point to accommodate new or changed stimuli. It might seem overly simple—and simple works. The beauty of the OODA loop is it's built for moments when shit doesn't go according to plan.

In lay terms:

- **Observe**—Something is happening: an opportunity, an obligation, a shiny object.

- **Orient**—Does this opportunity get you closer or further to your vision?

- **Decide**—Make the disciplined decision based on the structure that allows you to get where you're going.

- **Act**—Execute.

Then start over and observe the impact of the decision you made. You've been doing this all your life, whether you knew it or not.

The Trap of Success Without Strategy

You may find yourself in the completely opposite situation, raking in more cash than ever before. Having money doesn't mean you know what to do with it! The problem is that once the money starts coming in, it gets harder to make smart choices. You're thinking, *I can afford this!* And when you're on a roll, you say yes to everything. Unfortunately, when things are rosy, no one teaches you how to make decisions with clarity. In this situation, a different type of fear creeps in—of saying no, of missing out, of *I have to have this now*. And you begin believing this will last.

It starts innocently enough. A high-paying client wants work that's outside your wheelhouse. The money is too good to pass up, so you say yes. Then another similar opportunity comes along. Before you know it, half your business is work you dread, serving clients you don't like, in a market you never wanted to be in. The money is there, so you keep doing it, and before you know it, you're stuck in a shinier version of the very grind you were trying to escape. You're running a business you can't stand, making money you're terrified to lose.

Month after month, year after year, you dig deeper into this hole. You hire people to handle these profitable-and-wrong opportunities and build systems around them. Your reputation gets tied to work that was never part of your plan. Your lifestyle starts depending on that income, your ego gets hooked on those revenue numbers, and now you can't change or adapt. You feel like you can't say no, so you can't build what you want. You're too busy keeping the money machine running.

The most successful business owners flip the script completely. Not only do they not chase every shiny opportunity, they also get almost annoyingly picky about the ones they'll even consider. They can filter through all the noise because they have a vision so crystal clear that when something lands on their desk, they can cut through all the excitement and ask one brutally simple question: "Does this move me toward my vision or away from it?"

Though it sounds obvious, most people can't answer that question because they've never sat down to figure out what they really want. They've never started with the end in mind. They've been making decisions as they go, hoping it all somehow adds up to something good in the end.

The ones who seem to be killing it aren't necessarily smarter or luckier. They're simply playing a different game, where every decision gets checked against a clear picture of where they want to end up. When you know where you're going, it's amazing how much simpler it is to say yes to the right things and no to everything else.

Quick Win: Write Down Your Three-Year Vision

Grab a notebook, journal, or even a bunch of sticky notes. Give yourself 30 minutes, without distraction (no phone, tablet, laptop), to take your first cut at answering these two questions: "What do I want my business to look like three years from today?" and "What do I want my life to look like three years from today?"

◆ What brings you joy in your business?

◆ What do you want your ideal day at work to look like?

◆ Who are the customers you love working with?

◆ What work are you doing that's sucking the life out of you?

◆ When do you want to retire?

◆ What brings you joy personally?

◆ What are your personal and family goals?

◆ How many vacations do you want to take each year?

◆ Do you want to buy a cottage up north? A second home?

Don't worry about how you'll get there. Focus only on what you want. Let it be bold, big, and scary.

Then keep thinking about it, cementing it in your head, and rewrite it. Over and over.

This exercise shifts your brain from reacting to creating—and starts to give you something to move toward instead of away from. It's the first structural step in taking control of your numbers—and your future.

What's Your Next Step?

At the end of the day, your business works for your vision, not the other way around. Otherwise, you're not really a business owner—at least in the true sense—you're a stressed-out employee who can't call in sick. And you're probably feeling chained down to a business you're not even sure you want anymore. It doesn't have to be this way.

When you can clearly see where you're headed, you start making decisions that make sense. No more chasing every bright idea that pops up or mistaking being busy for making progress. Instead, you're building something that means something to you.

Once you are clearer about what you want in your business, you will naturally start pulling the right people toward you. Great employees want to work for companies that know their "why," not only their "what." Customers are drawn to businesses with a real purpose, not cool products. And investors aren't only betting on your idea; they're betting on you and your vision.

You have already proven you have guts. Starting your business took serious vision, hope, and creativity. Don't lose that spark now. Use it to build something that supports the life you want instead of it eating you alive. As you continue to explore this book, we'll connect those big dreams to the real money, choices, and systems that will get you there.

PART II

WHERE DOES THE MONEY GO?

"My accountant told me I'd made $100,000. Where the hell is it?"

It's the first question we get. Every time we see a new client.

You're not imagining it—you're in fact making money. Good money, even. On paper, your revenue looks strong. Yet, somehow, you're still broke.

Every month, the cycle repeats. The revenue rolls in and you breathe a sigh of relief. For a moment, you think you're safe, maybe even rich! Then reality hits—all those things you mentally keep track of, and sometimes completely forget about, come due. After bills, vendor payments, credit cards, and other obligations, the money vanishes as quickly as it arrives. And you're left staring at your bank account and wondering why you're living in financial uncertainty instead of enjoying the regular paycheck you used to get before starting this freaking business.

You're not the only one. Countless owners are grinding harder than ever while quietly asking themselves the same desperate question: "Where the hell is all the money going?"

At some point, you've likely found yourself in this position. You had a great month, only to admit, "I still can't pay myself." Sound familiar? Then this section is for you.

Here's something else no one talks about. Your business can look profitable while you, the owner, stay poor. We have seen owners build six- and even seven-figure companies while personally surviving on ramen noodles and suffering through sleepless nights. They tell themselves they're being responsible by reinvesting everything back into the business. They believe paying themselves is selfish. They promise they'll take care of themselves "when things get better."

Even when you tell others you started a business to make the best muffins, let's be honest now. You built this business to get paid—and it's time to start acting like it. Your business exists to serve you, not the other way around. Every dollar that flows through your company needs to have a purpose. And the first purpose is putting money in your pocket—not later, not someday after you've hit an imaginary milestone—now!

This section is about creating a system in which you pay yourself first, understanding exactly where your money comes from and where it goes, and stopping the hemorrhage of cash because of distractions. This isn't about spreadsheets for the sake of spreadsheets. It's about clarity, control, and finally getting paid for the work you're pouring into your business. You didn't risk everything to stay broke. You did it to build freedom, wealth, and stability.

You've already done the complicated part: you built something that makes money. Now let's make sure you get to keep more of it.

What's Next

In the chapters that follow, we'll start by tackling the importance of paying yourself first with a real salary that reflects your value. Then we'll guide you through an exploration of money in and money out, showing you where the money comes from and where it all goes. Finally, we'll show you how to stop the bleeding and expose the leaks you've justified for too long—unused subscriptions, overpriced vendors, random team bloat, and emotional spending. It's death by a thousand cuts. Together, we'll guide you to plug the profit leaks and build a business that truly pays you what you're worth.

CHAPTER 3

PAY YOURSELF FIRST (YES, FIRST!)

We'd bet money that you're not paying yourself enough—or anything at all for that matter. And no, taking whatever is left over at the end of the month doesn't count as paying yourself. That's not a salary. That's hoping for any remaining scraps.

Think back to when you had a regular job. Every pay period, your paycheck hit your account like clockwork. Your budget was basically done for you—predictable and simple. You knew what was coming in, to the dollar, and what you needed to pay from it. As a business owner, that luxury is gone. No steady paycheck, no automatic deposits, and no financial safety net.

That's why the old employee mindset doesn't work anymore. You can't spend what comes in because you don't always know in advance how much and when it's going to come again. Now you get to flip the script—you get to create your own budget first, then go make the money to support it. That means setting a real target, not some fantasy number or whatever feels right in the moment.

To do so, a lot of business owners jump into systems like Profit First.[7] And though it's awesome, Profit First assumes that you've got some financial chops and are already scaling. Most business owners aren't there yet, and you might be one of them. You'll get there—after you nail the basics first. That's what this chapter is about. We're going to teach you how to understand what you actually have and what you really need before you start paying for things randomly.

Whatever big vision you have for your business, it's going to take cash. That means you need real profits, and you need to pay yourself first. So let's dive into a straightforward system to stop the financial chaos and start taking control of your money. It starts with you.

Why Aren't You Paying Yourself?

Let's get this point out of the way: not paying yourself is one of the worst long-term business decisions you can make. Yet almost every business owner has done it.

Maybe you're doing it right now. And maybe, deep down, you've justified it with some warped badge of honor. You probably tell yourself something like, "I haven't earned it yet," or "Why should I pay myself when I'm going to put it right back in the business?" or "I'll get paid after everyone else does."

Sound familiar? That's not strategy; it's a scarcity mindset. That's martyr mode. And it's a fast track to burnout, resentment, and financial chaos. Not paying yourself is the same mindset that says, "I can't take a vacation," or "I can't afford a day off." It's the belief that **you**—the person who is writing the checks, doing the work, carrying the risk, and keeping the whole thing afloat—are the least important part of your business. That's insane. Besides, no one else works for free (or considerably less than they're worth)—not your team, not your vendors, and not your landlord. So why are you?

To add even more chaos, most business owners mix their business and personal money in an unhealthy or inconsistent way, transferring a little out when cash seems good, covering a personal expense on the business credit card, or maybe even paying business bills from their personal checking accounts.

Everything is all mixed up, messy, and emotional. And they're fooling themselves into thinking they're being responsible by not having a regular paycheck.

You need to treat your pay like you do any other expense: predictable, budgeted, and nonnegotiable. It will never be based on leftovers or tied to any specific project. Projects are too unpredictable to create steady income. Instead, you need to set a monthly amount you can count on (maybe not what you want!), maybe a fixed dollar amount or a percentage of revenue. Then bonus yourself responsibly when you exceed your financial goals. This isn't selfish; it's smart business. You want to develop the habit of rewarding yourself.

You need to treat your pay like you do any other expense: predictable, budgeted, and nonnegotiable.

Your personal bills don't care whether your business has had a good month or bad one. They're due either way. Paying yourself properly will take discipline to start. Once you get the hang of it, though, paying yourself becomes as automatic as paying rent—and equally as important.

The Simple System

We're going to say it again (and will say it throughout this book): you don't need to be an accountant or a "math person" to get your cash under control. You only need a system that makes it harder to screw up. That's where "Hillbilly Math" comes in. One application of these Three Steps to Success in action is our own version of Profit First. It's a simple strategy for tackling something that can easily become complicated, with the goal of getting things close—not down-to-the-penny accurate.

Create Your Buckets—Hillbilly Math

Most business owners run everything out of one checking account. The result? A complete fucking mess. They pay invoices in full when the money is there and forget about taxes. They take money out for themselves randomly when it seems like there is enough in the account. They swipe their cards for something that feels like a business expense because there is an account balance. That doesn't work, and it isn't going to pay you, the Internal Revenue Service (IRS), or the rent.

Andy

This is part of my Three Steps to Success:

- **Redneck Logic**—An educated man will find a problem to a solution; a naïve man will find a solution to a problem. Lean in on your naïveté.

- **Hillbilly Math**—What are the basic data, rules, or understanding you need to determine whether you're on track or off track? Pick a destination and go!

- **Kentucky Windage**—When you're hitting to the left of the target, aim to the right. No need to overcomplicate it; make adjustments along the way.

  "Good enough" is better than "paralysis by analysis." Something is better than nothing. My more educated con-temporaries call this a "minimally viable product."

With our tried-and-true Hillbilly Math system, when money comes in, you don't let it sit in your checking account and later pay everything from there. On a weekly or biweekly basis, you divide revenue into different buckets: profit, owner's pay, and taxes. Whatever is left gets moved to your operating account for you to pay business bills.

Yes, there will be less money in the operating account, and money is going to feel tight. Most owners experience this. It doesn't mean you will stop paying yourself or setting aside money to cover other things. It does mean you will need to get a better handle on money coming in and money going out. You might need to make some changes that we'll talk about much more in Chapters 4 and 5.

To make the system even simpler, we tell our clients to open separate checking accounts for their buckets. We have one client who pulls cash out weekly and puts it into envelopes to be saved up and used later for taxes, big purchases, and a "family bonus" for trips. Because one thing we know is that when they throw everything into one operating account, they will spend it. Period. It's natural that when your brain sees money, it assumes it's available. It's not.

Being in possession of something doesn't automatically make you the owner. That's the premise of this whole thing: stop spending money that doesn't belong to you. In other words, money coming into your business account isn't necessarily "yours." Some of it belongs to others: vendors, employees, banks, the IRS—you get the picture.

By dividing the money that comes in, you get a much clearer picture of where your money is going. Separate accounts make it harder to "accidentally" spend what needs be going to taxes, payroll, or rent. Even better, open the profit account at a completely different bank—hide it from yourself. Trust us here; we've been in your shoes. The fewer temptations, the better. However you choose to set it up is fine. The key is to set something up—be proactive.

We once had a client who actually had seven different bank accounts: one for inventory purchases, one for profits, another for short-term reinvestments, another for taxes, and on and on. Excessive? Maybe. And guess what? He always had the money when he needed it because he wasn't pretending the balance in one account was **his** money.

Maybe you're thinking this sounds too simple—that's exactly why it works. When your numbers are a disaster, this is the easiest way to get in a better spot quickly without too much

work. You don't even need perfect numbers to start—only percentages that make sense for your business. The following is a general baseline that will vary depending on your industry and your business:

- ◆ Profit: The goal is for 1–10% of revenue to be allocated to a profit account.

- ◆ Owner's comp: Allocate 11–50% of revenue to cover your own compensation.

- ◆ Taxes: A typical allocation is 5–15% of revenue (sales tax and use tax come off the top first).

- ◆ Operating expenses (OPEX): The remaining percentage—anywhere from 25–85%—is to be used for day-to-day business costs.

Solopreneurs will be on the high end in the first three buckets and lower in the OPEX bucket, whereas businesses with employees will be the opposite.

You probably noticed that the percentages above are ranges. Sometimes, these trip people up and they get stalled moving forward. They don't know what numbers to decide on, so they don't decide on anything. Don't let this happen to you. When you're first implementing this system, the goal isn't perfection—it's improvement.

Let's take the pressure off the decision. Your percentages will adjust over time as you get to know your numbers better and make important changes in the business. When you see that you have more room to pay yourself, bump up the percentage. And when you want to save more money in the business, increase the profit percentage. It's that simple.

Don't Be Afraid to Flex—Kentucky Windage

We know what you're thinking: some months suck and you don't bring enough cash in to pay yourself. We get it. That's the life of a business owner. Some months you'll need to flex, especially in a cash-heavy business. The difference is that when you have a basic plan and a few good habits in place, you'll at least know why you're flexing and how to bounce back.

Going forward, when there is a month you can't pay yourself what you planned or one when you must put more money into the business, that's okay. Keep track of it because the business still owes you. And when you know there will be more rough months ahead, have some money set aside. Keep a standing record for when this happens so you're not eating the loss; you are tracking it like any real company would.

This is all about smoothing out the crazy ups and downs of the financial roller coaster you're probably riding. It doesn't mean that every month will look exactly the same. It means that when you have a system in place, you can plan ahead and breathe a little easier—whether you're inching your way up to the top or racing back down. You're planning and taking control.

Quick Win: Use Hillbilly Math, Get Real Results

The key here isn't to become rigid. It's to build muscle memory. Start small. Hell, pay yourself 1% of your revenue to start the habit. Because the habit is what creates the result. Get your brain and your budget used to the idea that you matter—that your work deserves compensation, not leftovers. Do this every week, biweekly, or on the 1st and 15th of every month. Or choose whatever schedule works for you and keep it consistent. Make the choice.

Want more data? Go deeper than Hillbilly Math.

- ◆ **Step 1**—Know where your money's going. Pull the numbers from the last 12 months—yes, 12. You need to see the full cycle, including seasonality. Don't look only at one good month or one bad one. You want the big picture.

- ◆ **Step 2**—Convert dollars into percentages. You're not only looking at what you spent; you're also looking at how you spent it. Turn every dollar into a percentage of total revenue. How much went to operating costs? Owner's pay? Taxes? Profit? You might be shocked at the results.

♦ **Step 3**—Let the data guide you to make your decisions. You're not doing this to judge yourself—you're doing it to qualify or disqualify how you're running your business. When you're spending 70% of revenue on random overhead and paying yourself 2%, it's time to make a change. Immediately.

♦ **Step 4**—When you are completely lost in how to do this, get some help from your bookkeeper, a friend, or anyone else you know. Then go back to Step 1 and start again!

Consider This an Early Intervention

When you're a business owner or entrepreneur, nothing is fixed. You don't have a capped salary, you don't have a premade budget based on a paycheck that comes every two weeks, and no one else is dictating your financial future. That's both your gift and your trap. Without structure, most business owners stay trapped in chaos, living month to month, hoping it works out.

You have the power to change everything by rethinking how money flows. And you do this when you stop letting your income be an afterthought and start treating it like the priority it always needed to be. You're not a victim of your business— you're the architect of it.

This book isn't here to overwhelm you. It's here to guide you as you go. Nothing is permanent, and that's the point—you have room to grow and flex. We don't want you to worry that you need to track every penny forever. We want you to get clear enough to course-correct fast. You can't make smart money decisions without knowing what is actually happening. Look back, break it down, and then look forward with a smarter plan that includes paying yourself first.

We'll say it again (because it's worth repeating): you don't need to be a "math person," and you don't need complex spreadsheets. You need clarity, percentages, and guts. Make one change today—that's a win. Keep stacking them.

Get clear, get moving, and get paid. We have more to build.

CHAPTER 4

MONEY IN

Money started flowing into your business the minute you opened your business checking account. That may be the easiest money you'll ever get. Now the real work begins.

We all know you "shouldn't" avoid your numbers. And the one that will keep you up at night, especially early in your business, is how much money is—or isn't—coming in. In this chapter, we show you how to think differently about this number, and how to have more control over it.

There are only three ways money comes in the door of your business: (1) your own personal money, (2) someone else's money (loans or investors), and (3) the money the business generates, also known as "sales" or "revenue." For the sake of this chapter, we're focusing on the third. We talk more about the other two later in the book.

Yes, you might invest your own savings to get things off the ground. And sure, you can borrow to cover startup costs or scale more quickly. Over time, though, the bulk of your cash—the money that keeps your business running and growing—needs to come from the sale of your products and services to your customers.

Before we go any further, let's do a quick reminder on terms. Money coming in from sales is revenue. You'll also hear it called "income," "top-line sales," or simply "sales." Whatever you call it, it is the lifeblood of your business. Whether you're selling products, services, experiences, or ideas, this is where you start turning your work into dollars.

Money that flows in from sales flows out as you pay business bills, hire help, pay yourself, reinvest in growth, and take that next big step. The most important thing, for the purposes of this chapter, is to remember that **revenue is not profit.** Profit is what the business makes after paying all expenses. Not even close to revenue!

Money In Is Variable, Not Fixed

We said it in the last chapter, and it bears repeating: goodbye, steady paycheck. Welcome to business ownership—where variable revenue is the name of the game, especially in early growth mode. As a business owner, your income is dictated by the work you perform, the clients you serve, the contracts you land, and when those clients pay you. That means your revenue will vary—by day, by week, by month, and by year.

Though that unpredictability scares the hell out of a lot of people, it's also one of the best things about being a business owner. When you're in charge, the sky's the limit. You have the power to grow, pivot, scale, and earn more than you ever could in a traditional job. Your new role is to manage this variability by anticipating how much is coming in and planning your spending accordingly.

Every Business Is Seasonal—Yes, Even Yours

No matter what industry you're in, your business has some degree of seasonality. For some, it's clear-cut: tax-prep firms peak February–April, landscapers are slammed in the spring and summer, and retailers crush it during the holidays. Even with businesses that feel steady, there are still patterns and external factors (the economy, weather events, holidays, or industry shifts) that cause slowdowns or surges.

Take, for example, a restoration business that does flood and fire remediation. They can go for months without much activity, then get completely overwhelmed after a string of storms. The work is unreliable, and it comes in waves. Spring and summer are the time for floods. Fires, on the other hand, can happen at any time. These businesses need to be ready for whenever that wave comes rolling in.

Paying Yourself—Not Too Much, Not Too Little

Such variability can make it difficult to know how much to pay yourself, especially in the early years. Some owners underpay themselves (or don't pay themselves at all) to keep the business afloat, whereas others take too much too soon.

One client we worked with had a habit of pulling money out of the business when revenue was high, then putting it back in later to pay expenses when revenue was low. She never had a clear grasp on how much money was actually coming in— because there was no clear system for managing cash or paying herself consistently.

This is where the structure we talked about in Chapter 3 comes into play. Set a rhythm for reviewing your finances and determining how much you can afford to pay yourself each month. Stick with it—even when revenue varies. It's better to pay yourself a reasonable amount regularly than to go on a spending spree after one big win and then scramble to cover bills during a slower stretch. We recommend that business owners take a sustainable percentage of revenue early on in their business when fixed expenses are low.

The key is to remember not to overspend when business is booming and not to panic when things are tight—keep the rhythm regardless of the season. Build predictability into your system so you can make smart decisions and stay calm no matter what your bank account looks like on any given day.

Get comfortable with the fact that revenue will always vary. That's the nature of business ownership. Your job is to smooth it out over time by paying attention to your numbers and preparing.

Sales Has Two Main Factors

Two factors primarily impact your revenue. The first is the volume your business is doing. How much are you selling? Pretty straight forward, right? The second tends to be more confusing for some business owners—and that's pricing. How much are you charging?

Volume Is Determined by Sales Activity and Capacity

Remember that numbers reflect your company's decisions and behaviors. When it comes to generating revenue, there are endless strategies about how to promote your business, a host of things you need to know about customers, and choices to make about how you approach sales. All your sales activity creates sales volume, which is the number of products and/or services you deliver.

> **Remember that numbers reflect your company's decisions and behaviors.**

A business's sales come down to how well you meet customer needs and the decisions that customers make about your business. Buyers actually make two core decisions: what to buy and who to buy it from. Think about a car. Once you decide on the model you want, you have a choice of dealers.

With this in mind, no matter what business you're in, there are only four ways to grow sales. There are only four activities a (productive) salesperson can do each day. And each of those activities ties directly to one of the four decisions that customers make about your business. We refer to this alignment between business activities and customer decisions as RAPS.

Capacity is how much you can deliver. For solopreneurs and small businesses, landing a couple large clients can present real challenges. While enjoying the revenue boost, doing all the work can bring other critical activities like marketing and sales to a halt. When the sales are done, the pipeline is empty. Unfortunately, this is a lesson many people have to learn a couple times.

Sales volume is based on your capacity. When you're already at full capacity with staff, equipment, and other resources, more volume isn't the solution to growing revenue. Trying to add more could actually create more problems than it solves. You'll either need additional staff, more efficient systems, or better infrastructure before you can grow. Trying to take on too much without those things in place can overwhelm your team, damage your reputation, and cost you both money in the short term and opportunity in the long term. Growing too rapidly is dangerous to businesses, especially when numbers are ignored.

On the other hand, when you're **not** at capacity, increasing your volume is a great way to generate more revenue. More sales means more cash coming in—as long as your business can handle the demand. In this way, you have some control. Though you can't guarantee results, you can influence demand by ramping up your sales and marketing efforts, running targeted ads, optimizing referrals, and working the channels that bring in more leads. Don't be afraid to invest in some marketing expertise. Much like DIY finance, DIY marketing too often fails.

Volume isn't the only revenue lever to pull though. You can also increase revenue without increasing volume by raising your prices (arguably the fifth way after RAPS, not something you can do every day). Fewer clients at higher rates can be equally profitable—sometimes even more so—especially when you're offering high-value products and/or services.

Lynn

I learned the concept of RAPS from a great sales director I worked with for years:

◆ Retention—Keep the customers you have

  • Existing customers decide to buy or stop buying from you

◆ Acquire—Get new customers

  • New customers decide to start buying from you

◆ Penetration—Get customers to buy different things

  • Existing customers decide to buy something else

- ◆ **S**ame sales—Get customers to buy more volume
  - • Existing customers decide to buy more or less of the same items

When it comes to acquisition and retention, this often reflects the personality of your people. Some salespeople are hunter-killers: they love to bring in new business. Others are farmers—great at maintaining relationships. They both tend to sell the things they like to sell, especially when that's what they get paid to sell.

Penetration happens once you have a customer. Think of it this way. You have 10 different things to sell. How much time is spent trying to sell 3, 4, 5, or all 10? When you're at a restaurant, a great server doesn't ask whether you'd like dessert. They tell you, "Even though you're stuffed, our chocolate cake is to die for! Would you like to split a piece?" You'll surely end up ordering one, plus two coffees!

Sales increase when you show your customers how to use more of what they are already buying.

When you're planning your growth or designing a sales-incentive system, use RAPS to reward the behaviors and results needed to reach your total sales goals. It's hard work that will pay off when done well!

Sales RAPS - The Four Ways to Grow Sales

Retention

Acquisition

Penetration

Same Sales

Pricing

Andy

I pitched a keynote address once at $5,000. The client quickly agreed and mentioned that their budget was double that. Shit! The next time, I made the same pitch for the same amount to a different person and got flat-out rejected. Another time, the client said yes and that it was exactly what they were budgeting. Same product, same price, three completely different reactions.

There's an old saying in business: Good. Fast. Cheap. Pick two. Most successful businesses strive for good and fast and stay away from cheap. Because when people pay more, they often value it more. Be aware, though: when you're charging premium rates, the expectations will be higher. That's not a bad thing. It means you've stepped into the role of a premium provider.

Setting prices is an art, not a science. Though there are no universal right answers, there are three proven strategies to guide you to find the right one for your business. We recommend going through all three of the following approaches. Don't pick only one. Your best answer is likely going to be triangulated from the data you gain doing them all.

1. **Competitive analysis**

    Regardless of your industry, there is going to be a range of price points. That's why researching your competition is usually your first best move. What are others charging for similar products or services? From there, you can decide where you want to land on the spectrum. Are you offering something better, faster, more customized—or is your offer more entry-level, more accessible, or geared toward a niche audience?

Think about how you want to set yourself apart. Want to charge more than your competitors do? Go for it—make sure your offer communicates a premium value. Want to price a bit lower to gain traction as you start out? That's great too—don't undercut yourself so much that people question your quality. Remember: no one gets excited about the prospect of eating a $5 steak.

There's no single "right" price. Whatever number you pick will feel expensive to some and like a bargain to others. And that's okay.

2. Cost-plus model

With this approach, you want to figure out all your costs and then add your desired profit. We like to use Hillbilly Math here.

It all comes down to knowing your numbers.

3. How much do you want to make and how much do you want to work?

This is where your pricing strategy meets your lifestyle goals. It's simple math—and it's also very powerful. Start with what you want to earn and how many hours you want to work in a year. That will help you figure out what your hourly rate needs to be.

Let's say your goal is to make $100,000 per year. You plan to work 20 billable hours per week and take two weeks off annually.

50 weeks x 20 hours per week = 1,000 working hours per year

$100,000 ÷ 1,000 hours = $100 per hour

Now let's say you're dreaming big and want to hit $1 million. To do that, you'd need to generate $1,000 per hour working 20 hours a week (assuming a similar amount of time off).

Is that doable? Maybe. It's going to require a different strategy—higher-ticket offers, scalable products, or leveraging other people's time and talent. In other words, you're working 20 hours per week managing others, not doing everything.

Here's the simple formula: revenue goal ÷ hours you want to work = how much you need to charge per hour.

Don't think of this as a rigid rule, more as a starting point. You can adjust from here based on your industry, your business model, and what feels right for you.

At the end of the day, the market will let you know what it will tolerate. Start with a plan and raise prices or value accordingly. (Three Steps to Success methodology at work!)

We know what you're thinking: *this is "just" a math exercise.* No argument here. Say you tell your business coach, banker, or even yourself that you want to make $150,000. The next question will be, "How?" You have no idea until you run the numbers. What are the options (assumptions) you can change? Annual dollar goal? Number of weeks you're going to work? Number of hours per week you plan to bill? Your price? The chart below shows how this works for a consultant who bills by the hour. She earns $100,000 doing Plan 1. She already plans to raise prices, and is willing to work more hours. She'd also love to take more vacation. Looking at the numbers, her best bet is to raise prices by $50, bill the same hours, take 4 weeks off, and increase revenue to $144,000!

Your Sales Goal Depends on Your Plan					
	Plan 1	Plan 2	Plan 3	Plan 4	Plan 5
Price	$100.00	$150.00	$100.00	$100.00	$150.00
Hours per Week	20	20	30	20	20
Vacation Weeks	2	2	2	4	4
Total Hours Worked	1000	1000	1500	960	960
Price	$100.00	$100.00	$100.00	$100.00	$100.00
Annual Sales Goal	$100,000	$150,000	$150,000	$96,000	$144,000

Two restaurants with two different stories. Which do you want to be?

Andy

In high school, I worked for Marko's Pizza. The owner, Mark Caldwell, taught me a lesson that holds true today. He took his food cost and multiplied it by three. Five dollars in ingredients turned into a $15 pie. From there, he had $5 to pay staff and $5 to cover operating expenses. The goal for him was to maximize efficiency with staff and reduce operating expenses to make a profit because he had little control over the cost of ingredients.

To use this model, you need to know your numbers, especially your expenses, which we'll talk much more about in the next chapter.

Lynn

I worked with a coffee-shop owner who told me she thought she needed to raise her prices. Her reasoning? "Everyone says my prices are so reasonable."

When I asked her about her food costs, she told me that she hadn't looked at them in a few years, even with inflation driving everything up. This was where we needed to start. She couldn't realistically decide how much to raise prices without knowing her costs first. We ultimately determined that with rising food costs, she was in fact barely breaking even on certain dishes.

You can put numbers to anything you sell. To earn $100,000 building websites at $5,000 per site, you'll have to sell 20 each year. Walking dogs twice a week for rich people at $250 per month? Prepare to keep 33 families happy and walk nine dogs a day, rain or shine. Bonus—you can expense the shoes! Making custom bird houses for $15? You need to make and sell about 700 every month—and with all the supplies you'll need, your car will never fit into your garage again. Even in these quick examples, numbers make your business come alive, don't they?

Getting clear on the math first points to what options you have and gives you the information you need to make confident decisions.

Look at Your Pricing Regularly

You can't set your prices once and expect them to stay forever. Pricing isn't a "set it and forget it" situation. When you don't look at your prices regularly, you risk leaving money on the table. Make it a habit to review pricing at least once a quarter.

Start by looking at your bestselling products and services. Ask yourself, "Are these the ones I WANT to sell the most? Am I putting in more work than I'm getting paid for?" You may be undercharging or offering more than what's included. One client of ours realized that she was paying her subcontractors hourly while billing clients at a flat rate, even losing money on some projects. By switching to a project-based rate for her team, she instantly improved her margins—without raising client prices.

Pay attention to your sales conversations too. When everyone says yes right away, you're probably charging too little. When they tell you it's a great deal or is "very reasonable," chances are you could be charging more.

And remember: not all price increases feel the same. Some are barely noticed by customers. A car going from $20,000 to $25,000? That's a big jump. They'll wait longer to buy it. Windshield wipers going from $20 to $25? No one flinches. They need wipers to drive safely. Small increases on essentials like this often go unnoticed, and they can quietly improve your margins.

Here's another tip for restaurant owners: make sure prices end in a 9. Why sell a soft drink for $1.95 or slice of pizza for $4.95? No one will even think about the extra four cents—and for you, they will add up!

Annual Increases

We recommend raising your prices by at least 6% every year. Why? Because it keeps you ahead of typical inflation of around 2–3%. More importantly, you're not the same business owner you were last year. You've gotten better. More efficient. More experienced. Maybe even more in demand.

Andy

I picked this up from my tattoo artist. One day, I noticed his hourly rate had gone up. When I asked why, his answer was simple and honest: "Because I'm better."

And he was right. His skill had improved; he did my tattoo better and faster, and with that came the confidence to charge more. I ended up paying about the same amount of money for a better tattoo done quicker than expected. Win-win!

As your reputation grows and your processes improve, your pricing needs to reflect it. Staying stagnant doesn't only cost you money; it undervalues everything you've worked to build. Set a reminder to review an aspect of your prices quarterly and increase your prices regularly—annually at a minimum. There are a few ways to do this. You can do a straight 6% raise across the board once a year, increase 3% twice a year, or raise 10–15% on certain products quarterly. The goal is to raise your revenue 6% year over year without working more.

You also want to avoid lowering your prices. Things don't usually get cheaper. Your expenses won't go down. You probably won't pay people less. Lowering prices and discounting your offerings is a slippery slope that eats into profitability, and potentially your reputation for quality.

Not All Revenue Is Great Revenue

Sure, more money coming in sounds like an automatic win—except when it comes at the cost of your sanity, your team's morale, and/or your business's long-term health. Sometimes the stress, time, or resources a customer demands isn't worth it. We call these folks PITA (pain in the ass) customers, and every business has them.

Take this example from the owner of a pizza place. They had a customer who ordered pizza every Friday. And every Friday, like clockwork, she'd call to complain about cold pizza, late delivery, too much sauce, not enough cheese. The owner finally had enough. He looked up her history of complaints in their system—which he accessed by pressing a literal "PITA" button—and decided to act. The next time she called, he politely suggested that she find a pizzeria that would make her happier. And guess what? She stopped complaining and kept ordering!

At the end of the day, it's okay to fire a customer. In fact, we encourage it. You have the right, and the responsibility, to protect your business, your team, and your energy. When a customer consistently drains more than they contribute (financially or emotionally), they're not worth it. Great revenue supports your business. Bad revenue erodes it from the inside.

Quick Win: Analyze One Product/Service

Take one product/service you offer and work through all three strategies:

1. Competitive analysis

2. Cost plus

3. How much do you want to make/work?

Your natural inclination may be to take one strategy, like a competitive analysis, and run it for all your products. Avoid doing this. It's better to take your #1 product (volume, passion, etc.) and do the deep dive on it with all three strategies.

Get Comfortable...and Confident

Pay attention to your money coming in. Whether your business is generating $5,000 a month or $500,000, how it comes into your business sets the tone for everything else. The more comfortable you get with your numbers, the more confident you'll feel. You'll stop reacting and start anticipating. You'll be able to ride out the slow months without panicking—and take full advantage of the heavy ones. When you stop ignoring your numbers, more money will start flowing in!

MONEY OUT

Healthy expenses build your future; unhealthy ones drain it. This chapter will guide you in learning to tell the difference.

Business owners love seeing sales roll in. Your employees see the products going out the door. To them, you're swimming in cash. What they don't see is where the money goes after it hits your account. Unfortunately, from what we've seen over the years, neither do most owners.

Let's talk about all those checks you're writing, the ACHs you authorize, every swipe of a credit card, and the Venmos you send. How do you think about them? There are two different lenses for looking at expenses, and each one tells you something useful about where your money is going.

The first is the traditional accounting lens. Each transaction is sorted into a specific account within neat categories like "Cost of Goods Sold" and "Expenses" (more on those later). It tells you what it was for and can group spending in different ways, including which are fixed (pretty much the same each month) or variable (changes based on how much work you perform).

Then there is the emotional lens. You'll never hear about this view from your accountant or anyone else. It comes down to this: how do you feel when you write each check? Some expenses make you genuinely happy, such as paying a bonus to a rock-star employee who makes your life better. Others make you want to throw your computer across the room, like that software subscription you never use and keep forgetting to cancel. Those emotions guide you in figuring out whether an expense is healthy or unhealthy. Basically, is it investing in your future or draining your present cash?

Let's say you're a florist and you need to spend $800 on fresh flowers for the week. Through the accounting lens, that's cost of goods sold and a variable expense because how much you spend changes based on how many arrangements you're making.

Emotionally, you're probably feeling pretty good because needing more flowers means you're selling them, which also makes it a healthy expense. What about those days when you realize you've bought too many and tossed a few hundred dollars away? Each perspective tells you something different about whether that money is working for you.

Here's one thing we know for certain: expenses have a sneaky way of multiplying when you're not looking. One day you think you have all your shit together, and the next you're finding supplies that somehow doubled in price and mysterious charges that appeared out of nowhere. When you can't see exactly where each dollar is wandering off to, those little leaks add up fast.

Or what's even worse? When you finally wake up after seven months and realize you paid a shit-ton of money for the wrong business coach, marketing service, or employee who never was a good hire. And yes, both of us have made the same choices!

The truth is money walks out of your business every single day without you even thinking about it. You have to stop ignoring your numbers. This chapter is going to change how you think about every dollar leaving your business.

The Accountant's Categories of Money Out—Expenses

Every time you swipe your business card, cut a check, or hit "send" on an electronic payment, that's a transaction. Unless you are buying something of significant value (a building, a vehicle, higher-value equipment) or making a loan payment, you're paying for an expense. We'll get into a deeper accounting discussion in PART V. For now, we want you to think of expenses as being in one of two groups:

1. **Cost of Goods Sold (COGS)**

    COGS is the direct cost of everything it takes to produce or deliver what you sell. It includes materials, labor, packaging, and production costs that go into the product. As sales increase, COGS also increases. For example, you make your own candles. Direct costs are the price of materials, a glass container, and a packing box. Add in time to make the candles, put them in boxes, process orders, label the boxes, and ship them. You calculate the total cost at $7 each. When sales grow from 10 to 20 units, your COGS rises from $70 to $140. When your business doesn't sell physical products, the direct costs of a coach who works for you, or using a contractor to build websites, are COGS.

2. Overhead

Overhead, a.k.a. General Expenses or Operating Expenses (or whatever your accountant calls it), is basically everything that isn't COGS. That means it's not directly related to the individual products or services you sell. It's all the other spending you need to keep your business running: utilities, advertising, rent, phone bills, taxes, insurance, and office supplies. Overhead will probably increase as your sales increase incrementally over time with scaling, not month to month (rent expense will go up when you need more space to increase production). When overhead expenses are increasing faster than sales, it's time to take a real hard look at spending. This is something that even the largest companies deal with.

Before we go on, let's get into another thing accountants never talk about: investments in the business. Accountants think of costs only as COGS or overhead. You, as a business owner, need to think differently. In your daily decisions, you will spend money on things to improve your business, become more productive, and keep your business safe. You may hire a fractional CFO or business coach. You will want to do employee training. You must have insurance and anti-virus software.

From a business-management perspective, you need to think of this type of expense as an investment in yourself, your team, and your operations. Investments provide a positive return as long as you take the advice, apply the training, and/or learn a new technology. Remember: your bookkeeper will call all this an "expense." This is the healthy type.

One more point about investments and other money that leaves your business. Investments that your accountant talks about are usually physical things you buy, including inventory (material and products in the warehouse you haven't sold yet), higher-value equipment, buildings, etc. Another big "money out" goes to repaying money you borrowed. COGS, expenses, investments, and payments are all money out. We'll talk about physical investments and loans in Chapter 17.

Expenses: Which One Is Which? It Depends

Let's get back to COGS and overhead. How do you know which is which?

Confused? You're not alone. That's because some expenses are clear-cut, and others can be a bit tricky.

Let's look at some examples to help clarify the type of expense:

◆ In nearly any type of industry, an administrative assistant is overhead, and project-based independent contractors for specific jobs are COGS.

- For a restaurant, the manager's salary is overhead since they're running the whole operation, and the cooks and servers are directly tied to serving customers, so they're COGS.

- For a manufacturer, raw materials and factory workers are COGS, whereas the rent, accounting, marketing, and salespeople are overhead.

- A chiropractor's treatment supplies and direct patient-care staff are COGS, whereas the receptionist and office rent are overhead.

- In a pet-grooming business, groomer wages and shampoo used are COGS, whereas appointment scheduling software is overhead.

- For a catering company, food ingredients and server wages are COGS for each event, whereas commercial kitchen rent and business insurance are overhead.

- Cleaning supplies, lubricants for production equipment, and other "consumables" are usually considered expenses because they are not tied to a specific use (unless it's a cleaning company that uses those cleaning supplies to perform a service the company gets paid for).

See the difference?

How you look at things depends on your business and what information you want to get out of your numbers. The main thing is to make sure you're in sync with your bookkeeper and that they record things consistently.

Not understanding the difference between COGS and overhead can cause major problems with your numbers. Practically speaking, when you don't know how much it costs to make a product, there is no way you will ever know how profitable it is.

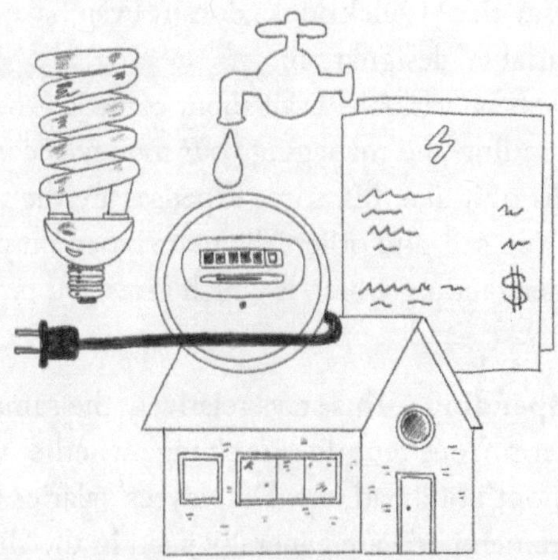

You may be looking for "right" answers: What's the "right" profit margin for COGS? How much overhead is too much? Sorry, there are no magic numbers that work for every business. It depends entirely on your industry. Instead of chasing some perfect ratio, look at your own numbers over the past three years. Take your time. Understand more about where your money is going. What's going up? What's staying steady? What's eating more of your revenue than it used to?

Maybe your COGS is creeping up because your suppliers raised prices. Maybe your overhead is ballooning because you're paying for services you don't need anymore. We've seen owners who've run their business for years without really understanding where their money goes, and it always leads to trouble. When you understand which bucket your expenses fall into, it guides you to price jobs correctly and manage operating expenses.

Fixed vs. Variable: The Control Factor

Every expense dollar leaving your business, regardless of whether it's COGS or overhead, is also either fixed or variable. Sounds like more accounting nonsense, right? It is—and it's not.

Why do we say this? QuickBooks doesn't even have a built-in "fixed" or "variable" designation!

"Fixed" versus "variable" is all about control. Once you get this, understanding and managing your money becomes a lot simpler. Think of it like this: some expenses are the same no matter what you sell, and others fluctuate based on your sales volume. Understanding which is which gives you power over your cash flow.

- **Fixed spending**—This stays relatively the same in the short term. Your rent doesn't change whether you have a good month or a bad one. Employees' salaries (including yours, remember?) are generally fixed in the short term and variable over the long term. Sure, utilities may go up and down over time; month to month, they are relatively fixed. You still pay them every month even though the amount may change. You need some level of spending on office supplies. Employee-benefit programs, insurance, and spending on repairs and maintenance are all required and fixed.

- **Variable spending**—These move with your business activity. We've already shown you that COGS spending is variable. Other things indirectly move with sales including credit-card fees, commissions, advertising/marketing, and sales tax.

The value of understanding fixed versus variable costs is the insights it gives you as you review your performance. Understanding your fixed costs in both COGS and overhead supports understanding what your true fixed costs are and the minimum sales you need to break even.

The Mindset Shift—Is It Healthy or Unhealthy?

Spending money isn't a bad thing. It all depends on what you're spending on: healthy or unhealthy expenses. This brings us back to the emotional side of spending. Healthy expenses are investments that either make you money or save you headaches down the road. Think about paying for a great tax planner instead of a cheaper tax preparer, working with a marketing expert to better tell your story, or hiring that employee who will free you up to focus on bigger things. These feel expensive in the moment, yet they're building something of value down the road.

On the other hand, unhealthy expenses are the ones that drain your cash without giving you anything back. Think about the extra interest you pay because you're always behind on bills, the late fees charged when you forgot to pay something, or fines because you tried to cut corners. One client of ours kept

Lynn

A friend of mine owns a distribution company, and for the longest time, he would spend hours in the warehouse packing customer orders. He genuinely loved it. It was hands-on work that provided a nice break from the office.

One day, I pointed out to him that he was basically valuing himself at $20 an hour. That was his lightbulb moment. Now he has someone else handling the packing while he is out there landing new customers or working on growing the business. He still misses the zen of packing sometimes; his bank account doesn't mind the change, though!

Successful business owners understand this. They know that some expenses are investments that will bring in more revenue. And they double down on them. Before you start cutting everything, figure out which expenses are helping you make money and which ones are bleeding you dry.

inventory in his backyard to save on storage costs—then got hit with city fines that cost a lot more than a warehouse would have.

Healthy expenses make sense. You can explain why they're worth it and how they support your business. The unhealthy ones make you feel annoyed. The real test is whether you're looking at an expense and asking yourself, "What the hell am I paying for?" That's usually unhealthy spending.

We see this in practice all the time. Clients will ask us how to reduce overall expenses, and we don't always agree that they need to. Instead, we dig deeper and look for opportunities to spend healthier so the business can make more. These are the expenses that make the business better: productivity tools, efficiency upgrades, employee training, the cost of hiring a fractional CFO, or (gasp!) even lawyer fees. This is where you spend money to make money.

Marketing/advertising is a big expense people feel conflicted about. Whether business is booming or tanking, you need to be marketing because that is how you get sustainable sales. Most business owners we talk to think, *When business is great, why do we need to invest in marketing? When business is slow, we don't have the money for marketing!*

Another example is employee training. We tell clients to treat it as an investment. Remember: accountants will say to limit spending to increase profit. It's a healthy expense because the goal with training is to make people as efficient, productive, and safe as possible.

Lynn

Even at marketing-driven P&G, I saw marketing budgets cut when sales were slow to protect profit. Isn't that counterintuitive? And here we are, the "frugal, anal" CFO types, advising owners that they need to consistently invest in marketing and advertising initiatives.

Then we'll get the inevitable question, "What happens when I invest in training my employees and they leave?" Our answer is always, "What happens when you don't train them and they stay?" This is a common adage played out in real life with real money. The fact is untrained employees who stick around are a lot more expensive than trained ones who might leave.

We also recommend that you, as the owner, look at how spending money can create more time for you. For example, a virtual assistant can save hours (and money, along with energy) managing your email inbox and calendar.

Quick Win: Sort Expenses into Buckets

Make a list of everything you spend money on. Don't worry about dollar amounts yet—brain-dump everything. Start by asking your bookkeeper to export the details of every account on your income statement. Review every account, listing every vendor, every subscription, and every product or service you pay for. Once you've got everything down, sort it into two buckets:

1. **COGS**—Everything directly tied to making your product or delivering your service.

2. **Overhead**—The everyday costs that keep your doors open: rent, utilities, software, insurance, all that necessary stuff.

Do they align with how your bookkeeper is tracking your money out?

Next, mark which expenses are fixed and which ones are variable. Seeing your spending laid out this way will give you instant clarity on where your money is going. No spreadsheets, no complicated math—a simple list that makes your next financial decisions simpler.

The Bottom Line

Most business owners are shooting in the dark when it comes to money out. They wonder why they're not profitable while hemorrhaging cash on things that don't move the needle. For you, that stops now.

Reducing expenses needs to be the result of becoming more efficient, not cutting for the sake of cutting. When you have the right processes, your expenses will naturally decrease while your productivity increases. You need guardrails, and to invest in making things better. Over time, you'll figure out where you get the best return. And that only happens when you stop avoiding your numbers and start tracking, paying attention to, and treating your money out as strategically as you treat your money in.

You may not know exactly how much things cost in the beginning, and that's okay. Remember: there are no "right" answers. Our guidance will help you focus instead on getting closer to the answer by asking yourself some important questions. The next chapter will guide you to understand more about expenses and how to mitigate them.

CHAPTER 6

STOP THE BLEEDING

Cash beats profit every time, so stop the bleeding!

When clients first start working with us, many of them are already at a breaking point. They don't know what is going on with their numbers, and they still know something isn't right.

Though our solutions depend on their specific situation, our top priority is almost always the same across the board: stop the bleeding. That means identifying and stopping the most immediate financial losses and/or harmful practices putting the business at risk: unnecessary expenses, outdated subscriptions, billing oversights, inefficiencies that are quietly draining profits. Once we get that under control, everything else becomes a lot simpler to manage.

What most don't understand is that though your business might be profitable on paper, it can still be bleeding cash. This happens when more money is going out than you realize. What's even worse is that you may not even know what cash is going out the door! Think about it. Your bookkeeper or accountant pays bills and assigns them to an account, and two to three weeks after the end of the month (best-case scenario), you see the income statement, which you tend to ignore.

A profitable business that runs out of cash is a dead business, even when it was profitable. Yes, you read that correctly.

Profits are important, for sure, and they still lose to cash every time. Cash is the lifeblood of your business. You can't deposit "profit" into the bank, and you can't pay your team or the rent with it. You need real money (actual cash in the bank) to survive.

Cash is the lifeblood of your business. You can't deposit "profit" into the bank, and you can't pay your team or the rent with it. You need real money (actual cash in the bank) to survive.

Our client Sarah demonstrates this reality. She owns a marketing agency that had its best year ever: $2.3 million in revenue and a 15% profit margin—nearly $350,000 in profit. Being up 40% from the year before, she was killing it, at least on paper.

In reality, Sarah was panicking. She was days away from missing payroll, shuffling money between accounts, and felt completely confused. The numbers didn't make sense to her. How could she have record-high revenue and profit and still have no cash? Where did the money go?

Does any of this wondering sound familiar? *Revenue is great, so why does my bank account barely have any money in it?* Then this chapter is for you. We're going to guide you to get clear on where your cash is going, how to stop the bleeding, and how to make sure your business can sustain itself day to day, week to week, and month to month. This chapter is the Band-Aid your business needs.

Where's the Bleeding?

Think about your own life for a second. Have you ever signed up for a free trial that quietly started charging you monthly after 30 days and you didn't realize it for six months? And before you knew it, that "free" trial ended up costing you $300. Businesses do the exact same thing, except the line items are bigger and the impact is often far worse.

In your business, cash doesn't simply hop from your clients' hands straight into your pocket. It takes a little detour. Once it lands in your bank account, it's been sliced and diced like a late-night infomercial, paying salaries, vendors, and taxes while buying software, services, supplies, and insurance. Many of these expenses are justified; others are not. Unless you're paying careful attention, you probably won't realize the difference.

A few of those unjustified expenses (a.k.a. where you're bleeding from) include hidden fees, forgotten subscriptions, late-payment penalties, high interest rates, forgotten/expired/dead inventory, waste, and inefficiencies. Maybe you're paying for software no one uses anymore. Maybe you're over-ordering supplies, paying rush fees because of poor planning, or getting hit with bank charges you didn't even know existed.

Sometimes it's as simple as inefficient processes that eat up labor hours, or clients who consistently pay late without consequences. Two other big sources of missing cash are the money that customers owe you and too much inventory that hasn't sold.

The real question is whether the cash flowing out of your business is going somewhere useful or vanishing into thin air because you got stuck paying for things you don't need. This comes down to asking yourself whether an expense actually helps you get where you want to go (OODA loop). When it does, great. When it doesn't, it's one of the places where you're bleeding. It's not fun to figure this out, and it's still necessary. Because when you don't know where the bleeding is happening, you can't put a Band-Aid, or in some cases a tourniquet, on it.

Stopping the Bleeding

You have to be smart about stopping the bleeding. That means cutting out the tools no one uses, getting rid of recurring charges for things that aren't driving value, and actually scrutinizing every dollar that leaves your bank account. You need to figure out what the essentials are in your business. Everything that isn't an essential needs a damn good reason to stay. Even when there is a reason, that's not the end to all this.

You need to look at everything you're paying out and ask yourself, "Can this be reduced?" "Can it be removed?" "Can it be replaced?" You'll be surprised at how many things are quietly bleeding you dry, including some from those with a built-in level of trust, like professional service providers.

Lynn

I worked with a coffee shop and asked why there were Walmart charges every few days. It turned out that an employee would constantly have to leave the store to pick up something that was out of supply. They would turn the receipts in, with no one asking, "Why does this keep happening?" The employee's time plus higher retail prices equaled bleeding cash. The Costco receipts were another issue. The external bookkeeper was putting them everywhere: "Dues & Subscriptions," "Auto Repair," and, worst of all, "General Shop Supplies." The owner never saw this level of detail, and never knew.

We worked with a client once who was trying to stop the bleeding, and when we looked at her P&L, we were shocked by how much money she was paying her accountant each month. It was at least double what we typically see for a business of her size, and she had no idea what a fair rate was. She told us they weren't even doing a very good job. She decided to let them go and hire someone else. When she told the accountant she was being let go and part of the reason was her high price, the accountant offered to cut her monthly bills in half. In half! It was confirmation she had indeed been overpaying that whole time. Don't let this happen to you. Shop around for all your vendors. Get quotes from their competitors.

Being smart also means getting crystal clear on what is personal and what is business. A $41 Walgreens charge? When it's personal, it doesn't belong on your business card. When it's business, you're still not in the clear because you probably overpaid for something you could have gotten for less from Amazon or a commercial vendor. Either way, you're bleeding money. Tighten this up and set the standard for your business.

Now let's talk about another smart strategy: being proactive with those fees and expenses. Here are some general rules to follow:

◆ When you can pre-pay something at a discount, do it.

◆ When you can invest now to have more later, do it.

◆ When you're carrying a high-interest balance, look into 0% APR transfers or call your credit provider and ask for better terms. Sometimes they offer a break for something as simple as setting up automatic payments. Most people never ask and end up paying thousands more over time.

These small steps buy you time, reduce stress, and free up cash. And freeing up cash is how you survive long enough to grow.

One smart thing is not being cheap. We see it all the time: owners who nickel-and-dime themselves into a corner. They'll spend $10 on 10 things that don't matter and skip the one $100 investment that could actually move the needle. Tripping over dollars to pick up dimes is not how you stop the bleeding. That's how you stay stuck. Think of it like this: being cheap is a short-term play, whereas being smart is a long-term strategy.

It's a Joint Effort

Your people are out there every single day, seeing and hearing things in your business without any context. When they only have half the story, they'll fill in the blanks with whatever they think is happening. Their assumptions are usually way off and not particularly helpful.

Why not tell them what's going on? A little radical transparency goes a long way here. Show them what it actually costs to keep the lights on. Let them see that payroll is your biggest line item. When they know the real numbers, they stop guessing about everything. When you tell them why things are important to you, they will probably even help you find the bleeding. Sharing some of your financial information can really get them involved.

Show them a complete picture and trust them with the truth. Ask them where they see waste. Ask why you're using three different vendors instead of one that offers a 5% rewards program. You can even design an incentive to reward participation and engagement. You'll be amazed at how much smarter everyone's decisions become.

Andy

Our average daily revenues in junk removal during the peak summer months was $12,000—four trucks, each pulling in about $3,000. The guys would see the money come in, as they collected checks and ran credit cards. From their perspective, we were killing it; from my perspective, it took a minimum of $9,000 every day to make that $12,000. The guys had no idea, of course. To them, we were rolling in dough. With that frame of mind, who would be worried about helping us save money?

We decided to get brutally honest. We didn't share percentages or vague numbers; we shared cold, hard dollars. We showed them it costs $6,000 a day to walk in the building and turn the lights on (fixed expense). And then we pay wages, put fuel in trucks, and pay disposal fees at the end of the day (COGS). Now we could start talking about profit, actual cash, assuming people pay their bills on time.

Everything shifted once they saw the real picture. Suddenly, they were spotting ways to save money and being more careful with resources. One guy even found us a better supplier that cut those costs by 15%. They started brainstorming improvements, talking strategy with each other, and thinking like owners instead of employees.

Your Quick-Start 24-Point Bleeding-Control Checklist

Once you've found where your business might be bleeding cash, it's time to act. This doesn't mean you need to make drastic cuts that hurt your operations. It means you need to be intentional with where your money goes. Think of this guide as a systematic sweep through your business to find the leaks you didn't even know existed. Some of these will save you a few hundred dollars; others might save you thousands. The key is going through each item methodically and asking yourself, "Is this still serving my business the way forward?"

Employees/Contractors

- **Review salaries/fees**—Is anyone underpaid or overpaid? People are your biggest expense, so this matters.

- **Manage overtime**—Who's creating it? Do you really need to allow early or late punch-ins?

- **Employee perks**—Meals, celebrations, gifts—though they may be valuable, be mindful.

Expenses/Fees

- **Review everything over $500 annually**—Combine services for reduced rates. Rethink vendors. You'll be shocked by what you find.

- **Audit your credit card**—Who's spending and why? Set some limits.

- **Subscription check**—Kill anything that isn't critical. Be ruthless.

- **Interest payments**—Are you paying for old debt that doesn't benefit you anymore?

- **Bank fees**—Ask your bank to wave them. Or switch.

- **Biggest line items**—Comparison shop your top five expenses.

- **Fees and fines**—Hunt down the reason behind every single one.

- **Utility-bill audit**—Use services like Schooley Mitchell to find savings.

- **Insurance**—Shop it annually. Prices change more than you think.

- **Refinance loans**—Lower monthly payments equals more breathing room.

Vendors

- **Supplier negotiations**—Ask about early pay discounts. Extend the terms when you need to.

- **Quote everything**—Trash, landscaping, cleaning—get three quotes for everything.

- **Vendor terms**—Are you paying early and not getting the discount? Fix that.

Clients

- **Late clients**—Call anyone 30+ days behind. Add interest and fees to your terms.

- **Fire bad clients**—When they constantly demand discounts or complain, cut them loose.

- **Menu/product costing**—Prices rise. Are you keeping up?

Efficiency

- **Waste**—Look for scrap—whether it's on the floor or in the cloud.

- **Update systems**—Could new software simplify tasks and actually lower costs? How could you use AI to make things more efficient?

- **Inventory loss**—Audit your shrinkage rates.

- **Portion control**—Ingredients, drinks, supplies—watch the waste.

- **Employee time**—Do you have too many meetings, or meetings with too many people?

Don't want to do this alone? Talk to your bookkeeper or accountant and let them guide you to dig through the numbers, or check out apps that will scan your financials and show where you're bleeding cash (we'll cover those in Chapter 18).

There are companies out there that will audit shipping, utilities, credit-card fees, waste-disposal charges, and a variety of other spending for free. You only pay when they recover or save you money!

Quick Win: Stop the Bleeding

Grab your phone and open your banking app or pull up your last credit-card statement. Look for any recurring charge: subscriptions, memberships, software services, anything that auto-renews. You'll probably find at least two or three things you'd forgotten about or don't use anymore. Cancel them immediately.

This one action could save you $50–200 or even more each month with literally five minutes of work. It's the fastest way to stop bleeding cash and see immediate results on your bottom line. Hell, this chapter alone will pay for this book!

The Train Station

Stopping the bleeding isn't exactly the glamorous side of business ownership—no one is making inspirational LinkedIn posts about expense audits—yet this is how you stay alive long enough to do what really brings you joy. That's why we had to guide you to clean up the mess before we went any further. This is your turning point—where you stop playing detective trying to figure out what went wrong and start knowing exactly what needs fixing and how to fix it.

In PART III, we're going to introduce you to the people who can support your business moving forward. After we introduce you to your financial team, we'll jump into the data and key performance indicators (KPIs) that will guide you to make smarter decisions. This is the train station where you hop off the "information train" and catch the "action express." Roll up your sleeves and get to work.

PART III

YOUR FINANCIAL TEAM

Whether you like it or not, you are the captain of your financial team. The saddest part about this? You probably never thought you even had one!

You've undoubtedly heard the phrase, "You're only as good as your team." When it comes to your finances, this couldn't be truer. You might be crushing it at what you do best—good for you! Without the right financial backup, you'll eventually hit a wall—no matter how successful things look from the outside. You've probably thought, heard, or said:

"I can't afford it yet."

"I'll figure it out myself."

"I'm not big enough for a CFO."

"I'll use the same person I use for my personal taxes."

And you'd be dead wrong. This line of thinking is going to bite you in the ass. Many "successful" businesses fail every day because they don't pay attention to their numbers. Does anyone wake up on Thursday morning and realize, *Oh, shit! We're out of cash!* No, you can feel it coming. No business owner was ever surprised when they ran out of cash. Your gut feels the pending doom. And your numbers will warn you well in advance when you pay attention. This isn't a scare tactic. It's your wake-up call.

You pee your pants a little? Good. It's time to get serious.

You need a team of six. The truth is that, even though most business owners think they can handle everything on their own or with an accountant, you need up to six different professionals to manage your business finances and also your personal wealth. Haven't hired them, then guess what? You're filling those roles yourself. No CFO? You're it. No bookkeeper? That's you too.

It always feels totally doable—until it's not. A lot of owners cruise along thinking they've got it handled, then bam!—cash flow is a mess, the tax bill is way bigger than expected, and those financial reports might as well be written in ancient Greek. And trying to find good help when you're already in panic mode? That's even more stressful than the actual money problems.

Here is another hard truth: even once you have them, none of these professionals are losing sleep over **your** business. They're service providers with specific responsibilities, not your partners or miracle workers who will solve all your money problems. Your bookkeeper isn't worried about how they categorized your expenses. Your accountant isn't strategizing how to improve your profit margins. Your banker isn't thinking about your Q4 cash flow. That's all on you.

Here is another hard truth: even once you have them, none of these professionals are losing sleep over your business.

The good news? (Yes, there is some good news!) You don't need to become an expert on all things financial. You do need to at least know what they do and don't do before you need them so you can hire people with the right skills to manage your money, ask the right questions, and know when someone isn't doing a good job.

Think of yourself as the general contractor of your business. You don't need to install the wiring—you do need to understand the blueprint and schedule well enough to know what's happening.

What's Next

In the next chapters, we'll break down the six key financial roles:

- Bookkeeper

- Accountant

- Tax planner

- CFO

- Banker

- Personal financial or wealth advisor

You'll learn what each person does, how to work with them effectively, and how to dodge some expensive, ill-informed choices. There is a huge difference between an okay bookkeeper and a rock-star one. We're talking thousands of dollars in savings and maybe even avoiding those fun IRS penalty letters.

Now, this doesn't mean you need six separate people on speed dial. Sometimes your bookkeeper also does your taxes, or maybe you have a different accountant handling different pieces. Some business owners are pretty solid at the CFO stuff themselves when they have good data to work with.

We'll share some real stories—the good, the bad, and the "Wow, I can't believe they fucking did that!" Plus, you'll learn the right questions to ask before hiring anyone and the red flags that will make you run the other way. The bottom line is that your financial team isn't another business expense you're wanting to cut. It's more like investing in really good equipment—it pays for itself when you do it right.

CHAPTER 7

THE BOOKKEEPER

Your bookkeeper will be among the first services you buy—and the most important. Choose wisely.

Think of your business as a house. No matter how impressive the structure appears above ground—vision, sales, marketing, innovation—it will only stand the test of time when it was built on a solid foundation. In your financial house, this foundation is your bookkeeper.

A solid foundation means every dollar gets tracked properly—where it comes from, where it goes—and everything balances out. Though these daily entries might seem boring, they're literally creating the story of your business.

When that foundation gets wobbly, everything else starts falling apart. Your reports are off, your tax prep is a nightmare, and you're making decisions based on bad information. Small, ill-informed choices turn into big problems fast—missed deductions, IRS penalties, or worse, choosing the wrong direction for your business because the numbers are wrong. Sometimes, one little fix can put thousands back in your pocket—or cost you thousands when you miss it.

This isn't some cautionary tale. It's every Tuesday for a lot of business owners. Bad bookkeeping doesn't only cost money; it puts you at risk. That's why bookkeeping matters so much. It

Andy

I was working with a client in my role as a fractional CFO. She came to me looking for strategic financial guidance— big-picture stuff like growth planning, budgeting, and cash-flow strategy. Before we could begin, I needed to review her books to get a baseline understanding of where her business stood. That's when any talk of strategy stopped.

Her books were such a mess that I didn't trust any of the numbers. Categories were all over the place, transactions were misfiled, and some important financial activity was missing altogether. This was more than a mess; it was a potential liability. I asked her to hop into QuickBooks with me and go line by line through her transactions.

Even with a basic understanding of some of the underlying problems, we were both surprised when we uncovered a major error. There was a large expense that had been miscategorized. Instead of being marked as a deductible business expense, it had been tucked away under a vague, nondeductible category. Fixing that single line item in one conversation about her bookkeeping put $7,500 back in her pocket in the form of tax savings.

Missing details like this can end up costing a lot of money. Though this particular story ended up benefiting the client, think about the reverse. Say she had taken a deduction when it wasn't available. She would have inadvertently underpaid her taxes, putting her at risk with the IRS. All because the bookkeeper she trusted didn't do their job properly.

shows you what's happening with your money and what's really making your business tick.

In this chapter, we cover why bookkeeping has the biggest impact, what your bookkeeper needs (and doesn't need) to be doing, what good looks like, and when it's time to stop trying to do it yourself.

The Most Underrated Role in Your Business

The second you filed for your LLC and paid your first fee is the second you needed to start tracking everything. Can't afford a bookkeeper yet? Congrats—you're it!

Don't wait until you're "bigger" to hire help because cleaning up messy books costs 5 to 10 times more than doing it right from the start. When a $50- or $75-an-hour bookkeeper screws things up, you'll eventually pay a $250-an-hour certified public accountant (CPA) or CFO to fix it. Even though the bookkeeper might be the least expensive member of your financial team, their performance is critical because everyone else depends on it. Think of them like the nurse taking your vitals. When they get your blood pressure and temperature wrong, the decisions your doctor makes based on that information will be way wrong. It's the same thing here. Bad books mean your accountant can't do taxes accurately, your CFO can't create a good strategy, and you can't make good decisions.

Your bookkeeper is basically your business historian, recording what actually happened. We can't say this enough: when they mess up, everyone else is working with garbage data. Bookkeepers might not have fancy titles, and yet they're the most crucial. The problem is most people don't really get what they do (and don't do), which leads to expensive choices and major headaches.

What a Bookkeeper Actually Does

Good bookkeepers stick to established accounting principles, keep clean records, and catch issues before they turn into disasters. Here is what they do for you:

- **Transaction recording and categorization**—Make sure every financial transaction is recorded and correctly categorized in accounting software, including revenue, expenses, asset-tracking purchases, loan payments, and equity transactions.

- **Bank, credit-card, and other account reconciliations—** The top priority is to compare accounting records against bank, credit-card, and loan statements so everything matches and nothing is missing. Typically, they connect your accounts to their software to make reconciliations easier. The same verification is needed for accounts receivable and payable, taxes, and other accounts. Oh yeah, every single month!

- **Accounts-receivable management—**Track money owed to the business, send customer statements, and flag overdue payments.

- **Accounts-payable processing—**Track bills, ensure timely payment, and maintain vendor relationships.

- **Financial-record maintenance—**Maintain organized financial records, including receipts, invoices, and financial statements.

- **Financial reporting—**Generate monthly financial reports, including P&Ls, Balance Sheets, and Cash Flow Statements.

- **Software management**—Maintain accounting software so that it is properly set up for business needs.

- **Alerting you when something looks off**—Now and then, things will happen that seem out of the ordinary or are a blip in your performance. A great bookkeeper will highlight these for you before you ask (sometimes you don't notice them at all).

For businesses with under $2 million in revenue, a good bookkeeper usually spends around 10 billable hours per month managing your books—roughly two hours a week, plus a couple additional hours to close out the month. The actual time will depend on how many transactions and how complex they are. Hourly rates across the country range from $35 to $125 (most are between $50 and $75) per hour. This is money well spent when the bookkeeping is done correctly.

What a Bookkeeper Doesn't Do

Here's where people get confused: bookkeepers don't handle everything money related. Knowing what they don't do is as important as knowing what they do. Your bookkeeper isn't responsible for the following:

- **Establishing your bookkeeping procedures**—How your books are organized depends on the type of business and what's most important to know and be tracked.

- **Financial-statement analysis**—Most bookkeepers stop at the "what happened" in their reporting to you. Some may get to the "So what?" and point out what's important for you to understand. They rarely get into the "What's next?"

- **Financial planning and analysis**—This is a "corporate" term for all the forward-looking work completed by financial (not accounting) experts. It includes budgeting, forecasting, pricing analysis, cost management, business/ investment evaluation, product and customer profitability, and business analysis that goes beyond dollars and cents.

♦ **Tax planning and strategy**—Though they provide the data needed for tax preparation, developing tax strategies is the job of a tax-planning expert or your CPA.

♦ **Business strategy**—Though good bookkeepers understand your business model, they're not business consultants.

♦ **Accounting compliance beyond basic bookkeeping**— They will follow accounting rules; however, complex accounting compliance is not their expertise.

Expecting your bookkeeper to handle these responsibilities is setting yourself up for disappointment—or worse, financial disaster. It's like asking the nurse who takes your vitals to prescribe medication or perform lifesaving surgery.

Bookkeeper vs. Accountant; Tactical vs. Technical

One of the most common oversights that small business owners have is expecting their bookkeeper to act like an accountant. Repeat after us: "Bookkeeping is not the same as accounting."

Bookkeepers handle the day-to-day or tactical side of your finances—entering transactions, balancing accounts, categorizing expenses. Most learn through QuickBooks training or on-the-job experience. Though they're great at tracking what happened, most don't analyze or give advice.

Accountants usually have formal degrees and deeper training (we'll talk more about them in the next chapter). Many are CPAs who can actually interpret your data and give strategic guidance. Though an accountant can do bookkeeping, it doesn't work the other way around. Both are important, and they do different things.

As you continue through this chapter and the next, keep in mind that there are not always clear lines between bookkeepers and accountants. A lot of bookkeepers don't prepare taxes; some do. A CPA firm may offer bookkeeping/accounting services and tax preparation, with the work divided between two or three separate people. Understanding this is important so you can figure out what you really need.

Your Books, Your Vision: Why One Size Doesn't Fit All

Here's what catches most business owners off guard: there is no cookie-cutter way to do bookkeeping. Your setup needs to match your business, where you're headed, and what you want to know. Your bookkeeper records what your vision is; they don't create it. You need to decide things such as, *How many accounts do I need? How detailed do my reports need to be?* For example, when you have three revenue streams, your bookkeeper may be fine dumping everything into "Sales," whereas you'll want three separate accounts. They need to know what goes where.

Bookkeeping also isn't a "set it and forget it"–type thing. When you don't know what good looks like, you won't catch problems. Period. Even great bookkeepers need clear direction from you to do their job well. You're still running the show, even when someone else is crunching the numbers. Though we are not saying you need to be an accounting expert, there are three things you must do:

1. Have a basic understanding of how accounting works and what your statements mean.

2. Clearly communicate to your bookkeeper what you expect.

3. Review your statements to make sure you know what they mean.

Hiring a Bookkeeper

Too many business owners make big decisions—hiring employees or launching products—without knowing their real numbers. It's like knowing your salary and having no clue what you spend on clothes or restaurants, except with way higher stakes.

Most owners try DIY bookkeeping to save money, then eventually throw up their hands in frustration and hand it off to whomever is available—a spouse, an admin, or someone fresh out of online courses. Sometimes, this crashes and burns. Other times, it can work out—if you're smart about it.

Andy

I started out as the bookkeeper for my business, getting a crash course in QuickBooks Online (QBO) from the University of YouTube and QBO tutorials. Eventually, the business grew to a place where I could hand it off to someone internally. I gave it to my office manager, who told me that she had previous experience. She was terrible with the structure I valued. She was a total disaster as a bookkeeper. Next, I gave the bookkeeping to my virtual assistant after noticing that she was detail oriented and great at following directions. I trained her myself, and she became an amazing bookkeeper because I had set clear expectations from the start. Same company, same owner, two totally different results.

Not All Bookkeepers Are Equal

Hiring a bookkeeper involves finding someone who gets your business and can keep your financial foundation solid. Don't get distracted by fancy websites or big firm names—what matters is the actual person you'll be working with. You could end up with a rock star or someone totally unqualified, and either way, it's going to impact your business big time.

The fact is different industries need different skills. When you run a coffee shop and your bookkeeper only knows life-coaching businesses, you're asking for trouble. Make sure they've handled stuff like inventory or depreciating assets when that's what you need. A bookkeeper might be amazing with one type of business and completely lost with another. That's why you need to interview them like you would any other key hire.

Andy

I was recently looking for a bookkeeping firm for a restaurant client and reached out to a company that I had used in the past. The first question I asked was, "Have you worked with any bars or restaurants?" They responded, "No, not typically. We do limited-service places like Subway and Culver's, not full service. That industry is a beast, and the fastest way to lose money is to not watch your margins. I've worked with them before, and I know I don't want to work with them again." At least he was honest, right?

Questions to Ask When Hiring a Bookkeeper:

- What types of businesses do you typically work with?

- When do you deliver month-end reports?

- Have you worked with a business like mine (industry, size, inventory, etc.)?

- How do you prefer to communicate, and how often will we meet or check in?

- What software do you use, and what kind of access will I have to my records?

- How do you handle categorization questions or ambiguous expenses?

- Can you walk me through how you would set up the Chart of Accounts for my business?

Remember: Your Bookkeeper Works for You!

Don't forget that you're the boss here, not the other way around. A good bookkeeper will be proactive about keeping you informed and helping you understand what's happening with your money. Here's what you need to expect from the relationship:

- You can set expectations (e.g., "I need my books on the fifth workday of the month; ALL accounts must be reconciled.")

- They review your monthly statements with you to point out key results or changes.

- They can educate you on your statements so you know what they mean.

- You can ask them questions.

When they don't meet your expectations, complete the work on time, or educate you on your results…look for a new one.

Lynn

I worked with the owner of two coffee shops. She had been with a large regional CPA firm and paid them $1,000 per month for nine months. She knew she wasn't getting the service she was paying for and didn't know how to express what was missing. The second time we got together, we sent four pictures from her QuickBooks to her CPA with a note requesting a chat about a refund. She never got a call, an email, or a text. Three weeks later, she received a check for $6,000. Four pictures were beyond damning.

Quick Win: Assess Your Bookkeeping Today

Before moving on, take 10 minutes to think about and answer the following questions. Whether you've hired a bookkeeper or you're still doing it yourself, this is your chance to make an immediate adjustment that could save you time, money, and stress down the road.

Ask yourself:

◆ "Do I feel confident that the person doing my books understands my business model and goals?"

◆ "Do I understand my business model and goals from a financial perspective?"

◆ "Do I know exactly how much money came in and went out last month?"

◆ "Am I getting monthly reports I can actually use to make decisions?"

◆ "Am I receiving my monthly financials in a timely manner?"

◆ "Is my bookkeeping current (are all transactions consistently categorized)?"

◆ "Are my bank, credit-card, and all other accounts reconciliations up to date?"

When you answer no to two or more, it's time to act—whether that means hiring help, finding a new bookkeeper, or simply getting more involved in the process. Your financial foundation starts here. Make it strong.

The Bottom Line

At the end of the day, your bottom line tells the whole story. And that story starts with your bookkeeper. Sure, hiring one might feel like something you can put off—and when you do, you're basically gambling with your entire financial picture. Miscategorized expenses, missed deductions, wonky reports— this stuff adds up fast. Your bookkeeper isn't only recording what happened yesterday; they're literally creating your financial reality. Get it wrong and everything else becomes a house of cards. Get it right and you're setting up your whole financial team to help you succeed.

That's the thing about numbers: they fucking matter. And no one influences the quality of your numbers more than your bookkeeper. Who is ultimately responsible? You.

CHAPTER 8

THE ACCOUNTANT

Now that you understand the role of a bookkeeper—the person providing the foundation for your financial house—it's time to meet their counterpart, the accountant.

Before we go further, so you understand the definition of "accountant," here's some help:

- Merriam-Webster: One who is skilled in the practice of accounting or is in charge of accounts.

- American Heritage Dictionary: One who maintains and examines the business and financial records of a person, company, or institution.

- Oxford American Dictionary: A person whose job is to keep or inspect financial accounts.

Clear as mud, right? A bookkeeper who provides these services is an accountant. So are accountants on your payroll. So is your CPA.

For our purposes, an accountant is someone who has a two- or four-year degree in accounting, deeper technical skills, and more responsibility than a bookkeeper. They also cost a lot more. CPAs are accountants who earned their professional certification through extensive experience and ongoing education in technical accounting and tax preparation. Naturally, they are the most expensive accountants.

To summarize, though bookkeepers do accounting work, not all are considered accountants. All accountants do accounting (insightful, isn't it?) and are more skilled than bookkeepers. All CPAs are accountants; not all accountants are CPAs. Now that we've got that settled...

In the last chapter, we covered how bookkeepers keep your financial house tidy. Now let's talk about accountants—what they actually do (and don't do) and how to find a good one so you know exactly where they fit into your financial puzzle.

Accountants make sure your books follow all the rules that matter for taxes, loans, and reporting your financials to anyone who cares about your numbers. Think of your bookkeeper like you would the person changing your oil at the quick lube and your accountant as the certified mechanic who figures out what's wrong when your engine starts making weird noises. Whereas a bookkeeper keeps things running, an accountant gives you the deeper knowledge so you don't end up with an expensive problem. The key is finding the right one.

Andy

When I started doing my own bookkeeping, I quickly realized that I was in over my head. Though I could categorize expenses in QBO, I still wasn't always sure which categories to use and why. I could follow the steps; I still didn't get the reason behind them. *Was that lunch actually a deductible business expense, or was it just wishful thinking?*

What's the difference between tools, job supplies, and equipment? And why does it matter? I was making it up, dropping expenses in buckets to clear out the queue—not exactly a sustainable long-term financial strategy. I knew that someone somewhere was smarter than me. I was missing a key part of my financial team: an accountant. Understanding that I needed someone in that role was only half the battle; finding the right person was the other half. In retrospect, I was looking for someone who had three things (I didn't know this at the time exactly): (1) a similar risk profile, (2) an understanding of my business, and (3) a willingness to embrace technology.

The first person I hired, who had done my personal taxes in the past, said that she specialized in "everything" accounting (not exactly special). She was an old-school bookkeeper—manilla folders, pieces of paper all over her desk, paper-receipt requests for every purchase. The next guy was someone I'd met at BNI (Business Network International, a networking organization) who owned his firm. He was overly conservative, telling me all the reasons he wouldn't write off what I considered to be business expenses. The next guy was a token military veteran who did everything he could to screw over the government—an "all they do is waste it anyway" type. His advice was to do more cash jobs and split the cheddar with my brother 50/50.

I went from one end of the spectrum to the other. Like Goldilocks, I finally found an accounting firm and someone who felt right. He asked thoughtful questions about what my goals and vision were. He explained tax implications in plain language. He appreciated the transparency that QBO provided versus using the QuickBooks desktop version that most of his company used for client work. And he respected how I wanted to run my business today and in the future. He gave me options to decide from instead of me making it up on the fly.

I've been working with his team for years now, and I'm thankful to have him in my corner. We speak the same language when it comes to my books, financial goals, and personal wealth, creating an invaluable part of a positive, long-lasting relationship.

Technical Mastery and Collaboration

Accountants bring the technical know-how to lock down your financial foundation and make sure nothing falls through the cracks. They keep your records lined up with tax laws, accounting standards like Generally Accepted Accounting Principles (GAAP), and all those regulatory requirements, while giving you a clear view of your cash flow and overall financial health. Think of them as your compliance partner—they catch reporting issues, keep you audit-proof, reduce your risk, and set you up to plan with the rest of your team.

Whereas bookkeepers focus on daily transaction entry, accountants step in to interpret, verify, and fix that data. It's like having a quality-control layer. These roles need to work together seamlessly—your accountant backs up your bookkeeper, answering questions and solving problems behind the scenes. This teamwork prevents errors and makes sure your monthly books close cleanly.

Accountants also play middleman with other service providers. They coordinate with your payroll company, insurance folks, and legal team so everyone is working from the same accurate financial data. This keeps your whole business ecosystem in sync and ready for whatever growth you've got planned.

What an Accountant Actually Does

Good accountants take your clean bookkeeping and turn it into bulletproof financial compliance. They've got the technical chops and attention to detail to help you dodge expensive choices and keep your financial house in order. Though bookkeepers and accountants both handle some of the same stuff, including month-end bank reconciliations and credit-card matching, it's really the accountant's training and expertise that you need for the following:

- **Depreciation schedules**—Manage depreciation schedules for assets, like equipment and vehicles, spreading out their costs over time.

- **Payroll-tax oversight**—Though your bookkeeper or payroll provider may run payroll, your accountant is the one who makes sure that payroll taxes are calculated and filed correctly.

- **Tax compliance for sales, service, and employment taxes**—Accountants make sure that you're filing and paying the correct Department of Revenue taxes—including sales tax, service tax, unemployment tax, and workers' compensation.

- **Audit support**—When you get audited by the IRS, unemployment office, or general liability insurance or workers' compensation insurance, you want your accountant by your side. They help prepare documentation, represent your interests, and work to resolve any issues efficiently and with minimal penalties.

Unlike big corporations that need full accounting departments, smaller businesses don't need nearly as much hands-on time. When you're doing under $2 million a year, you're probably looking at three to five hours of accounting support per month. Don't let those few hours fool you, though—they're absolutely crucial for getting your books closed right and avoiding expensive screwups down the road.

What an Accountant Doesn't Do

As important as understanding what an accountant does is knowing what they don't do, including the following responsibilities:

- **Daily bookkeeping**—Though accountants know how to do bookkeeping, it's not usually part of their day-to-day responsibilities as experienced staff—especially CPAs. Hiring them to enter transactions or track receipts is not only inefficient—it's also unnecessarily expensive.

- **Business or financial analysis and strategy**—Accountants focus on past performance and compliance, not forward-looking decisions. Don't expect them to help you with pricing, growth planning, or deciding when or how to expand. This is the work of business financial experts like those in the financial planning and analysis departments in larger corporations.

- **Proactive tax planning**—Most accountants are reactive. They are working with the numbers your bookkeeper gives them. They will rarely guide you on how to reduce your tax burden throughout the year.

Even though accountants are important for your financial operations, it's good to know where their expertise ends. Sometimes accountants will say that they can also do fractional CFO work. Be careful there. The CFO role is totally different and needs a strategic mindset that we'll get into in Chapter 10. When someone crushes it as an accountant, it doesn't mean they can naturally jump into being a finance person or CFO. When you really need CFO support, you're almost always better off finding someone who specializes in that and isn't trying to juggle your accounting too.

Your Accounting Team Changes as Your Business Grows

There is a natural progression of your accounting support as your business grows:

- **DIY (or something close to that)**—In the beginning and early growth stage, the owner, a family member, or friend does the bookkeeping. A CPA may or may not review before taxes are prepared.

- **Outsource**—As the volume of accounting work grows as the business grows, it makes sense to hire a bookkeeper or CPA firm (that employs bookkeepers or accountants) to manage the books.

- **Bring in-house**—Eventually, there is enough work to bring accounting in-house. Accounting clerks or entry-level accountants replace the external bookkeeper. Accountants get promoted to senior accountant and eventually controller (the top accountant). A CPA with more business-focused experience is used for technical advice and tax preparation.

Hiring an Accountant

When you're ready to hire an accountant, look for someone who understands more than accounting rules and tax codes—they need to get your industry too. You need proactive and clear communication and experience with businesses your size and complexity. CPA credentials are nice to have, especially when you're dealing with audits or need GAAP-compliant reports. They're not always a must, though. What really matters is finding someone who is detail oriented, responds when you need them, and plays well with your bookkeeper and other financial team members.

Questions to Ask When Hiring an Accountant/CPA

- **What types of businesses do you typically work with?** Make sure they're familiar with your industry and the unique accounting, tax, or reporting issues it involves.

- **Do you specialize in compliance, tax planning, or both?** Clarify whether they are primarily compliance focused or also offer strategic tax guidance.

- **How do you prefer to communicate: email, phone, virtual meetings?** Communication preferences matter for ongoing collaboration and efficiency.

- **What software do you use, and are you familiar with my system?** Compatibility with your existing bookkeeping or accounting platform (e.g., QuickBooks, Xero) means a smoother working relationship.

- **Can you coordinate with my bookkeeper, payroll provider, and/or legal advisor when needed?** A good accountant will be comfortable acting as a liaison with other financial partners.

- **What is your availability throughout the year?** Make sure they're accessible when you need them most, especially for quarterly filings or year-end support. There's nothing worse than finding your CPA "too busy" when you're panicking about taxes!

- **What is your billing structure: hourly, monthly retainer, or flat fee?** Understanding the cost up front will help you budget accordingly and avoid surprises.

Treat hiring an accountant like you are bringing on a key team member, even when they're external. Remember: the right accountant doesn't only check boxes; they also help you understand what's happening in your business and ensure that your numbers hold up under pressure and your foundation stays strong.

Quick Win: Schedule a Financial Check-In

Instead of waiting for tax season or year-end to review your financials, block off 30 minutes this week to meet with your accountant—or review your records on your own when you are not working with anyone yet. Use this time to ask questions, flag anything that looks off (we'll cover how to spot these in PART V: Financial Statements), and confirm that your books are up to date.

You can use this check-in to do the following:

◆ Have them provide a complete review of your financial performance, including annual and monthly trends. Ask them to explain the numbers you don't understand.

◆ Ask them for one improvement you can make this month (e.g., automating reconciliations, updating your Chart of Accounts).

◆ Confirm that all recent expenses and revenue are recorded.

◆ Review your current cash flow and upcoming obligations.

◆ Ask about any red flags or overdue tasks.

A regular check-in doesn't have to be long or formal. The primary goal is to catch small problems before they turn into big ones. Doing this, you are less likely to miss out on important details that can protect your business from financial risk.

Closing the Books

When you're building your financial house, getting the details right really matters. Your accountant makes sure your foundation can actually hold up everything you're planning to build on top of it. Without that technical oversight, poor choices slip through the cracks, taxes get screwed up, and you miss opportunities.

Your accountant isn't there to tell you how to run your business—they're making sure the road behind you is clean, well documented, and legally solid. They've got your back on costly choices and keep things running smoothly behind the scenes.

Once your books are dialed in and your accounting process is humming, you're ready for the next piece: tax prep. Because when it comes to taxes, what you report matters as much as how you recorded it—and that's where your tax pro steps in.

CHAPTER 9

THE TAX PLANNER

My accountant said I made money. I don't know where it is, and I always need to come up with more to pay taxes. Why?

A lot of business owners start thinking about taxes at the end of the year. Maybe even the end of January when W-2s are due to employees. Maybe you even have a big red circle around March 15 on your calendar, the day business taxes are due. Or April 15, the due date for personal taxes.

Whatever caught your attention, you're now thinking about meeting certain deadlines and completing your tax return on time. This is called tax filing, another accounting activity related to the past. Filing taxes is the final chapter of last year's financial story.

The real game-changer? Tax planning.

Why? It's the first time we're shifting your perspective from the past to the future. Tax planning (or tax strategy) is way more than merely filling out forms by April 15. You can think of it as the bridge between your bookkeeper and accountant (who handle the past) and your CFO and financial advisor (who plan for the future).

Real tax planning happens all year long, not when taxes are due. Looking ahead with a tax pro can lead to smarter tax decisions and more money back in your pocket. The problem? Most small business owners aren't even aware that there's a difference between filing taxes and planning for them. And honestly, why would they? Too many "relationships" look like this: you agree to use the same people as last year and they file your taxes, call you to say they're done, and ask you to sign. Done.

A tax planner will proactively share changes in the tax laws that may affect your business and ask you a variety of questions as your business evolves:

- Are you expecting any significant changes in your business next year? Sales and profit growth?

- Do you plan to buy or sell equipment or buildings?

- Do you want to talk about the pros/cons of being taxed as an LLC versus an S Corp?

- Do you have any children under the age of 18?

- Have you thought about offering a retirement plan to your employees?

- Do you have a home office?

- In addition to your salary, are you also taking distributions?

- Have you ever heard about the Augusta Rule (a US tax provision that lets homeowners rent out their personal residence for up to 14 days per year without having to report the rental income on their federal tax return)?

- When do you plan to exit your business?

Jennifer, a client of ours, had been running a thriving consulting business for 13 years. She is creative, detail oriented, and had built a strong reputation in her local market. And without fail, as the tax season approached each year, she somehow started to feel like she didn't know a thing about her company.

Over the years, she'd worked with a handful of different tax companies and every experience went about the same way.

Automated email for the engagement agreement, another automated email to upload documents to their portal. She'd stumble through it, worried she was missing something important, and could never actually talk to anyone because they were always drowning in other clients' returns.

She got it: tax preparers are MIA from mid-February to April 15. She kept wishing she had gotten organized earlier so maybe she'd get some actual support. And each year it played out exactly the same as the previous one.

Then, after filing, she would get a letter saying that she was getting a small refund and was "fortunate" she didn't owe anything. Why was that the case? She had no idea! She didn't know what factors went into her tax calculation or whether her firm was doing great work or totally screwing up. After years of running a successful business, taxes were still a complete mystery to her.

Any of this sound familiar?

Many small business owners think exactly like Jennifer: taxes are a once-a-year thing. Returns are filed and they find out what they owe or how much they'll get back. That's the extent of it. The issue is that filing is not strategic advising—and that's where business owners like Jennifer get stuck.

The tax professionals she worked with over the years did their job (as far as she knew). They filed everything correctly and on time. Yet none of them helped her understand how her accounting showed up on tax forms, let alone plan ahead. From their perspective, the job was done. From hers, she was still in the dark—no clearer on what was going on with her taxes than she was before.

And the worst part? When you sign your returns, you are certifying that the returns include everything and were prepared correctly! Let us repeat that—*YOU*, not your CPA or other tax preparer, are signing. You are the one with skin in the game—and have no idea what you signed.

Let's clear up the mechanics of filing returns and the strategy that helps you pay less in the future. Tax filing is about compliance. Think of H&R Block or similar services, or a lot of CPA firms. Data is entered into "the system" and out pops an answer. During a wrap-up conversation, you might hear, "Sign at the X. You owe ____."

Though we don't want to get too far into the weeds, there are a couple things to keep in mind:

- There are blurry lines. Like we saw blurry lines between the bookkeeper and CPA, they also exist between different tax preparers, which we'll get into shortly.

- Taxes are prepared from the information your bookkeeper or accountant gives them. Remember when we mentioned what could go wrong when they screw up?

- CPAs wear many hats. They prepare and review financial statements, do audits, set up accounting systems, consult, and, of course, prepare taxes. Because the tax code changes every year, when you want the best tax service from a CPA, find one that focuses primarily on taxes.

Tax planning is about being proactive. Tax-planning professionals go beyond basic filing. You might hear in a conversation: "Let's look at this line by line so you understand how to reduce what you owe next year."

Who else can provide tax services? There are several alternatives:

- **Enrolled agents (EAs)** are tax experts. All they do is taxes. Though CPAs can offer several services, EAs are specialists. They file taxes and help you plan for what's ahead. They are licensed by the IRS and can represent clients who are being audited by the IRS. Not all, however, offer strategic tax planning, so asking questions before hiring is important.

- ◆ **Tax attorneys** specialize in high-level tax strategy, estate planning, trusts, and business structures. They're going to be more expensive and are great when things get complex. They are less focused on tax preparation and more on strategy.

- ◆ **Financial planners / wealth managers** can help you manage taxes when it comes to investing, retirement-account strategies, income timing, limiting capital gains, and gifting. They sit at the intersection of your business and personal wealth.

- ◆ **Tax-preparation franchises** include H&R Block and others. They are good for filing personal returns—not your best bet for business or serious planning.

- ◆ **Bookkeepers with tax training** can help identify deductions to support tax planning. Keep in mind, they simply do not usually have a detailed, working knowledge of tax regulations.

The bottom line is this: look for the **right person, not the right title**. First, clearly identify what you need, then find someone you're comfortable working with. No license is required for taxes, so anyone can offer their "advice." The only people who are going to do tax planning well are those with deep knowledge, current training, and strong ethics.

It's also important to remember that no matter which type of tax professional you hire, you're still ultimately the one responsible to the IRS.

What a Tax Planner Actually Does

A lot of business owners fall into the trap of thinking their CPA has them covered when it comes to all things taxes. Too often, we find that's not the case. A CPA files for you and often has ideas and recommendations for lowering your current year's taxes. This may be a great idea—that may be poorly executed.

Instead of only looking at what has already happened (e.g., your tax preparer), a good tax planner focuses on the road ahead.

They help you make smart, forward-looking decisions that reduce your tax burden and support your long-term goals. For example, maybe they'll walk you through the pros and cons of pre-tax vs. post-tax savings options so your retirement plans will be aligned with your current income. They can also help you structure how money flows through your business or investments to be more tax efficient, whether that's in how you pay yourself, reinvest profits, or shelter income legally. You might even explore lesser-known strategies, like paying your children through your business. When it's done right, this can shift income into a lower tax bracket and teach your kids about money.

Your tax planner will also help guide you in choosing (or switching to) the best entity type—LLC, S Corp, or C Corp—for your unique situation, because each one comes with different tax rules, benefits, and ways you can pay yourself. It may be appropriate to set up different legal entities. Though doing so creates additional administrative complexity that can cost, it can yield significant savings.

> **Lynn**
>
> I worked with a profitable landscaping company. Every year
> for five years, they bought a new truck for $50,000–70,000
> based on advice from their CPA. Because they could deduct
> (expense) the full amount from income, they would lower
> their current year's taxes. They didn't need new trucks, so the
> money spent created no wealth.
>
> Imagine how much the $60,000 would be worth years
> later after the CPA instead said, "Let's set up a plan where
> you can still take the deduction and put it in savings that
> would grow tax-free." When the $60,000 or so had been
> invested each year at 5%, $300,000 would grow to nearly
> $450,000 over the next 10 years! This is why you need a tax
> planner.

Most importantly, a good tax planner helps you get ahead
of things so you're not caught off guard when it's time to file.
No last-minute scrambles. No missed deductions. Only smart,
proactive planning that puts you in control instead of reacting to
a surprise tax bill.

What a Tax Planner Doesn't Do

Like with other roles, there are many things a tax planner does
not do. They don't manage your investments or advise where
your money needs to go—that's your financial advisor's lane.
And when it comes to tracking expenses, reconciling transactions, or organizing receipts, that stuff is below their pay grade.

Though a tax planner will help you spot opportunities to
reduce your tax burden and make smarter decisions for the long
term, they won't make those decisions for you. They'll give you
insights, options, and strategy—at the end of the day, though,
you're still the one in the driver's seat.

Plan for Taxes Like You Plan for Growth

When you're avoiding your numbers and are lost when it comes to accounting, you certainly don't have a background in tax law. The great news is you don't need one. What you do need is someone who can give you guidance that connects your business needs with the tax code. You also need a basic understanding of three important rules taught to Lynn from Tim, a great tax planner. He was fond of saying that the tax code is equivalent to seven bibles and 30% of the words change each year. We cannot confirm or deny this is true, but knowing that tax rules continually change, it certainly seems reasonable!

Tim's Three Rules of Taxes

1. **It depends.**

    When it comes to taxes, there are rarely black-and-white answers to complex situations. The tax code is full of rules written with phrases like "reasonable," "ordinary," and "necessary," leaving a lot of room for interpretation—and also for confusion. That's why it's so important to work with someone who can explain the nuances. This shows up when you hear about tax preparers who are very conservative or very aggressive in making decisions about your taxes.

2. **One size never fits all.**

    Tax advice isn't one-size-fits-all, and what works for one person or business might be a terrible fit for another. Your income level, business structure, industry, family situation, and even long-term goals will all affect what strategies make sense. Trying to copy someone else's approach—especially based on a social media post or something you overheard—can backfire. A good tax strategy is personalized to your unique situation. Again, tax laws are written with a lot of vague language exactly because there are so many variables.

3. **The fine print giveth, and the fine print taketh away.**

The tax code offers a lot of opportunities, and most of them come with strings attached—rules, timelines, documentation, and exceptions buried in all the fine print. Though you might be allowed to deduct an expense, when you don't follow the correct procedure or keep the right records, the IRS can—and often will—deny it. Remember that audits can go back seven years, and fines and penalties start whenever a violation occurred, not when it was found!

Smart tax planning takes all this into account and looks at the big picture for growth. Are you using the right business structure? Are your transactions timed and reported in a tax-efficient way? Are you leveraging retirement plans and other tax-advantaged tools? Are you paying yourself last and paying the IRS first by setting aside 15% of your money in for taxes before making spending decisions? These aren't once-a-year questions to ask in March or April. They are questions that demand ongoing attention.

Ready to Hire Someone?

Finding the right tax person can make your life a lot simpler. Less stress, more time, and ideally, more money in your pocket. To find the right fit, it helps to ask the right questions. Here are a few you can keep in your back pocket to figure out when someone's going to help you move forward—or will only look backward.

1. Where did you get your training and your license? (No license, no hire!)

2. How much of your practice is focused on planning vs. preparation and compliance?

3. What examples can you provide of strategies you have implemented with others, and what was their impact?

4. How do you stay up to date with tax changes?

5. How often and when will we meet to talk about the year ahead? (Ideally, at least quarterly.)

6. How can you show me different scenarios for different strategies for the upcoming year?

7. How will you work with my financial planner?

8. How long will you typically take in reviewing my returns with me? (When they say "it's easy" or "just a few minutes," RUN!)

Remember Jennifer from our opening story?

She finally realized she had been missing a whole piece of her business puzzle, even though she'd been paying someone to do her taxes for years. When she met with a new tax firm, it was like finally someone actually understood what she needed. Instead of the usual yearly scramble, she had a real two-hour conversation about how her business worked, where she was headed, and how to be way smarter about taxes. They gave her some solid moves she could make right away that were going to seriously help her bottom line.

Now she has quarterly check-ins on the calendar plus a deeper planning session every January, instead of crossing her fingers and hoping she's doing things right.

That's what happens when you stop treating taxes like an annoying chore and start thinking of them as part of your business strategy. With the right people and a little planning, tax season can actually help grow your business instead of being a total fire drill.

Quick Win: Create a Tax System That Supports Strategy, Not Only Filing

Want a simple way to start turning tax filing into tax planning?

First, talk with an expert to completely understand your prior year's taxes. Have them explain current deductions and what type of documentation is needed for each. You're already thinking ahead.

Then, set up your own tax-prep system to stay organized and make smarter moves all year long. Create a digital folder system (or old-school file box if that's your thing) with categories for common business deductions: travel, meals, car expenses, software, education—whatever might be deductible. When receipts come in, toss them in the right spot. Set a monthly reminder to clean it up and stay on top of it.

Here is the smart part: share this system with your bookkeeper and tax advisor early in the year, not only during tax season. When they can see your spending patterns in real time, they can spot trends, opportunities, and potential problems while there is still time to actually do something about them.

Closing the Tax Loop

Filing your taxes is about staying compliant. Planning for your taxes? That's when you get strategic and actually save money. A tax planner helps you think ahead so you can keep more of what you earn and dodge those nasty surprises.

Your numbers are powerful when you actually use them—and expensive when you don't. It's time to stop thinking of taxes as boring paperwork and start treating them like the business tool they really are. When you ask better questions, work with someone who gets your goals, and make tax planning a regular thing, everything shifts. Your bank account will thank you.

CHAPTER 10

THE CHIEF FINANCIAL OFFICER (CFO)

I need a CFO. Chances are that idea has rarely crossed your mind. What's going through your head right now is more like, *Oh, shit! I'm learning what I don't know, and I need help!*

Those two thoughts? Well, they really mean the same thing.

Most business owners don't think about needing a CFO. It sounds too fancy or corporate. You picture someone in a suit, locked away in a glass office, analyzing spreadsheets you don't understand. It feels expensive, intimidating, and entirely out of reach for your business. And besides, your CPA, banker, tax planner, or someone else certainly has your back, right? Wrong!

As two professionals who live and breathe numbers and know what CFOs do, we can say without a doubt that old-school image is outdated. Having a CFO isn't about status. It's about strategy.

Why Every Growing Business Needs a CFO

The CFO is the only management partner focused on the financial future of your business. We can say this for two reasons:

1. Accounting (begins with A) is about "actuals" and "ago." By definition, it records and reports the past. Finance (begins with F) is about the "future"—it's "forward focused."

2. The CFO is the only one who connects the dots between all the other senior advisors to create a clear, unified financial path for your business.

There's a reason why the CFO is typically #2 behind the CEO or president of a larger company. Their work is strategic, spans every other part of the business, and provides value-added guidance that helps your business be more profitable while mitigating risk. That's why we say every business needs a CFO.

> **Lynn**
>
> I was catching up with a friend who suddenly shared, "Someone in my family needs you." His cousin was struggling after taking over not one but two family businesses after her dad passed. One was the chocolate and ice-cream shop he ran for 37 years, the other a 16-year-old coffee shop that had recently been expanded. She stepped into her father's role with courage and soon realized she was alone and overwhelmed. Considering the following, it's no wonder:
>
> - Dad had no transition plan.
> - She had little coffee-shop experience.
> - Neither business had processes to follow.
> - Both businesses shared one income statement.
> - She had no knowledge of business finance.
>
> She assumed a lot of responsibility without a lot of sound business practices in place. And the family had one question after he passed, as often happens: "Where's the money?" Dad left little business or personal wealth.
>
> For decades, everything looked fine from the outside. Both businesses seemed to be doing well and had provided

 a good life for the family. They had a beautiful home, took family vacations, and Mom loved the diamonds she received. Dad and his CPA were the only ones who looked at the numbers.

I worked with them for almost three years. The first priority was to financially separate the businesses so we could see the sales, costs, and profit contributions from each. We streamlined the income statement by creating groups of related accounts so we could look at 10 key lines instead of 60 accounts in alphabetical order. We also got her financials caught up. We started together in June, and just the week before, she finally received her March statements from her CPA!

The second priority was to establish financial and operational KPIs for both businesses. These were tracked for the next 18 months, giving us real data to see what was working and what wasn't. It turned out the coffee shop was actually losing money and dragging down the entire business. The third priority was to bring in additional tax expertise. They got forward-looking advice to unravel the very complex, and costly, legal entity structure their lawyers had implemented.

The family had been pouring time, energy, and money into keeping both businesses running for all those years, thinking it was all working. In reality, the coffee side had been quietly draining resources the whole time. Because everything had been lumped together before, including bank loans for the separate businesses, no one had realized it. There was literally no way to see it. All those long days, late nights, and sacrifices. And the hard truth? It didn't need to happen that way. That realization was frustrating. And heartbreaking.

In the end, she made the difficult decision to close the coffee shop and sell the building to pay off debt. Over the years, she grew as a CEO and gained financial experience. She is now focused on her passion, profitably growing her chocolate business and creating both business and personal wealth.

Sooner or later, you must begin thinking strategically about the financial management of your business. All your other finance team members handle specific tasks. Sure, you have relationships with your bookkeeper, accountant, banker, and tax planner. Are they helping you get better at running your business? Your tax planner and wealth advisor only become critical to have once you've grown successfully.

Like most small business owners, you probably keep the financial side pretty close to the vest. It's not something you discuss with your team or bring up with friends or other business owners. Money feels too personal or complicated to talk about. Silence can be expensive.

Without someone to bounce ideas off of, big financial decisions start feeling overwhelming. You're making calls that affect your business and personal life with no real sounding board. Though you might get occasional advice from a business coach, banker, or well-meaning relative, how much do they understand about your day-to-day reality?

That's why so many business owners hit a wall. On paper, things look fine—they're making money; sales are coming in. So why does it still feel like such a struggle?

We see this constantly: businesses that are technically profitable and still can't seem to get ahead. Maybe cash is tight even after a great month, or they're wondering when they can afford to hire or expand and there is no clear answer. They're stuck making guesses in the dark.

A CFO changes everything. Finally, you have a right-hand partner with expertise at looking across your entire organization from both an operational and financial perspective. Financial management is not only about spreadsheets; it's also about understanding, optimizing, and confidently leading your business. When done well, you'll achieve both real peace of mind and improved actual financial results.

What a CFO Actually Does

Your CFO is the financial expert who truly has your back. They are the quarterback for all the other advisors discussed in earlier chapters. Unlike other financial roles working **on** your business, a CFO works alongside you **in** your business. They do two key things: (1) ask smart, sometimes tough questions and (2) give you the right information to make more-informed decisions.

For example, let's say that although your profit margins look great right now, your pricing hasn't kept up with rising costs. Your CFO can tell you when, and by how much, it is going to drag down profit. Or maybe you're proud to tell everyone about your best-selling product. What happens when that product is the least profitable? We're going to point out that you need to fix the problem or focus on selling the most profitable products.

A CFO is also the person you turn to when you're facing those make-or-break questions: *Can I afford to hire another team member? What will happen when we lose one of our biggest clients? How much of this year's profit will I invest back into the business?*

Maybe even more important than the technical stuff, a great CFO doesn't merely care about your business—they care about you. They're thinking beyond your revenue or your margins; they're asking questions that impact you on a personal level:

- Do you want to grow this business to sell in five years?

- Do you want Fridays off to spend more time with your kids?

- Are you okay taking on some financial risk, or does that keep you up at night?

- Are you willing to sacrifice the life you have to get the life you want?

CFOs help ensure that your business supports the life you want to live. We had a client once whose business was extremely profitable. Great, right? Well, he was completely burning out working 70-hour weeks. We helped him step back and ask, "Is this really how I want to live?" It wasn't, so we helped him create a plan. In this case, it meant hiring more support—so the business worked for him, not the other way around.

Your CFO's job is to make you a smarter, more successful business owner. This means they play two roles: strategic financial partner and teacher. They make sure you understand your finances and numbers and notice when you're merely nodding along and pretending you get it. When they make recommendations, they'll walk you through why they're suggesting one option over another. Most importantly, they keep you focused on the big picture instead of getting lost in the weeds.

What a CFO Doesn't Do

It's understandable for some to mix up what a CFO does versus your bookkeeper, accountant, or tax advisor. Yet they're completely different roles. A CFO is your strategic partner, not your admin person. Don't expect them to enter receipts, balance your bank account, or chase down invoices. Same goes for payroll or paying vendors. Of course, they could do work they are overqualified to do. Honestly, though, paying a CFO for it is like tearing up $100 bills.

They're also not filing your taxes or handling tax strategy. Though they may work with your CPA to spot opportunities or catch problems early, they're not the ones hitting "submit" on your return or keeping up with the latest tax-law changes.

One more thing: CFOs don't do magic. They can't wave a magic wand to fix messy books or broken systems. When your accounting is behind, that needs to get sorted first; otherwise, we're all making decisions in the dark. And when things are messy, it takes a long time to untangle.

Asking "Why?"

You've probably seen this in some way—whether it's *The Office* with its painfully awkward budget meetings or in movies where the CFO is the buttoned-up buzzkill shutting down every big idea—it may seem that a CFO's job is simply to say no. No to spending. No to high-end coffee. No to risk. No to meals. No to anything that might threaten the bottom line. When you hear of a CFO who sounds like this, do not use them!

In real life, a great CFO isn't the fun police. They help you say yes to the right things, the things that will drive return on investment (ROI). They think like scientists running experiments. *What happens when we do this or that? What are the outcomes?* They measure the results and adjust accordingly. To do so, they ask, "Why?"

By asking why, they know which levers to pull (a lot more of these in Chapter 20). This situation happened recently with a client of ours. They didn't hit their revenue goal. Why? Because they weren't doing enough jobs. Why? Because they didn't do enough advertising. Why? They had pulled back on advertising because they were over capacity and didn't have enough people.

After all the questions, we found the real problem wasn't that they missed their revenue goal because of sales. It was that they didn't have enough people.

We figured out how much it would cost to hire five more employees so they could do more work and bring in the money the company needed to make. At first, they were unsure, thinking only that when each new person costs $4,000 per month, that would be $20,000 in extra expenses. We explained that though that was true, that same $20,000 would help them hit a $120,000 sales shortfall. That's a 6x return and a no-brainer investment.

The budget allocated for advertising got moved to recruiting for the next 30 days, which was enough time to recruit an additional six employees. Then the budget got moved back to advertising to increase the number of leads. When those leads converted into projects, the now-trained employees were able to take on additional work. Within days, we had designed a plan that took weeks to implement and delivered financial results within months.

Finding the Right CFO for Your Business

You didn't start your business to be a CFO, so why are you acting as one?

In an ideal world, every business would have a CFO from day one. In reality, most businesses don't. And when you don't have one, then guess what? The CFO is you—and let's be honest, you probably didn't sign up for that job and are likely not qualified for it.

Most business owners bring in a CFO only after something forces their hand. The trigger moments usually fall into one of three camps:

- **A moment of crisis**—Cash flow dries up, an unexpected tax bill lands, or your finances suddenly spiral and you have no idea why.

- **A period of growth**—Business is booming, and you're overwhelmed. You need systems, forecasts, and someone to help keep it all from unraveling.

◆ **A creeping sense of shame**—You start to admit you need to understand your numbers better, and every financial report seems like it's written in another language.

Finding the right CFO doesn't have to be overwhelming. You probably don't need someone full-time, only the right person for your current stage. Most small businesses can start with a fractional CFO who puts in a few days to get you on track, then maybe a couple hours monthly after that. It's an investment in your business. Even without an ongoing contract, you need someone to call for advice on big decisions. At around $250–500 an hour, think of it like hiring a lawyer—you bring them in to protect your interests and make smart moves from the start, not after everything falls apart. A CFO provides the same value.

When you're talking to candidates, find someone who has worked with businesses like yours. Ask about what size companies they typically support, what industries they know, and whether they've helped other owners with similar challenges. You want someone who connects your numbers to your goals, not merely hands you spreadsheets. And run from anyone promising huge savings or instant results—this stuff takes time.

Think about what your business actually needs, because there are two main types of CFOs:

◆ **Former accountants**—CPAs who've left firms or controllers who got promoted. They are naturally focused on making sure financial statements, payroll, and taxes are bulletproof—and are great when you need more accounting expertise.

◆ **Former financial leaders**—People, like both of us, who either grew up as financial business partners or have run their own businesses. We bring a more strategic perspective to help you actually manage and grow your business.

Finally, trust your gut. This isn't only business; it's personal. Your CFO will see all your financial wins, losses, and everything in between. There will likely be conversations about your family finances as well. Whoever you work with, you want to feel comfortable asking the "dumb" questions you think you "should" already know (there aren't any). You're not hiring someone to judge you; you're hiring a partner who meets you where you are and helps you move forward with confidence.

Quick Win: Go CFO Shopping

For those who have never worked with a CFO, start by talking to a few. Prepare by defining the problem(s) you want solved, the level of support you need, and the budget you're comfortable investing. Be honest about where you're stuck and whether you want strategic guidance, hands-on work, or both.

After pulling this together, reach out to three to five fractional or full-time CFOs and ask them how they support business owners like you. You're not committing to anything—this is a learning exercise.

Ultimately, you want a CFO who fits your style and works with you, not strictly for you. Ask each of them the following questions to start your assessment:

- Is your experience predominantly accounting or finance?

- What is your approach to strategy?

- How do you help owners make smarter decisions?

- How do you think about risk, growth, and profitability?

This will help you get familiar with how CFOs work and what kind of personality or approach might be the best fit for your business. It's also a great way to build confidence and clarity before you decide to bring someone on. Think of it as "CFO shopping" with no pressure to buy.

Looking Forward

In the end, your financial results are simply a mirror of your past decisions and behaviors. A great CFO makes sure those decisions are smart and serve your long-term success. They're there to help you move forward—with peace of mind and a clear plan. They don't simply tell stories—they help you write a better one.

CHAPTER 11

THE BANKER

When you need money and haven't talked to a banker yet, you're too late. Most businesses that fail were profitable; they simply ran out of cash.

Most business owners haven't talked to an actual human who works at their bank in a while. Between mobile deposits, online bill pay, and automated everything, walking into a bank—or even knowing someone at your bank—may feel like a thing of the past. Unless you're dealing with a loan or a problem, you likely haven't had much reason to meet with a real person. And yet building a relationship with your banker is one of the smartest business decisions you can make.

Your banker isn't only someone who stamps checks or processes wire transfers. They're a potential powerhouse on your financial team—right up there with your accountant, tax planner, and CFO. The banker is the one who can open the doors to much-needed capital.

You've probably heard, "You need money to make money." Old-school wisdom? Sure. Any less true? No. Running and growing a business takes cash. Whether it's to buy inventory, pay your team, invest in marketing, upgrade equipment, or keep things steady during a slow period, it all takes money.

Bootstrapping can work for a while, though there will come a point where your next big step may be out of reach.

You Can Wait...

Sure, you can wait until your business earns enough money to make that next move. You can save up for new equipment, wait a year to launch your next product, or hold off on hiring that extra help you desperately need. And sometimes, that's the smart move. Other times, waiting holds your business back. It keeps you stuck in survival mode, trying to get through the month, instead of stepping into growth mode.

Let's say you run a small bakery and you know that adding a second oven would allow you to double your output and meet demand. Do you wait until you've saved enough to buy it outright—while missing out on all that potential revenue in the meantime? Or do you look at the numbers, run the projections, and realize that with the right financing, that oven will pay for itself in six months?

Think about it from a personal standpoint. Would you wait to save $500,000 to pay cash for a house? You'd be dead by then. With a banker's help, you can buy the house today. Even though it will cost you more money, you'll have somewhere to live now and an asset in the future.

Debt is not a dirty word. Yes, mismanaged debt can sink a business. What about strategic debt? That's a growth tool. The right kind of debt—used at the right time—can be the smartest move you make. The key is to know your numbers. Can you afford the payments? How long will it take to see a return? Is this debt helping your business grow or helping you survive?

Money can solve most problems. It can accelerate growth through sales and marketing. You can buy time by hiring an assistant. You can buy machinery to reduce COGS. It smooths out cash flow. It helps you grab opportunities. A business line of credit, even one you never use, gives you peace of mind. That's where the right banker—and the right relationship—comes in.

You're Not Only Asking for Money—You're Building a Relationship

When it comes to banking, business owners usually show up late to the conversation and in crisis mode. Maybe they mixed personal and business finances (a big no-no!) because they never opened a business checking account—a day-one task, along with getting an employer identification number (EIN). Maybe they've run out of cash (the reason most businesses go under) waiting for customers to pay them, waiting for inventory to sell, or mismanaging personal or business debt. By the time they decide to go to the bank, they are already underwater. It's probably too late for the banker to do anything at that point.

That's why building the relationship before you need it is so important. When the shit hits the fan—and it always does—you want to know someone you can trust is already in your corner. Like all good relationships, the one with your banker takes time to develop. Build it early. That means **before** you need money.

The best time to ask a banker for money is when you don't need it. Maybe this seems counterintuitive. Maybe you think you're fine. After all, you have money coming in and you're paying expenses on time—things look good. Get a loan or line of credit when your accounts receivable (AR is money people owe you) is the strongest and have money in the bank, not when you're desperate to make payroll. Even when the money sits there for a while or is never used, at least it's available.

We know one business owner who was able to get $160,000 approved and in their account within 48 hours—because the banker already knew them and had seen their books. Another, with a thriving law firm, was able to take a line of credit to prep for tax season to bridge the gap between earning and reporting income. A construction business used its line to buy equipment ahead of client payments. A retail business leveraged 80% of its receivables to make payroll. These are the real-world examples of how a banker, and the bank's money, can keep you in business.

Andy

My parents have been in business for over 30 years without ever having established a solid relationship with one banker. They were at the same bank the whole time—never with the same banker, though. Every time they needed money, they repeated the same song and dance: go to the bank, ask for a commercial banker, sit in the uncomfortable chairs, and wait their turn like everybody else does, even though they are business owners depositing more money than the average bank customer ever would. The banker would ask them for their life story, financials, etc., and my parents would get frustrated going through the same process every time.

When I first started my business, I thought that's how it always was. I went to the same bank at which I'd deposited my first communion check. I told them I wanted to open up a commercial checking account and credit card with my EIN. That was pretty much it—a transactional relationship. For the first year or so in business, that was plenty fine: I would deposit checks, give a friendly wave to the guy that set up my accounts, and move on with my life.

And then I wanted to do more than run my business; I wanted to grow it. I needed more than a transactional relationship from a big-box bank to join me on the journey of purchasing my first building. I needed support. I needed someone who would see the big picture. I needed someone to think strategically. I no longer needed products; I needed a partner.

What a Banker Actually Does

At a basic level, bankers handle relatively routine—and still critically important—stuff. They help you borrow money, buy financial products, and manage your day-to-day business banking with your checking, savings, and merchant accounts. They offer term loans, lines of credit, and Small Business Administration (SBA) loans. Whether a bank or SBA loan, they'll usually want your last three years of tax returns and financials because your history is considered a good indicator of what you'll keep doing, and their main concern is making sure you can pay them back.

A good banker is way more than transactions, though. They're a resource, a sounding board, a guide. They can help you figure out the best type of loan for your situation, check when you're financially ready, spot potential problems, time your application when your numbers look strongest, and connect you with resources you didn't even know were out there.

What a Banker Doesn't Do

Bankers don't perform miracles. A lot of business owners think bankers can step in and offer funding no matter what—even when their business is underperforming or they lack basic financial discipline. That's not the case, even when you have a strong relationship with their bank.

When you go to a bank with no plan, poor financials, and no demonstrated effort to clean them up, you're not going to get the green light. Bankers will give you advice and provide resources. They won't fix your business for you.

A banker once shared a story with Lynn about a customer who applied for a $200,000 loan to remodel their retail shop.

Despite having a solid history with the bank, he had to tell them he couldn't help them. Why? Their sales and profits had declined every quarter for eight straight quarters. The owner had no idea! "That can't be right; my CPA is one of my best friends!" He learned some hard lessons that day. He didn't know his financials. He had trusted someone too much. He didn't understand the story behind his numbers. And he was not getting a loan.

Banking Isn't Monogamous

When it comes to banking relationships, feel free to play the field. You're not expected to be loyal. Bankers know this. Date a few. Find the right fit for where you are right now and understand that things can change. Diversify where your money lives—when your banker isn't loyal to only you in your industry, don't feel the need to be loyal to them.

One of our clients met a banker at a regional bank who specialized in local real estate and took a risk with him with an SBA loan. Great. When he went back a year later for more capital, they turned him down. "Too risky," they said.

Lesson? Shop around. And when you do, think about the differences. Big banks are great for their technology, credit cards, and automation, yet it can seem tough to build a personal relationship with one. Though mid-sized banks may lack the flash, they are often more flexible with loans and credit lines. Local banks and credit unions offer great personal service and niche products like auto loans, equipment loans, and a home-equity line of credit (HELOC)—however, they might lack technology, a cash-back credit card, or accessibility outside of a metro market.

Note of Caution: Predatory Lenders

When a traditional bank says no, there are always alternative sources that are willing to lend you money. Some are decent—nontraditional lenders that move fast, sometimes approving unsecured loans in under 24 hours, usually at higher rates. Others? Not so much.

Stay away from loan sharks and hard-money lenders. Some will lend for real estate deals or flipping properties at brutal costs—we're talking 20% interest with repayment due in months. When timing doesn't go perfectly, you're in trouble fast. Also avoid payday-loan-style lenders that charge around 30% interest or more. Sure, they'll approve you quickly, and the cost will eat any profit and only put you deeper in the hole.

We've seen business owners take these loans out of desperation and get trapped in cycles that are hard to escape. One client took a loan with daily repayments that drained their cash flow so badly they couldn't cover payroll without more debt. It spiraled quickly.

Bottom line? Desperation is expensive. Plan ahead by building a relationship with your banker, and get your finances in order so you don't end up borrowing from a lender that profits off your lack of options.

Quick Win: Build Your Banking Relationship (Before You Need It)

When you've never worked directly with a banker, this may feel overwhelming. You're probably thinking, *Whom do I even call? What do I say? Do I need an appointment? Am I going to look dumb?*

Let's make this simple:

- **Start with the bank where you already have a business account.** Call the main branch or walk into your local branch and ask, "Who handles small business relationships?" or "Can I set up a time to talk to someone about business banking products?"

- **When you don't like the bank you're at or don't feel supported, shop around.** Ask other business owners who they bank with and trust. Not all banks—and not all bankers—are created equal. You're looking for someone who gets small business, will listen to your goals, and will offer you solid advice that's tailored to your needs.

◆ **Before the meeting, prepare.** Take a good look at your financials, notice the trends, and think about how much you might need. You know we have to say it again: "Know your numbers!"

◆ **When you do get a meeting, here's what to bring:**

- A recent snapshot of your financials (P&L, Balance Sheet, and Cash Flow Statement)

- A short summary of what your business does

- A list of any upcoming investments you might need capital for

◆ **In the meeting, ask:**

- What types of credit products would I qualify for today?

- What would help improve my eligibility?

- How does my cash flow look from your perspective?

- Are there services I'm not using that could help me manage my money better?

- Would I qualify today for a line of credit?

Keep in mind that you may get turned down by several banks. It can be frustrating. You sit down with a banker for an hour to go over everything and hear how much they want to earn your business. Then they call you to say you aren't approved. Don't get discouraged. Your inability to get a loan right away doesn't mean you've failed. At least you know where you stand and what you need to work on.

One of the smartest things you can do right now is ask your banker, "What do you need from me today to eventually approve me for a loan?" That question alone will put you ahead of most business owners.

Build the Relationship

A banker is more than money. Even though it may be hard to see right now, your banker is one of your best allies. They can connect you to other professionals, give insight into trends in your industry, and even alert you to other opportunities. Don't wait until you're stressed out, behind on bills, and desperate for a quick fix to think about banking.

Find a banker who sees you as a partner, not merely an account number. Get curious. Ask questions. Build the relationship, ask for what you need **before** you need it, and use the bank's money to accelerate your growth.

CHAPTER 12

THE FINANCIAL ADVISOR

You started your business because you wanted the freedom to make the best muffins ever, didn't you? Let's be honest. No, you didn't. You wanted the freedom to make money. Yet many business owners focus so much on day-to-day business challenges they forget this fundamental purpose: to build personal wealth and achieve financial freedom.

Planning to sell your business for a big payday? Smart move! Don't bet your retirement on it. Even the best businesses don't always deliver the exit their owners dreamed of. The key is balance. Instead of pouring every dollar back into operations, consistently funnel money you take out of the business into personal wealth-building investments. And definitely work with someone who really knows their shit! Your future self will thank you for not putting all your eggs in one basket.

Samantha was in her early 20s when she opened a 401(k) account through her employer. When she left that job, she rolled the account over into another fund. To do this, she worked with the financial advisor her parents had used for years. She had a small amount of money, typical for someone starting their career, and trusted the advisor to increase her investment. After a few years, Samantha (finally!) checked on her account, and what she discovered shocked her. Her 401(k) was actually getting smaller over time instead of growing.

When she called her advisor to ask what was happening, his response was even more disturbing: "Well, I thought you wanted to keep the account." The annual management fees he was charging exceeded any interest the small account was earning. In other words, Samantha was paying him to lose her money—and he never thought to mention it. She realized that day that no one would ever care about her money as much as she did. And the same will hold true for you!

Samantha's story gets worse. This same advisor failed to advise her parents to diversify their investments and pull money out of stocks as they approached retirement. When the 2008 recession hit, they lost a significant portion of their wealth at the worst possible time—too close to retirement to recover.

Maybe Samantha's situation sounds familiar. Maybe it sounds to you like it's in another language. Either way, it's important. In Chapter 1, we identified your destination—your vision for your financial future. This chapter focuses on how to get there by ensuring that some of the money you earn through your business transitions into personal wealth.

As a business owner, you'll have more options to earn tax-advantaged money than those who work as a W-2 employee for someone else:

- **Retirement plans**—For you, explore a solo 401(k). When you have employees, you can set up an SEP IRA (simplified employee pension individual retirement arrangement) or a simple IRA without the complexity of a 401(k). The next level is to offer a 401(k) plan.

- **Health savings accounts**—These offer opportunities for tax deductions, tax-deferred growth, and tax-free withdrawals for expenses.

- **Equity and profit-sharing plans**—These include everything from simple employee bonuses and profit sharing all the way to an employee stock-ownership plan (ESOP) as part of your exit planning.

♦ **Executive benefits for owners or key employees**—These include deferred compensation and cash-value life-insurance plans.

♦ **Real estate investment**—This can be business related or personal (e.g., buying the building your business leases).

The specifics of most of these are well beyond the scope of this book. We simply want to increase your awareness of the possibilities out there. Unless you have a great wealth advisor or tax planner, or go looking for them yourself, you may never hear about these opportunities. Our goal today is to get you started on creating personal wealth for the lifestyle you want.

The Numbers Behind Your Personal Wealth

Want to grow your personal wealth? All you have to do is invest money in things that do well over time, for a long time. In the finance world, the amount you invest is called "principal." How quickly it grows is called your "rate of return." Say you put $100 of principal in a savings account with a 5% rate of return. Over one year, it will grow to $105 [$100 + ($100 × 0.05)]. The next year, it will grow to $110.25 [$105 + ($105 × 0.05)]. Your original $100 will increase every year through the power of compound interest. The earlier you start, the more you end up with. This is why you want to start building your personal wealth as early as possible.

Let's go back to Samantha for a moment to see how this works. Had she invested $1,000 when she was 26, achieved a stock-market average of an 8% rate of return, paid 1% in fees, and did nothing else, by the time she was 65, that $1,000 would have grown to $14,974.

Let's say she developed a habit of saving $1,000 more every year. At 65, she would have had $200,615. Had she waited to start saving until age 36 and wanted to have the same $200,615, she would have had to have added $2,210 each month instead of $1,000. Waiting until age 46 to start, she would have needed to have saved $5,264. By the time she was 56, her monthly saving requirement would have soared to a whopping $16,584!

Where you invest is complicated. There is a wide variety of investments you can make, and every one has different factors that will affect your returns, including taxes, inflation, and the economic cycles.

These same factors add to the uncertainty of the future value of your business, which is why we urge you to use earnings from your business to also create personal wealth. This will help you retire with the lifestyle you want when your business doesn't sell for what you wish, hope, and pray it will be worth!

Understanding Basic Investment Accounts

Think of investment accounts like different types of piggy banks for your money. Each savings plan has its own rules about when you can access it, what tax benefits you get, and how much you can put in each year.

Once you have plans set up, you need to decide what to put inside: generally stocks, bonds, and mutual funds. A stock is a small piece of ownership in a company, a bond is essentially a loan you give to a company or government, and a mutual fund is a collection of stocks and/or bonds managed by professionals. One type of mutual fund that passively tracks a market index like the S&P 500 is an index fund, which gives you market exposure without trying to pick individual winners.

New business-owner investors can stick with low-cost index funds in tax-advantaged accounts like 401(k)s and IRAs. Think of a 401(k) as your employer's retirement plan (often with free matching money—take it!) and an IRA as something you set up yourself. Though both offer tax perks, you can't touch the money without penalty until your reach age 59½. Traditional accounts save you taxes now; Roth accounts (more on those later) save you taxes later.

Major brokerages like Vanguard offer low-cost index funds with minimal fees. For individual stocks, you can buy fractional shares of established companies directly. Set up these same retirement plans for your business and people—they're gold for attracting and keeping good employees while helping you save too. When the DIY approach starts feeling overwhelming, that's your cue to call in a financial advisor who can sort through the noise for you.

What a Financial Advisor Actually Does

No matter what kind of support you're looking for, a traditional wealth advisor will usually start by helping you analyze your current financial situation and investment accounts. They may have you fill out detailed information about how you make money and where it all goes. Then the advisor will ask about your future goals—maybe buying a house in 5 years, saving for your kid's college in 10 years, or retiring by age 62. Next, they will help you figure out how much money you'll actually need to hit those goals and what strategies could get you there.

Traditional firms generally stick to conventional investments like stocks and bonds. Depending on the firm, they may have various financial products that could work for your situation. They'll walk you through their recommendations, help you set up new accounts, and create a strategy for funding those accounts.

What a Financial Advisor Doesn't Do

A lot of financial advisors tell potential clients that they can be a one-stop shop for all their financial needs. "Estate planning? We can help with that. Life insurance? We got you!"

Proceed with caution.

As you've learned by this point in the book, you want to hire people who are experts in niche areas. Estate-planning attorneys are a good choice for setting up trusts, wills, and other legal structures to protect and transfer your wealth. Not your financial advisor. Even though someone says they're able to serve in multiple roles doesn't mean they are your best option. For example, Andy has his life-insurance policy at a bank that also provides financial advisory services. Every time he has a yearly check-in call with the account manager who handles his policy, he says he wants to talk to Andy about his business-savings strategy. Andy tells him each year that he already has that covered. Beware of people in these roles trying to snap up extra business from you by managing everything you could possibly need.

How to Choose the Right Financial Support

Assuming you've thought about getting financial help at all, you've likely already encountered financial advisors. We meet some of these people every time we go to a business networking event. Of course, we also meet bookkeepers, accountants, and tax-prep people. Financial planners are a different breed. That's because their work is really sales. That's right—sales, not finance. Though many have valuable financial knowledge, their main job is to bring in new business, sell financial products, and retain clients. Other people in their company do the business analysis and actual investing.

Given these realities, how do you find the right financial support for your wealth-management needs? Here are some key considerations:

1. Identify What You Actually Need

Before hiring someone, clarify what aspects of personal wealth management you need help with. Are you struggling with retirement planning or investment management? Are you concerned about your tax strategy? Are you thinking about estate planning and insurance planning?

A financial advisor might not be the best person for estate planning (consult an attorney) or tax strategy (find a tax planner). Educate yourself as much as you can. There are plenty of educational resources on this, including the book *MONEY: Master the Game* by Tony Robbins, in which he notes, "You can't have a plan for your money without having a plan for your life. When you don't educate yourself, then you'll never get out of the trap."[8]

2. Ask What They Don't Do

One of the most revealing questions to ask someone is, "What services do you NOT provide?" The best thing they can tell you is what they don't do. Quality professionals are clear about their limitations and have a network of specialists they can refer you to. As we've talked about, be wary of those who claim to do everything.

3. Understand Their Compensation Structure

Financial advisors typically make money in three main ways: (1) percentage of assets under management; (2) commission; (3) flat fee or hourly rate.

Percentage of Assets Under Management (AUM)

In the most common model, wealth managers get paid a salary and charge you an annual fee of 1–2% of whatever they manage. When they're managing $500,000 of your money, you might pay $5,000–10,000 per year. The more money they manage, the lower the percentage.

Here is what you need to remember: a financial advisor charging 1% annually needs to help you beat the market by more than 1% for you to break even. Research shows very few fund managers consistently outperform index funds over time, and those who do usually work with billionaires, not small business owners.[9]

Getting somewhat investment savvy and creating your own portfolio of index funds is probably more effective than paying someone to actively manage your investments. Not everyone can do this, and that's totally fine! For example, when your money is sitting in a checking account earning 0% and an advisor gets it into an IRA that earns 6% minus their 1% fee, you net 5%—way better than before! But when you already have a self-managed IRA earning 6% and bring on an advisor, you'll probably net less than you did before.

The key takeaway: the less you pay in fees, the more money stays invested and working for you. Even small percentage differences compound dramatically over decades.

Commission

Some advisors get paid when you buy products they recommend—like earning 5–7% when you purchase a certain mutual fund. You won't see a direct bill because those commissions come out of your investment returns. The conflict of interest is obvious: they might push products that pay them the most rather than what's best for you.

There are a ton of these kinds of "advisors" out there. Hell, we get DMs on LinkedIn every week from these people. Here are some of the actual LinkedIn taglines that came up recently in our inboxes:

- "Stop your tax & financial chaos in 30 days! Helping service-based business owners ($200,000+ in revenue) find a path to financial freedom."

- "Empowering individuals to create their own tax-free or tax-advantaged banks for investment and ensuring a risk-free retirement that never runs out of money!"

Feels salesy, right? That's because it is.

One important thing to know is whether your financial professional has a fiduciary duty to you—meaning they're legally required to put your interests ahead of their own. A registered investment advisor is held to this standard. Honestly, the bar isn't that high. They only need to recommend products that are "suitable" for you based on your situation and goals—not necessarily the best option for you out there.

Flat Fee or Hourly Rate

Fee-only advisors charge either a flat annual retainer ($2,000–7,500 depending on complexity) or an hourly rate ($200–400 per hour). This approach minimizes conflicts of interest because their compensation isn't tied to specific products. However, you'll need to write a check for their services, which feels more expensive. Some advisors use a fee-based model that combines fees and commissions. This hybrid approach can be confusing—you might pay a lower percentage of AUM and the advisor still earns commissions on product sales.

4. Find Someone Who's Aligned with Your Goals

When you want to grow your wealth, find a financial advisor who works with people who have a higher net worth than you currently do. You want someone who can help you reach your future goals, not merely manage where you are now. Also consider age compatibility—when you're in your 30s, working with someone close to retirement might not be ideal since they may not stick around long. Turning this point upside down, working with someone who has seen more market ups and downs may have a greater perspective than someone newer to the industry.

Think about the type of firm too. Big names like Thrivent, Northwestern Mutual, and Schwab offer more standardized, one-size-fits-most options—like shopping at Home Depot. Smaller boutique firms are more like that specialty shop in town: more personalized, sometimes higher quality, usually pricier. Either can work well depending on your goals and how customized you want your investments to be.

Watch for Red Flags

When choosing a financial professional, watch for red flags that could signal trouble. When they can't clearly explain how they get paid, push specific products without showing you alternatives, or guarantee returns, be careful. The market doesn't make promises, and neither can they. Avoid anyone who gets annoyed by questions or only calls when they want to sell you something. A good advisor is transparent, works with you, and focuses on your goals—not their own agenda.

Quick Win: Create a Personal Wealth-Management Checklist

Don't let your business success come at the expense of your personal financial future. Take 15 minutes today to jump-start your personal wealth strategy with these steps:

◆ Define one clear financial goal that's only for you—not the business.

◆ Make a list of what feels confusing: investments, taxes, insurance, retirement. That's where you need support.

◆ Commit to interviewing at least one financial professional this month who understands both personal and business finances.

◆ Choose one tax-advantaged account [e.g., IRA or solo 401(k)] and start contributing—even a small amount.

◆ Set up a recurring transfer from your business account to your personal savings.

Final Thoughts

When it comes down to what you can do with your money, you really only have three choices. You can spend it/give it away, pay off debt, or save it. For most business owners, saving often (and mistakenly) comes last. We'll cover this in more detail in later chapters. For now, remember this important lesson: whether for your business or your personal wealth, no one will ever care more about your money than you do. Stay engaged, ask tough questions, and make your personal wealth management a priority—not an afterthought.

For now, remember this important lesson: whether for your business or your personal wealth, no one will ever care more about your money than you do.

As a business owner, you've already shown the initiative and courage to take control of your professional life. Isn't it time to apply that same mindset to your personal finances?

PART IV

DATA (YOU SAY "DATA," I SAY "NUMBERS")

You say you don't like numbers. We're calling bullshit!

Do you like to be on time? Do you know how much dinner at your favorite restaurant costs? Does your blood pressure matter? What about phone numbers? Your bank-account balance? Calories on that frozen-pizza nutrition label you pretend not to read while scarfing down slice after slice?

The fact is you live and die by numbers and data every single day. What's the difference between that and your business numbers? Simple: you were never taught how to use your business numbers. And because you weren't, and because the word "data" is scary, you avoid it like the plague.

You don't know where the hell to start. You don't know what to look for. You don't know how to pull the data. Maybe you're afraid of what you might find lurking in those spreadsheets— like discovering that your business has been bleeding money while you've been playing pretend CFO (forgot that was your job, didn't you?).

We're going to address all these things. Right here, right now.

Think about your health for a second. When you go to the doctor, the first thing they do is check your vitals: blood pressure, temperature, heart rate. There's a reason why they do that. They need this data to see where you are now and figure out what might be off before your condition spirals. The doctor uses these numbers along with the narrative you tell them to figure out the true story. Even without knowing the exact cause and effect of your numbers, you listen to the doctor when they say something is high or low.

Your business is no different. It has vitals too.

When someone tells you your profitability is down, it triggers the same gut reaction as hearing your blood pressure is too high: *that sounds bad*. But do you actually know what it means? Do you know what's causing it—or how to fix it? With your business, you're your own doctor. So where's your business stethoscope?

Your gut has gotten you this far. Maybe it's even helped you build something pretty damn impressive. But when you want to scale and want sustainability, you need more than instinct. You need your vitals—you need the data to be proactive instead of reactive. Think of it as regular checkups for your business. Early warning signs. Preventative care instead of only going to the doctor when something is wrong. You can't wait until the bank account is low, the invoices are piling up, or your team is burned out before taking a hard look at the numbers.

Now that you understand your business has vitals like you do, it's time to have a real conversation with the doctor.

What's Next

In the following chapters, we'll take a deep dive into the vital signs of your business—the data that matters. No MBA crap needed, no theoretical frameworks that look pretty in Power-Point and fall apart in the real world. We'll explore the difference between good data and bad data and cut through the noise to identify the key performance indicators that matter for your business.

CHAPTER 13

GOOD DATA VS. BAD DATA

Every day, business owners make hundreds of decisions—big and small, strategic and tactical. And far too often, those decisions are driven by gut feelings, fuzzy memories, or whatever opinion was loudest in the last meeting.

When we're working with clients, the difference between guessing and leading with clarity becomes obvious the moment we ask them to back up their decisions. When a business owner can instantly pull up customer-retention rates, satisfaction scores, and complaint trends, you see it: real confidence. They lean in, work their dashboards with ease, and speak in specifics. And when they can't? We get hesitation, vagueness, and decisions built more on instinct and memory than on insight.

"We know our customers better than anyone," a client will tell us. Then they'll bring up that nightmare customer who nearly killed their biggest product launch—they demanded 17 revisions, called the support team at midnight, and ultimately left a one-star review that still shows up first on a Google search. When we ask where that information is documented and where the patterns are tracked, we get a shrug. "I just remember it that way."

They recall it the same way they "remember" that customer segment being profitable. The same way they "think" that a specific marketing channel is working. The same way they are "almost positive" which product features customers actually use. Running your business on memory and vibes is like refusing to see a doctor until you're doubled over in pain. Sure, you might coast for a bit—and when something finally breaks, it's not a quick fix. It's an ICU visit. Maybe even surgery.

This chapter might humble you a bit. Honestly, you probably need it, because most business owners are making decisions like this—based on what they think they know, not on what's true. And that gap between assumption and reality is expensive. Bad data (or no data) creates bad decisions. Bad decisions cost you time, money, sanity, and sometimes the good people you can't afford to lose. The research backs this up. *Harvard Business Review* found that bad data costs US businesses over $3 trillion annually.[10]

Without solid data, every decision is like a coin flip dressed up as strategy. Your instincts might have helped build your business; they can't scale it forever, though. When that competitor launches, when sales dip for three straight months, when your biggest client threatens to leave, that's when gut feelings turn into panic decisions. Good data cuts through this noise. It keeps you steady during the high-speed emotional roller coaster that business ownership often is. When business is booming, data reminds you you're not untouchable. When things are rough, it shows you you're not doomed.

What Is Data, Really?

When we talk about data, what we're really talking about is evidence—the actual facts about how your business is running. It's like taking your pulse at the doctor instead of guessing how your heart feels. And it's not all spreadsheets and formulas like you might be thinking.

Three Types of Business Data

1. **The Stuff You Already See (No Numbers or Dollar Signs Required)**

   - Who showed up today?

   - What got finished?

   - Which team is drowning in work?

   - Names and addresses

   You see this everywhere—on whiteboards, in your project-management app, even in group texts. It's all data; you probably aren't thinking about it in terms of numbers or "scary" math. We call these "common-sense metrics."

2. **The Counting Game**

   This is your "how many" stuff. It can be jobs completed, leads that came in, new customers, inventory that moved—anything that can be counted. Maybe you are already keeping tabs on some of this. Maybe you're not—and that's okay (for now).

3. **The Money Talk**

   Here's where people tend to get nervous: the dollar signs. Your P&L numbers feel intimidating because they're not part of your daily routine. They show up when your accountant wants to have a "serious conversation" or when something is already broken. This tends to be the area that's avoided most. One client told us on her very first call with us that she felt like she was "walking into the principal's office."

The Four Cs: Good Data vs. Bad Data

Because you're reading this chapter, chances are you don't actually have the data you need—or at least not in a form you can trust or use. Some of it is buried in disconnected systems. Some of it lives inside someone's head. And some of it? It's there, and it's a mess—duplicated, mislabeled, out of date, or plain wrong.

We hear it all the time: "We can't use our data because it's so bad."

The truth is your data is bad because you're not using it. This is the cycle most businesses are stuck in. You don't trust your data, so you don't use it. Because you don't use it, it never gets cleaned up. Because it never gets cleaned up, you still don't trust it. And around you go—wasting time, missing insights, and making decisions in the dark.

> **The truth is your data is bad because you're not using it.**

Yes, your data might be messy right now. Honestly, we're betting it is. And no surprise here: When you start using it, things get clearer. Patterns emerge. Problems surface. Confidence builds.

Your data doesn't have to be perfect—it does need to be pretty darn good! And for it to be good, it needs to meet a similar standard as a diamond: the four Cs.

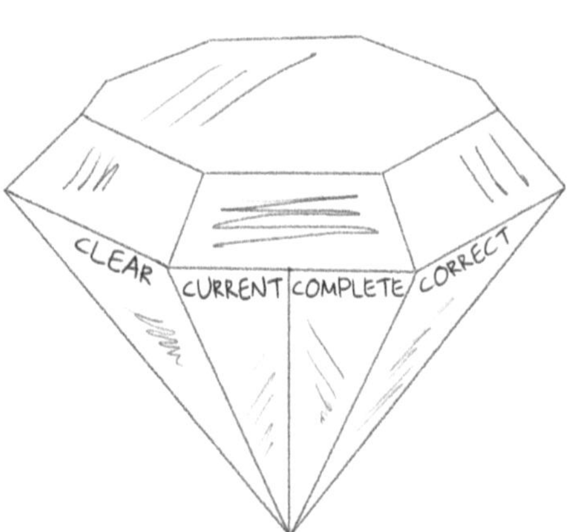

1. **Clear**—Everyone understands what it means. No guessing involved.

2. **Current**—It's up to date. Not from three or six months ago.

3. **Complete**—No missing fields, holes, or gaps. Mostly complete doesn't count.

4. **Correct**—It's accurate, verified, and trustworthy. It is or it ain't.

What Bad Data Looks Like in Real Life

You might be thinking, *Okay, but what does bad data actually look like in my business?*

Think about incorrect data showing up in typos and inconsistencies. One home-builder client had a model called "The Harrison" spelled many different ways—Harrison, H-son, The H-son, Harisson—with and without dashes. Looking at information from the company's system was a nightmare. You can't do anything until what's wrong is fixed. Outdated data might include information on clients from three years ago that no longer applies now. Maybe they've moved. Maybe they are no longer ideal clients for you at all.

Let's say you want to send an email to a prospect list of women business owners. Though you can easily pull up email addresses, do you have a male/female field in the database? You have missing information and incomplete data that someone must go through and fix. While they're doing that, they also have to check to make sure every email contact has a first name. There's nothing that makes customers and donors feel super valued more than getting an email that begins "Dear ," (first name left blank)! Right?

And then, of course, there's data that is unclear. Try to see where you're spending when $50,000 of everything is lumped together under "General Business Expenses" (or as we like to call it, "where good accounting goes to die") instead of being listed out in the correct expense categories. It's going to take hours to figure out what's there because things weren't done right the first time. You cannot make solid, data-driven decisions because you have bad data. Full stop.

The costs of bad data add up fast. Wasted hours cleaning and cross-checking information. Missed opportunities to double down on what's working. Blind spots in hiring, customer trends, and operations. Bad forecasting, bad marketing, and bad decisions overall. This is all because your systems aren't talking—or worse, because no one knows what "good" looks like.

Why Is This So Hard?

Why does getting data right feel like climbing Mount Everest in flip-flops? That's simple: because in most small businesses, it's no one's actual job. Well, no one except yours.

Then, when you dig into who actually owns the data, things get even messier. In bigger companies, sales has one system. HR has another. Finance has its own. They're all talking about the same customers, the same projects, the same people—from completely different angles, using completely different tools. (You haven't had fun in a meeting until you've sat in a big company conference room watching the arguments over whose numbers are right!)

The same type of chaos happens for small business owners, with fewer people. One person uses QuickBooks, another employee uses customer-relationship management (CRM) software, and yet another tracks hiring in a Google Sheet, while the owner keeps a mental list of everything in their head or inbox. Same problem, smaller org chart.

When those pieces don't connect (whether they're managed by teams or one overwhelmed founder), you end up with six systems telling eight conflicting stories. Same data, different definitions is exactly how errors pile up, trust breaks down, and decision-making gets fuzzy.

Think about it: big companies have entire departments dedicated to data. They have analysts, dashboards, and systems talking to each other all day. And a lot of them don't do data well either! In your business? That team is you. You're the only one with the full picture who needs to understand what matters, what's missing, and what questions actually need answering. Now, that's a scary thought, isn't it? And it makes it really simple to push this stuff off. You're busy. You're juggling a dozen things. And data cleanup is never the fire that's burning the hottest.

The truth is this isn't hard because it's complicated. It's hard because it's boring, and tedious. It doesn't feel urgent. It doesn't feel exciting. And it definitely doesn't give you that dopamine hit like closing a deal or launching something new does. We push it to "next week." Again and again. And the longer you avoid it, the worse it gets—and the more painful it becomes to unravel later.

The good news? You are not alone in this. Everyone is winging it. That business owner you follow on social media who seems to have it all figured out? They're probably as confused about their data as you are. And the even better news? It's never been easier to start—and believe it or not, there are things that are going well. Glimmers of hope.

When you're feeling a bit down, here's the good news: not all of your data sucks! Look at your primary systems:

- ◆ **Payroll**—This must be right or else your employees would be screaming. You have good data on payroll costs, including regular and overtime hours. Maybe what you need is to set up departments to see where the costs are going.

- ◆ **Accounting**—When your bank transactions automatically come into your system and your bookkeeper is reconciling cash accounts, all activity is at least in your reports. It may not be in the right spots; at least it is there.

- **Sales**—When you use Square or other point-of-sale (POS) systems, you can look at sales by hour or per item in quantity and/or by its value. You can quickly determine which ones to focus on to check pricing.

- **Invoicing**—Every invoice includes customer name and address, items, quantity, prices, and total value that can be accessed. Get this really messed up and your customers will be screaming (which is a completely different type of data that will actually demand your attention!).

- **Marketing**—Every email marketing campaign creates data on open rates, clicks, and bounces. When you send an email to 100 people and no one opens it, that's important data to know.

The point is we're way past the days of manually typing everything into Excel like some kind of digital caveman. There are tools now that do much of the work for you: they sync, connect, and even predict stuff—when you feed them good data. This is about leveling up your data, understanding why it matters, and getting better about maintaining the "good" kind so you can use it to track where you're going next.

We worked with a company that had a sales-incentive program. It was relatively simple. When a salesperson sold 1,000 items, they earned a 5% bonus. Clear, right? Sally sold 1,007, then one customer returned 15. Does she still get that bonus? Your sales manager says yes; your accountant says no. You have a data problem, a policy problem, and a human-resources problem. Make the decision, boss.

Before moving on, we have one final thought about data and numbers. When everyone understands them the same way, it becomes a common language for your business. We'll spend a lot of time guiding you through this idea in the next chapter.

Quick Win: Fix One Thing Right Now

Take a few minutes to think about the number-one question you have about your business right now. Something like:

- How much are we actually making on this service?

- Where do our customers come from?

- Why are we always behind on projects?

- How many leads did we get last month?

Now ask yourself, "Where does that answer actually live?" When your answer is "somewhere in my head" or "I think it's in three different places," you've found your starting point.

Set aside one hour this week to answer that question, clarify it, and own it. Make it pass the four Cs test. Get it clear, current, complete, and correct:

- **Clear**—Is everyone using the same format? Or does one person write "Smith, John" while another writes "john smith" and someone else puts "J. Smith?" No weird duplicates, typos, or "test entries" that nobody cleaned up? No customers named "asdfgh" or projects called "Bob's thing"?

- **Current**—Is this information actually up to date? Or are you looking at data from three months ago thinking it is for this week?

- **Complete**—Do you have all the pieces, or are there random gaps? Missing customer information? Projects with no end dates? Expense reports with no receipts?

- **Correct**—Is the data actually accurate? Does the billing match the services delivered? Are the numbers real, or are you seeing sales that never closed, customers who never paid, or employees listed who haven't worked there in months? Are addresses, contact information, and dates all verified—or assumed?

One area. One week. Four Cs. That's how you start turning chaos into clarity.

Once you experience the pain of going through a bunch of nasty data, you'll gain a new perspective on the cost of cleaning it up and the value of keeping it four-C quality. This is your time to feel the pain you have been putting off. Next time, "volunteer" the responsible party to have the opportunity of learning the importance of good data. That person will become an evangelist because they won't want to do it again later!

The Bottom Line

Good data doesn't start with fancy dashboards or complicated formulas. It starts with getting clear—clear on what you need to know, clear on who is handling what, and clear on where everything lives. Once you nail that part, the tools practically set themselves up. The tech is there. The automation exists. And when you start treating data like the valuable gold mine it is, decisions get simpler. That gut-wrenching "should we or shouldn't we?" moment becomes a quick look at the numbers. The late-night-worry spiral about whether something's working is replaced by actual answers.

You don't need to become a spreadsheet wizard or hire a team of analysts. You only need to start somewhere and stay consistent. Pick that one messy area, clean it up, and watch how much clearer everything becomes. Because once you have data you can trust, you can start identifying the numbers that actually move the needle in your business—the metrics that tell you when you're winning or losing before your bank account does.

That's where KPIs come in. Data is the foundation. KPIs are the comparison of the data that starts to tell the story of your business from a whole new perspective. They create your dashboard with the handful of numbers that tell you exactly how your business is performing and where you need to focus next.

CHAPTER 14

KPIs—THE OWNER'S GPS

You're probably thinking, *Great, another abbreviation I have no clue about.* Stop worrying. A KPI is only one number that gets compared with another number. Really, that's all it is.

Remember all that data we talked about? Data becomes numbers, then you identify your key numbers, then you start comparing them to something, and like magic, you have KPIs. They are the keys (clever, huh?) that show you what's really driving your business forward.

Still nervous? Don't be. You use KPIs every day—even though you would never call them that. Love football? Let's say the Packers score 21 points by halftime. Sounds impressive, right? Until you see the other team scored 27—the Packers' 21 suddenly doesn't feel so great. During halftime, the Packers coaching staff makes adjustments and the team goes on to win by a score of 49-30. That's a KPI in action—you compare two numbers, decide what you need to do, and make decisions about your next moves.

A lot of business owners get excited about one number, like total sales, without having any context to know whether it's good or bad. Or they focus on the wrong KPIs (tracking what's easy instead of what actually matters). Only thing worse? Not tracking anything at all. They end up making decisions without

the support of good information. When things go sideways, they're left guessing instead of knowing. Missed opportunities, wasted effort, and confusion are not far behind.

Here's the dirty secret: understanding your KPIs is more important than understanding your financial statements. We told you in PART III that accounting only records the past. Financial statements are not designed to help you grow; they tell you what already happened with your finances. KPIs help you figure out what's happening in your operations so you can decide what to do next.

> **Here's the dirty secret: understanding your KPIs is more important than understanding your financial statements.**

KPIs include both financial numbers (because yes, your P&L and Balance Sheet are full of KPIs in disguise) and non-financial numbers, like how many calls came in or how much downtime you've had on a machine versus its availability this week. These are insights you won't get from your bookkeeper.

This chapter will help you understand your KPIs better and identify the top ones to track. By the end of it, you'll start making smarter, more confident decisions based on the real story—not gut instinct.

What Your KPIs Are Really Telling You

Before we go any further, let's break down what "KPI" stands for, because don't forget: *Words Fucking Matter* too:

◆ **Key**—Only a few numbers truly matter. The important ones that move the needle.

◆ **Performance**—This is the evaluation of the "what's happening?" part. What the numbers say about how you are doing.

◆ **Indicators**—KPIs give you suggestions and hints, not the whole story. Think of them as clues, not conclusions.

Remember at the end of the last chapter when we said that numbers can provide a common language? This is where it comes true. KPIs tell everyone what is important, and they set goals and expectations. They'll tell you what's happening so you can figure out why and what to do next.

KPIs are only meaningful when one number is compared with the same number from somewhere else: a goal, a different time period, an important assumption about the business, or even an industry benchmark. Ideally, you will also review them as trends so you can view performance over time.

The good news is that the math involved in calculating KPIs is very basic—so don't panic! No complicated formula—we're talking grade-school addition, subtraction, multiplication, and division. You can use a calculator for everything. Hell, when you don't want to do the math, you can feed data into AI and ask it to run the calculations for you!

Your KPIs tell you something important, though not everything. Don't blindly follow them. Use them as your starting point, then look around for context or other confirming data. What else is happening in your business? What story are the numbers trying to tell you?

Here's a quick example of what we mean. You're walking in Washington, DC, approaching a busy intersection. The walk signal (your KPI) flips from the red hand to the white walking guy, so the data says, "Go." The light is the right color; the timing is perfect; everything checks out. What happens when you act immediately on these facts? You either cross safely or you're smashed by a car blowing through the red light because you didn't look left or right to confirm the data. That's exactly what happens when business owners follow numbers blindly. Even when they look great, you still need to lift your head up and see what is actually happening around you.

Lynn

I had a client, Paul, whose sales were up 13% (great!), yet gross margins were decreasing (bad) at the same time. I wanted to learn more. When we dug a little deeper into the numbers, the story became clear. We found that his largest customer had grown from 62% of his total business to 75%. That might seem like a win at first; it was actually a major red flag. Not only was this customer the least profitable (they earned volume discounts and deducted "marketing funds" from their payments), they also had a risky concentration problem. Meanwhile, smaller clients with better margins were being overlooked.

Using additional data helped us understand what was happening and gave us some options. Paul made a conscious decision to focus more energy on nurturing smaller, more profitable relationships. Within six months, overall profitability improved as those smaller customers' sales increased.

Tracking KPIs

When it comes to business metrics, everyone is looking for the "easy" button, which usually means they're tracking top-line revenue. We get it. It feels good watching revenue climb and seeing how much money is coming into the business. Here's an important reminder about getting too excited about sales:

◆ Revenue is for vanity; profit is for sanity.

◆ Revenue is for show; profits are to grow.

◆ Top line is where it starts; bottom line is what matters.

◆ And above all else, cash is reality.

Instead of tracking how much is coming in, ask the right questions and dial in on what matters most for your business. The key is to figure out what you're really trying to accomplish that will move the business forward, then link all the numbers to that strategy—and don't forget about the context.

A marketing company promises you 20,000 impressions to drive growth. That might sound good—is it? Is it above industry average? Is it for a day, a week, a year? Is it going to help you reach your actual goals? Or what happens when they promise you they will drive 20% more leads? Also sounds good—as long as they are the right leads. How many of those actually turn into sales? And what's the cost to acquire them? Without context, you have no way to know.

How Many KPIs to Track?

When you start tracking, cast a wide net, and then narrow your focus to the numbers that help you make better decisions. What is your main priority right now? Is it gaining more customers? Is it more sales through loyal customers? Improving profit margins? Speeding up delivery times? Your KPIs will reflect what matters most to your business at any given time.

Andy

One of my clients had one of those "aha!" moments that makes all the number crunching worth it. She was juggling different types of clients—some paying hourly, others on monthly retainers, and some on flat project rates. Though she kept good records on hours worked per client, she never really compared them. When we finally did the math, we discovered her effective hourly rate ranged from $17 to $133. That's when she made a bold move: she said goodbye to 8 of her 17 clients and doubled down on finding more like her top three moneymakers. That's what we call a "KPI-powered pivot"!

This doesn't have to be complicated. My business has 10 trucks. When none are in the parking lot, I know it's a good day. When more than two are parked, I know it's a bad day. That's a KPI. All I need to do is look out the window to see how the business is doing that day.

Imagine you bought a rental property to list on Airbnb. Your primary goal will likely be net profit. You randomly pick $18,000 annually. You've done some homework and concluded that your fixed costs will be $30,000 to cover your mortgage, utilities, cleaning, and maintenance. That means you will need total revenue of $48,000 ($18,000 profit + $30,000 expenses). An annual $48,000 sales goal over 12 months equals $4,000 every month. Your base nightly rate is $225, and since you offer discounts for weekly rentals, you're going to plan on an average of $200 per night. So to reach $4,000 per month, at $200 per night, you'll need 20 nights of occupancy. Congratulations! You have your first KPI goal: 20 nights booked each month. Now start tracking the number of nights rented.

From there, you can start to track other numbers that affect your performance. These may include the actual average nightly rate, overall occupancy rates, guest-satisfaction scores, and cleaning costs per booking. You now have a complete picture of operations, tracking actuals to goals and the key assumptions you've made. It's better to start with a decent list of KPIs and whittle it down as you learn which are in fact the KEY performance indicators.

When you're unsure where to draw the line when you're figuring out what to track, here's a good rule of thumb: when you can't influence it, don't track it. Sure, the weather might affect your sales—it's not like you can call Mother Nature and ask her to dial it down, though. Focus on what your team can control, like pricing strategy, costs, and customer retention.

> **Lynn**
>
> I once worked with a company that went completely KPI crazy. They wanted to track everything—every click, every social media stat, every time someone sneezed in the office. The result was analysis paralysis. With an overwhelmed team that was so busy tracking they barely had time to work, the business was stalling. After working together, we found the seven KPIs that were really important for them. When they ditched the rest and focused on what mattered most, the business started moving forward again.

Ever look inside the cockpit of a passenger jet? There are dozens of gauges grouped by the phase of a flight: startup, taxi, takeoff, climb, cruise, descent, and landing. Different information is used to monitor and control different things. Your business

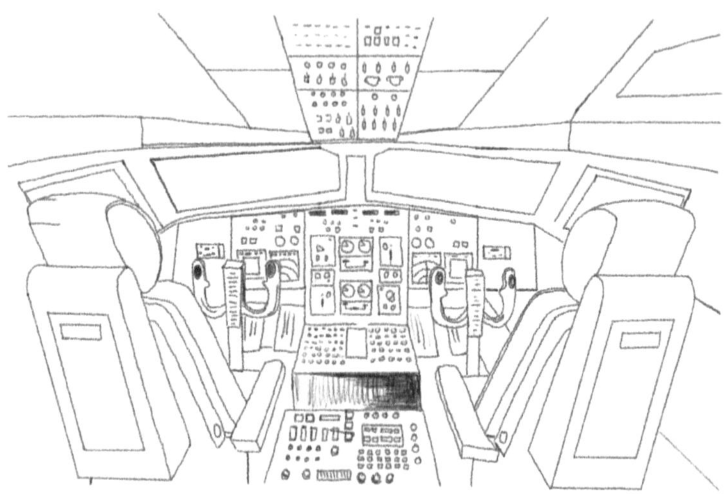

runs the same way. Each KPI shows your actual results compared against a goal and provides a simple way to track your progress.

Most businesses find that 5 to 15 KPIs are enough to tell them what really matters. Less is more when they're the right

KPI	What to Compare	Most Useful For
Sales per Square Foot	Total sales ÷ total square footage	Food & beverage, retail
Sales per Employee	Total sales ÷ number of employees	Service, retail, hospitality
Sales and Profit per Location	Sales and profit at each business location	Multi-location businesses, franchises
Average Ticket per Customer	Total revenue ÷ number of transactions or customers	Food & beverage, retail
Sales	Current sales vs. forecast or previous month, year	Every industry

ones. As your business grows and becomes more complex, you'll want to develop separate KPIs for each department (sales and marketing, operations, etc.)—three to five per department is ideal.

Once you decide what to track, make it visible. KPIs don't live in a hidden spreadsheet. They need to be on a scorecard (we'll walk through that in Chapter 20), reviewed and updated regularly, and shared. Your entire team needs to know what you're measuring and why it matters. In fact, the best-run teams are evaluated—and even rewarded—based on those key metrics.

Get Started—Common KPIs to Track

Still not quite sure where to start with KPIs? Here are some useful ones that work for many different types of businesses. Remember: you don't need to track all of them. Pick a few that make the most sense for what you're trying to accomplish right now.

Example	Why?
Bakery with $300,000 annual sales in a 1,000 sq. ft. space = $300 per sq. ft.	Helps compare performance across locations or justify rent
Salon making $500,000 annually with 10 stylists = $50,000 per stylist	Great for identifying productivity and setting performance benchmarks
Compares results across locations	Useful for spotting underperforming stores
Coffee shop has 1,000 transactions totaling $8,000 = $8 average ticket	Tracks when upselling or menu changes increase per visit spend
Compare Q1 sales with expectations or last year	Are you achieving goals, growing, flat, or declining?

KPI	What to Compare	Most Useful For
Discounts Given	Total discounts given ÷ total sales	Retail, service, freelance
Gross Profit Overall	Revenue – COGS	Product or service businesses
Gross Profit by Product or Service	Revenue – COGS from each product or service	Retail, food & beverage, software as a service (SaaS)
Gross Profit by Customer	Revenue – costs for serving that customer	Agencies, consultants, custom services
Gross Margin % Overall	(Gross profit ÷ revenue) x 100	Every industry
Gross Margin % by Product/ Service	Gross profit per product ÷ price	E-commerce, manufacturing, restaurants
Gross Margin % by Customer	Total profit from customer ÷ their total spend	B2B, agencies, freelancers
Sales Calls per Month	One month's calls ÷ the next month's calls	B2B, SaaS, agencies, freelancers
Close Rate for New Customers	Leads closed ÷ total leads	Retail, e-commerce, startups, growing companies
New Website Visitors	(One month's visitors – previous month's visitors) ÷ previous month's visitors	E-commerce, all industries with an online presence

Example	Why?
When you discount $10,000 out of $200,000 in sales, that's 5% in discounts	Useful to see when you're giving away margin unintentionally
You make $100,000 in revenue, and your COGS is $60,000; your gross profit is $40,000	Are you charging enough? Are direct costs too high? Why?
You make $15 on each cocktail and $3 on each appetizer	Focus on marketing and sales on what's most profitable
One client brings in $10,000 in revenue and costs you $9,000 to serve; another brings $8,000 and costs $4,000	Identify your ideal clients and fire pain-in-the-ass clients!
When gross profit is $40,000 on $100,00 revenue, your margin is 40%	Helps track profitability over time
$100 product costing $40 to make = 60% margin	Shows which items have the highest return
Two clients pay the same, and one requires more hours and revisions	You'll see who's worth keeping
Consulting firm scheduling 40 discovery calls in July vs. 20 in June = 50% increase	Tracks pipeline-building activity; when appointments dip, future sales often follow
Software company closing 20 new customers from 100 qualified leads = 20% close rate	Tells you whether leads are well qualified and how effectively your team handles them
E-commerce site gets 12,000 new visitors in August, up from 9,000 in July (33%)	Leading indicator of brand visibility and digital marketing success

KPI	What to Compare	Most Useful For
Customer Acquisition Cost (CAC)	Total marketing or sales spend ÷ number of new customers	Startups, e-commerce, B2B services
Customer Change Orders	Number of change requests ÷ total projects	Construction, design, consulting
Month-to-Month Trending	KPI values across months	All industries

Leading and Lagging Indicators

Remember that indicator part we talked about? Well, any KPI can be a leading or lagging indicator—it all depends on what you're measuring and what you're trying to learn. Leading indicators hint at what is likely to come. Lagging indicators show you what already happened. The truth is that most numbers moonlight as both.

Let's use our example about the Packers again and say they are up at halftime. That same score is whispering, "We need to make some adjustments going into the second half" (leading) and "We didn't practice great last week" (lagging).

Your business works the same way. Last week's "sales vs. goal" is a leading indicator to the leadership team on the expected financial performance for the month. It's a lagging indicator for the sales team's strategy for the current week. A great leading indicator for the sales team is the amount of capacity available to book in the coming weeks.

Look at your KPIs as your report card. Then look at net profit. Start looking for trends by comparing KPIs with each other. When sales have been going up every month and net

Example	Why?
You spend $5,000 on marketing and gain 50 new customers; your CAC is $100 per customer	When your CAC is higher than the lifetime value (LTV) of a customer, you're losing money
When 6 out of 10 projects have change orders, you have a 60% change-order rate	High change-order rates may indicate unclear scopes, poor initial planning, or misaligned expectations
Tracking gross margin or average ticket by month helps spot seasonality, growth, and/or decline patterns	Month-to-month trending helps you spot growth, declines, and/or seasonal patterns so you can adjust strategy, budget, and/or staffing accordingly

profit has been going down, something bad is going on. You need to figure it out now! Your KPIs become your crystal ball to show you what's coming.

Quick Win: Choose Three KPIs

Think about your number-one priority (and no, it cannot be top-line revenue). *What do I want to accomplish that will move my business forward?* Then look at the chart and pick three KPIs that, when improved, would have the biggest impact on getting you there. Write them down, track them, and share them with your team.

Making Smarter Moves

Though KPIs might feel overwhelming at first, remember that you don't need to track every possible metric. Pick the ones that will support you in making better decisions, and not merely giving you more numbers to stare at. The magic happens when you start listening to the stories these KPIs are telling you. As the stories become clearer, you can make smarter moves that drive the results you want.

PART V
FINANCIAL STATEMENTS

Take a deep breath; this isn't going to be as overwhelming as you think.

Like most business owners, you probably have a complicated relationship with your financial statements. You know you "should" review them regularly. Yet every time you try, the numbers swim around endlessly on the page and you end up closing each report feeling more confused than before. At least you gave it a shot. Many don't even look at them at all!

We've worked with countless business owners who started exactly where you are. They felt that same sense of being overwhelmed—that same urge to hand everything over to someone else and hope for the best. Let's make one thing clear: it's not all your fault! We recognize you're a smart cookie! (You're reading this book, aren't you?)

Here's the dark, dirty secret no one ever talks about: accounting is not designed to help you grow your business. The whole thing is set up to make it simpler to share your financial performance with outsiders and to pay taxes. You're taught from day one to outsource your bookkeeping because someone else understands it way better than you. Doing this, however, creates a big wall between yourself and you understanding your numbers. This makes it impossible to bridge the gap between accounting and the finance work that drives insights and value at bigger companies.

Clients we work with have the what, how, and why of accounting explained to them. They now confidently review their financial statements and use them to make better decisions for their business. You'll get there too.

For those of you wondering why you need this when you've already been successfully running your business for years, we get it: you've built something successful, and that's impressive. Even experienced business owners can hit a wall when they're not staying on top of where their money is going or spotting opportunities to get better (this may be a good time to reread Chapter 6: Stop the Bleeding). Understanding your financials helps you get smarter about what you've already built. It gives you the tools to keep your business running and to grow it with real confidence. And that's exactly what this part of the book is all about.

In this section, we're going to walk you through your Chart of Accounts and three key financial documents:

1. Profit & Loss Statement

2. Balance Sheet

3. Cash Flow Statement

Together, these documents paint a clear picture of how money flows through your business—where it comes from, where it goes, and what's happening along the way. The good news is you may not have to spend a lot of time with all three. Most businesses have one or two that matter most for their day-to-day decisions, while the third might need a quick peek every now and then. It's like having different tools in your tool kit: you'll reach for some more often than others.

What matters most is understanding the story your financial statements are telling when they work together. You'll need to invest time getting familiar with these documents and how money moves between them. The best approach is to have a financial professional walk you through all three statements side by side, showing you the connections and explaining what each number means in the context of your overall financial picture. Then, instead of only seeing rows of numbers, you'll begin to notice patterns. You'll catch yourself saying things like, "Oh, that's why cash was tight last month" or "Look how much that new marketing strategy paid off."

Cash vs. Accrual Accounting

Before we move on, there is a general accounting concept you must understand. When using QuickBooks or any other accounting software to track your business finances, there are two different ways it can report your results:

1. **Cash basis**—This reports your financial transactions based on when money moves. When you sell something in April and you deposit the customer's check in June, your reports will show the sale occurred in June.

2. **Accrual basis**—This reports transactions when they take place, regardless of whether any cash moved. When you sell something in April, the sale is reported in April, no matter when the customer pays. This approach provides a better picture of what really happened during the month, though it is a bit harder to manage as there is more accounting to do.

    Small businesses are typically managed on a cash basis. Their tax returns are also typically prepared on a cash basis. The following is a quick summary of the differences between the two approaches.

What's Next?

In the chapters ahead, we're taking the confusion out of your financial documents. We'll start right where you need to, with your Chart of Accounts (a.k.a. "Label Maker"). From

	Cash Accounting	**Accrual Accounting**
When revenue is recorded	When cash is received	When it's earned (invoice issued)
When expenses are recorded	When cash is paid	When they're incurred (bills received)
Focus	Actual cash in/out today	True profitability over time
Simplicity	Simple to track	More complex, requires extra entries
Best for	Small businesses focused on cash flow	Businesses seeking accurate financial performance and growth planning

there, we'll get into the P&L Statement, Balance Sheet, and Cash Flow Statement. By the end of the section, those once mysterious and intimidating documents will simply be valuable tools that help you run your business smarter.

CHAPTER 15

YOUR LABEL MAKER (CHART OF ACCOUNTS)

Think about your favorite grocery store. Everything has its spot: fresh produce in a specific area, breakfast cereals down one aisle, canned goods down another, and frozen foods in their own section. Within each area, items are grouped logically and labeled clearly so you can find what you're looking for.

You would think it weird to stumble across dog food mixed in with the bananas or find paper towels chilling in the freezer section, right? That's exactly the kind of sensible organization your Chart of Accounts brings to your business finances.

Before we can get into the three key financial documents, we need to start with their foundation: the Chart of Accounts—or, as we like to call it, your business's Label Maker. Like how a label maker brings order to chaos, your Chart of Accounts helps organize your financial data, so it makes sense. When it does, it's like opening an old-school filing cabinet where everything is neatly labeled, maybe even color coded, and clear at first glance. When it's a mess, it feels like trying to find an important file in a messy drawer full of unlabeled folders and loose paper. You waste time, get frustrated, and often give up before finding what you need. That's why understanding and actively managing your Chart of Accounts is one of the simplest—and most overlooked—ways to bring clarity to your finances.

This chapter is all about helping you understand your Chart of Accounts, including why organizing it the right way for your specific business is one of the best investments you can make in your business's financial health. Once you have this piece sorted out, all those intimidating financial statements will become much clearer and more helpful.

What Is the Chart of Accounts and Why Is It So Important?

Your Chart of Accounts isn't some intimidating accounting concept; it's simply the organizational system that keeps your financial data in order. Every business has one (even when you don't realize it or call it something else), working behind the scenes to give each dollar going through your business a home and every transaction a clear purpose.

Let's start at the beginning. Accounting is based on "accounts." Every account represents a specific thing. Remember the 4Cs? This is the "clear." Every account has a name that, depending on what it is, goes on either the Income Statement or Balance Sheet. Your Chart of Accounts is simply a list of all the accounts you've created.

QuickBooks and other accounting software basically take all your categorized (labeled) transactions and arrange them into those familiar financial documents. When your Chart of Accounts is set up correctly, your bookkeeper, accountant, and tax preparer have good data to rely on, your monthly reports make sense, tax season becomes less stressful, and you can make business decisions based on clear, reliable information.

Don't Rely Only on QuickBooks… or Your Accountant

Most business owners we've worked with have assumed that QuickBooks or their accountant is managing their Chart of Accounts. It's often running in the background, completely untouched. That's because when you first set up QuickBooks, whether that was six months or six years ago, the software took its best guess at what your Chart of Accounts will look like based on your business type. The problem is that guess was likely wrong, or at a minimum, not tailored to how your business works, and it has remained untouched ever since.

We've also met plenty of business owners who mistakenly assume that since they have an accountant, they're all set. What they don't realize is that their accountant needs to be asking them how they want things set up. And when those conversations aren't happening, you, the owner, need to start them. In the end, your financials need to be simple to understand and provide the information you need to manage your business finances.

We worked with an owner who, despite paying a lot of money to her accountant, felt like she needed a translator every time she looked at her financial statements. When we started digging around, we found that her accountant had set things up in the weirdest way possible, without ever asking her what made sense for her business. The accountant basically took whatever messy setup existed years before, made some random changes, and then operated like that for years. The result was a shitshow, including one sad little $15 office expense sitting all alone in its own special category. This wasn't exactly the kind of insight that was going to help the owner run her business better. We talked about her company and her goals and created a Chart of Accounts that made sense for her business.

Sound familiar? Do you feel like your financial documents may as well be written in ancient Greek? Please don't sit there feeling frustrated. Find out what's going on. Maybe your accountant figured you were fine with however things initially got set up and simply continued with it. Or maybe they let QuickBooks do its thing on cruise control. Whatever happened, the good news is you can, and will, take back control of your financials by asking questions and explaining your business and goals.

The Numbering System

Accountants love numbers—no surprise there! That's why the Chart of Accounts is taught to accounting professionals using a universal, numbers-based language that works the same way whether you're in New York or New Zealand. For example, revenue always lives in the 4000s category, while expenses hang out in the 6000s, and those rules stay consistent no matter what. Good accountants don't care whether you call something "Office Expenses" or "Office Supplies" because both live in the 6000s and get treated as expenses. For them, it's all about the number, not the name.

Things can get a little messy when you don't use the numbering system, as most accounting software (including QuickBooks) defaults to reporting types of accounts in alphabetical order, which is not exactly helpful when you're trying to make sense of your money. How much did you spend on marketing last year? Find all the numbers: Advertising, Google Ads, Graphic Design, Promotions, SEO, Website— whew! You picked through 40 accounts to find and manually add up 6! Doesn't it make more sense to have your bookkeeper group them? When it was a pain for Advertising, it's going to be true for People, Building/Facilities, Administration, Financial Expenses, and Professional Services. That's what this is all about.

The Standard Numbering Convention

You don't have to be an accountant to see how this system can make things easier and help you run your business smarter. Think of these number ranges as different neighborhoods in your financial world. Each one has its own identity and keeps similar types of transactions grouped together. Once you know the basic layout, looking at your financial statements becomes far less intimidating.

Before we go on, there's something we want you to understand. Let's say you recently bought a new building. You're going to have a ton of new accounts for the building, the mortgage, the rent your tenants will pay, utilities, etc. When you ask your accountant to set up the accounts, the first thing they must do in QuickBooks is pick 1 of 15 different types of accounts. Each of these has 5 to 15 different sub-types.

The combination of types and sub-types is mapped to your financial statements and tax-preparation software. When you're not careful, accounts for things you owe can show up where only things you own will be. Getting it right is important!

Lynn

I worked with a client whose accountant set up a new account for sales. Unfortunately, she didn't change that account type from Bank (default) to Revenue. Instead of money showing up in Revenue, it showed up as Cash. A mistake like this would have flowed right into their tax preparation. What a mess!

The standard numbering system helps you understand what group each account belongs to and what statement it shows up on. The following shows numbers in thousands, which allows lots of flexibility to creatively use groups—you'll see more of these in upcoming chapters.

- **1000s: Assets (Balance Sheet)**—Things your business owns.

- **2000s: Liabilities (Balance Sheet)**—Things your business owes.

- **3000s: Equity (Balance Sheet)**—Ownership stake in the business.

- **4000s: Revenue (Income Statement)**—Money coming in.

- **5000s: Cost of Sales/Goods (Income Statement)**—Money going out as direct costs to deliver your product or service.

- **6000s: Expenses (Income Statement)**—Money going out as operating costs to run your business.

- **7000s: Other Income (Income Statement)**—Money coming in from sources outside your main business.

- **8000s: Other Expense (Income Statement)**—Money going out that doesn't fit in your regular operations.

You don't need to memorize this like you're cramming for a test; knowing these basic categories helps you spot when things are in the wrong place. When your bookkeeper accidentally puts your office rent in the 4000s (Revenue) instead of the 6000s (Expenses), you'll recognize and be able to call them out on it. At the same time, this isn't to say you must do it this way or that everyone does.

In fact, you don't HAVE to use numbers at all. Quick-Books doesn't require it. The numbers do provide valuable clues, though. Say you are set up to have wages in both production operations and the office. Then you get a new bookkeeper. Numbers provide a clue as to where the costs will go. When you really leverage your numbering system, people learn that all building/equipment expenses belong in the 6500–6590 range. Now they know where to look! Remember when we talked about how data needs to be complete, current, correct, and clear? This is another example.

Andy

I never learned the number system like Lynn did, and therefore, I never used it with my business or my clients. He has a corporate finance and accounting background while I was self-taught—neither of us is right or wrong in this way.

All I want to know is exactly where the business is burning through the most cash. I rely on the account names and where they show up on the statement. I only want things to make sense for my business and clients. For me, it's simpler to not have another set of numbers my clients need to learn.

When I figured out in QBO that I could have the numbers on my P&L in descending order, it was life-changing. Instead of the accounts appearing alphabetically, I have them showing the largest numbers first. My highest-grossing revenue is right there on the top line, hence the "top-line revenue" you might hear people referring to. "Sales" comes before "Service" alphabetically, though in my business, Service makes up over 90% of my total revenue.

My military background taught me BLUF (bottom line up front): keep the most important things the most important. This was the way I solved my sorting problem.

How Many Accounts?

The number of accounts you use depends on two things: what you want to know from your business and what level of detail you want. Right now, you probably don't know the answers, and, as we've said before, that's okay. Your Chart of Accounts will evolve as your business changes.

The key is balance. Some business owners like to create a separate account for nearly everything. They end up with accounts for every small expense, which is not particularly helpful. Others take the opposite approach and dump everything into one giant "Office Expense" bucket that's equally not helpful.

When you have too many accounts, it becomes hard to see the forest for the trees. When you aren't sure how many is too many, here's a simple test we like to use: when a $25-or-less expense has earned its own special category, your Chart of Accounts is too detailed.

On the flip side, when you have too few accounts, your reports don't tell you much of anything useful. Everything gets lumped together into these massive, vague buckets that leave you scratching your head about where your money came from and where it went. Remember the "clear" part of good data?

The sweet spot lives right in the middle: you want enough detail to understand where your money is flowing and not so much that reading your financial statements feels like solving a puzzle. Keep this in mind: it is way simpler having your system add up several similar accounts than it is to go back and separate a financial junk drawer.

We also recommend creating "groups" of similar accounts. QuickBooks allows you to have a "parent" account that totals all the individual accounts assigned to it. For example, a "Building/ Facilities" parent would include the accounts for Rent, Utilities, Cleaning Services, and Maintenance Supplies. We'll revisit groups again in the next chapter.

Wherever you land, stay consistent with your categories and avoid the trap of putting things into the "Miscellaneous" category, even when you have every intention of going back to fix it later. The IRS doesn't like mystery money, so anything beyond a couple hundred dollars in "Miscellaneous" is going to raise some eyebrows. Keep it clean and well organized.

When Your Accountant Mentions a "Trial Balance"

Your accountant or tax preparer may mention something called your "Trial Balance." Don't worry too much about this because chances are you will never use it; they will. We want you to know that it exists.

The Trial Balance is simply your entire Chart of Accounts and the current amount of money in each account. Amounts are either a debit or credit, and the total debits must equal the total credits. They have to "balance"—hence, the name.

We're going to use a fictional restaurant called Great Eats! to explain your financial statements. Let's jump right in with the Trial Balance:

◆ Debits = credits. We're starting with everything in balance.

◆ The numbering system will work as follows: 1000–3000 are on the Balance Sheet and anything 4000 and greater is on the Income Statement.

Keeping things in balance is now built into accounting software, so it's generally not a problem you need to worry about. Your main worry at this point is to make sure everything is recorded, especially when you're running things out of your checkbook. Beware—you may not catch errors you made, and it may be costly to have someone recreate your accounting.

Quick Win: Get Familiar with your Chart of Accounts

Before you pull out your Label Maker, take a step back and ask yourself what you want to know about your business. Then peek at what's currently living in your Chart of Accounts. Do you see any of the following?

◆ A separate account for every bank account, credit card, or loan? When one's missing, add it.

Great Eats!
Chart of Accounts
October 31, 2025

	Debit	Credit	
1100 Primary Checking	$15,000		
1102 Operating Savings Account	$75,000		
1201 Accounts Receivable (A/R)	$18,000		
1301 Inventory	$120,000		
1351 Prepaid Expenses	$4,000		
1401 Equipment	$165,000		
1402 Vehicles	$50,000		Balance
1450 Accumulated Depreciation		$36,000	Sheet
2101 Accounts Payable		$15,350	Accounts
2102 Sales Tax Payables		$4,500	
2201 Credit Card - Office		$9,000	
2202 Credit Card - Production		$17,000	
2300 Total Payroll Liabilities		$8,900	
2600 Vehicle Loans		$47,000	
2700 Notes Payable		$75,000	
3100 Owner's Investment		$50,000	
3300 Retained Earnings		$161,900	
4100 Food Sales		$86,500	
4200 Beverage Sales		$20,750	
5100 Food Costs	$32,000		
5200 Beverage Costs	$6,200		
5300 Direct Labor	$20,600		
6100 Advertising	$1,000		
6200 Office Supplies	$450		Income
6301 Manager Salaries	$10,000		Statement
6302 Health Care	$2,100		Accounts
6303 Other Benefits	$1,500		
6401 Rent	$5,000		
6402 Utilities	$975		
6403 Repairs/Maintenance	$1,200		
6404 Building Supplies	$325		
6501 Legal & Professional	$900		
6502 Depreciation	$2,000		
6503 Dues & Subscriptions	$650		
Total	$531,900	$531,900	

◆ Any account names that make you wonder, *What would go in there?* Clarify and rename them.

◆ Accounts that look like they're collecting the same things (e.g., "Office Supplies" and "Office Expenses")? Check the details and separate into separate accounts.

We're going to ask you to take another look at your Chart of Accounts at the end of Chapters 16 & 17 (P&L and Balance Sheet).

Not sure how to make changes? Schedule a chat with your bookkeeper or accountant. Walk through it together, ask your questions, get their feedback, and set it up the right way.

Want to add account numbers or change account types or names yourself? Follow these steps in QBO:

1. Type "Chart of Accounts" in the search bar.
2. Find the account you want to edit and click the dropdown arrow on the right.
3. Select "Edit."
4. Make your changes to the name, detail type, or description.
5. Click "Save and Close."

Use Your Label Maker

A Label Maker doesn't organize your stuff for you—it simply gives you a tool to do it yourself. The same goes for your Chart of Accounts, and you have more control than you think. You get to decide what to name your categories, where to group things, and how detailed you want to get. Once you print those "labels" (a.k.a. account names and numbers) and your Chart of Accounts is in order, you're not only more organized—you're ready to make your financial statements work for you.

CHAPTER 16

PROFIT & LOSS STATEMENT

We're starting this chapter with some good news: you already understand the core idea behind a P&L. You've applied it personally forever; you haven't yet looked at it through a business lens.

Think about how you handled money before you became a small business owner. You had a job, someone cut you a paycheck, and from there, you covered the basics: rent, groceries, car payments, gas, and maybe some fun stuff. Whatever was left after paying for everything was yours to keep: pocket money, fun money, beer money.

Your business operates the same way. Your P&L is basically your personal budget all grown up and tracking a business. It shows what your business brings in (revenue) and what it spends (expenses). The difference between those two numbers tells you whether you're making money or losing it—straightforward, right? That's why, of all three financial statements, this is the one that probably feels the least intimidating to you.

In this chapter, we're walking you through your P&L in plain English—no accounting jargon needed. You'll learn what it really is, how to read it, and why you need to use it as the tool it is to help you make smarter financial decisions. It's time to start looking at your financial statements with confidence so you can make moves that help your business grow.

What Is a P&L? (And Why Do You Care?)

Though this financial statement answers to a few different names—Profit & Loss Statement, P&L, and Income Statement—they all mean the same thing. In plain terms, your P&L is your business report card for a specific time period, rather than a snapshot of a single day like your Balance Sheet (we'll get into that in the next chapter).

At its core, your P&L is grade-school math in action: Revenue - Expenses = Profit (or Loss). QuickBooks breaks this down into a few other steps:

- **Net Revenue**—The total of all sales (revenue), less discounts.

- **Total Cost of Goods Sold**—The sum of all COGS (or cost of sales) spending.

- **Gross Profit**—The dollar profit earned on net revenue minus total cost of sales.

- **Total Expenses**—The total amount of operating expenses or overhead.

- **Net Operating Profit**—Gross profit minus total expenses.

- **Other Income and Expense**—Money earned, or costs paid outside day-to-day operations.

- **Net Income**—Net revenue minus all expenses.

There is more to the P&L than a simple formula though. It tells you the story about whether your business is operationally successful and begins to answer the question that keeps every business owner up at night: where the hell did my money go?

The Three Main Sections of Your P&L

We've already mentioned that your P&L tells you a story. Now let's get into its three chapters (sections). In the previous chapter, we introduced Great Eats!, our fictional restaurant. We're going to use its Income Statement to walk you through this important report. Before we get to the numbers, let's do a proper introduction.

When you run the report, the first thing you'll see is the name: Profit and Loss, and your company name, in this case, Great Eats! Then you see the "period." For this example, we're looking at two months: the period of September through October 2025.

Profit and Loss Statement
Great Eats
September 1 - October 31, 2025

Header—P&L

Then you'll see some column headings. We recommend showing two periods and adding how much things changed in both dollars and percentage changes by clicking the "Compare" menu. These columns immediately give you additional information to help you review. When sales are down thousands of dollars and -20%, it's a red flag begging for your attention.

Ready to dive in?

1. Revenue—The "Top Line" (Money In) = Account 4000s

This is where the "money in" from your business we talked about in Chapter 4 shows up on your financials. It's the money you earned when customers bought something from you over whatever time period you specified. This is your top-line revenue in, not your profit, and certainly not cash either. Money that you put in and money from your bank does not belong here.

This section is where you want to track different revenue (or Income or Sales) streams. For example, let's say you owned a professional-services business. Your money in could be from Retainers, Consulting Projects, and Hourly Projects. For nonprofits, that might look like Donations, Grants, and Special Events. A distributor may have a different account for every major product category it sells.

Great Eats! is much simpler, with only two income streams:

	Sep-25	Oct-25	$ Change	% Change
Income				
4100 Food Sales	$80,000	$86,500	$6,500	8.10%
4200 Beverage Sales	$20,000	$20,750	$750	3.80%
Total Income	$100,000	$107,250	$7,250	7.30%

Revenue—P&L

4000 Income
- 4100 Food Sales

- 4200 Beverages Sales

Looking at these two-month results, you may want to explore why Food Sales were up 8.1% while Beverage Sales were up less than 4%, especially when historically they were much closer. Was there a price increase? Did you promote a more expensive offer?

In the case of a restaurant, it may also be beneficial to track sales by dine-in vs. take-out or delivery. Why? When thinking about the revenue streams you have, they may have a very different cost structure and different types of advertising or other expenses you need to assess results. **Why It Matters:** Organizing by revenue streams helps you see which products/services are selling the most, what customers want, where your growth opportunities are, and maybe even which products you need to stop selling. When deciding what key categories of sales you need to track on your P&L, keep in mind there is a ton of extra data in your POS system. You can always explore later!

2. **Cost of Goods Sold / Cost of Sales (Direct Costs) (Money Out) = Account 5000s**

Remember COGS (every dollar spent to directly make the product or deliver the service) in Chapter 5: Money Out? This is where it shows up. Ideally, you want your COGS breakdown to mirror your revenue breakdown.

Continuing our example from earlier, we have these COGS accounts:

	Sep-25	Oct-25	$ Change	% Change
Cost of Goods Sold				
5100 Food Costs	$30,000	$32,000	$2,000	6.70%
5200 Beverage Costs	$6,000	$6,200	$200	3.30%
5300 Direct Labor	$20,000	$20,600	$600	3.00%
Total Cost of Goods Sold	$56,000	$58,800	$2,800	5.00%
Gross Profit	$44,000	$48,450	$4,450	10.10%

Cost of Goods Sold—P&L

5000 COGS (no dollars show up in the heading!)
*   5100 Food Costs

*   5200 Beverage Costs

*   5300 Direct Labor

Remember how we said sales could be broken down to dine-in or take-out or delivery? Now think about the different costs. Food for delivery now needs additional packaging and comes with direct delivery labor.

Why It Matters: When your sales and COGS are closely aligned, you may see you need to raise prices—and you'll definitely be able to get an idea of which products and services are most profitable. In this example, recall food costs were up 8.1%. Now we can see food material costs were up

6.7%. In the case those were reversed, and the trends were consistent, a price increase would be called for.

In addition to Food and Beverage Costs, Direct Labor is an additional cost to get to full Gross Profit. Because labor can represent the largest costs to a restaurant, do you see how beneficial it would be for Great Eats! to break Direct Labor into three separate accounts, one each for Back of House (food prep), Front of House (waitstaff), and Delivery?

You can also see how quickly things can get complicated!

Understanding which products/services are most profitable is critical. Profitability shows you where to spend more time and where you're wasting effort. In other words, it's the efficiency of your sales! Understanding your "product profitability" also allows you to look at the profitability of individual customers, customer segment (types of customers—Great Eats! tracks individual vs. business sales separately), sales areas, etc. Bookkeepers don't do this type of analysis, so to get this type of insight, a great finance person comes in handy!

To bring this section to a close, Gross Profit is the difference between Total Income and Total COGS. Notice that profitability increased by 10.1% as sales grew faster than COGS.

3. **Operating Expenses (Keeping the Lights On) (Money Out) = Account 6000s**

The other "money out" we talked about in Chapter 5 was Operating Expenses, or everything else it costs to run your business other than COGS. Remember: Operating Expenses exist whether you sell 1 unit or 1,000 units. You'll see them listed based on how you organized them in your Chart of Accounts, which is typically by function.

The Income Statement for Great Eats! gives you a taste of how the account groups we mentioned in the previous chapter can work.

	Sep-25	Oct-25	$ Change	% Change
Expenses				
6100 Advertising	$1,500	$1,000	-$500	-33.30%
6200 Office Supplies	$500	$450	-$50	-10.00%
6300 Wages and Salaries				
6301 Manager Salaries	$10,000	$10,000	$0	0.00%
6302 Health Care	$2,000	$2,100	$100	5.00%
6303 Other Benefits	$1,000	$1,500	$500	50.00%
Subtotal Wages and Salaries	$13,000	$13,600	$600	4.60%
6400 Building Expense				
6401 Rent	$5,000	$5,000	$0	0.00%
6402 Utilities	$1,000	$975	-$25	-2.50%
6403 Repairs/Maintenance	$800	$1,200	$400	50.00%
6404 Building Supplies	$150	$325	$175	116.70%
Subtotal Building Expense	$6,950	$7,500	$550	7.90%
6500 Other Expenses				
6501 Legal & Professional	$1,000	$900	-$100	-10.00%
6502 Depreciation	$2,000	$2,000	$0	0.00%
6503 Dues & Subscriptions	$750	$650	-$100	-13.30%
Subtotal	$3,750	$3,550	-$200	-5.30%
Total Expenses	$25,700	$26,100	$400	1.60%
Net Profit	**$18,300**	**$22,350**	**$4,050**	**22.10%**

Expenses—P&L

Here is a broader example of both groups and how the numbering system can be used:

- **6100 Marketing/Advertising**—Anything to promote your business.

- **6200 Administrative**—Office Supplies, Minor Equipment, Subscriptions.

- **6300 Wages & Salaries**—Salaries, Benefits, Bonuses for Non-Production Staff.

- **6400 Building Expense**—Rent, Utilities, Repairs.

- **6500 Other Expenses**—Legal/Professional, Dues, Travel, Employee Appreciation, Bank Fees, Depreciation. Of course, when any of these begin to pile up, they need to be broken out separately.

Why It Matters: Using groups allows you to see how much you're spending in related expenses and simplify your P&L. Using the groups allows you to budget and review actual performance more efficiently. We've seen companies with more than 100 expense accounts. Which is easier to make sense of your spending, looking at 100 rows in alphabetical order or 8–10 group totals? The gory details are always there when you need to investigate one group and the individual accounts that go into them.

Finally, we get to Net Profit, the "bottom line," which was up $4,050 or 22.1%. This is what you want to see, and a good time to remind you of two things:

1. It's calculated by Gross Profit minus Expenses. For Net Profit to grow, Sales have to grow faster than Expenses.

2. Net Profit is why you're in business, so figure out how to grow Sales faster than Expenses.

Understanding your P&L really is that simple!

Remember how in the KPI chapter we told you that you must have a comparison to provide any type of context for the numbers you're looking at? The same idea holds true for your Income Statement. We showed you two months for Great Eats! to demonstrate how to read, understand, and use your P&L. Let's look at this from a slightly different perspective.

Three "Whats" to Using Your P&L

We like to say there are three "whats" to your Income Statement. Let's take a look at the full P&L for Great Eats!:

◆ **What?** Your accountant gives you a P&L each month that provides you with a lot of facts. October sales were

Great Eats!
Profit and Loss Statement
September 1 - October 31, 2025

	Sep-25	Oct-25	$ Change	% Change
Income				
4100 Food Sales	$80,000	$86,500	$6,500	8.10%
4200 Beverage Sales	$20,000	$20,750	$750	3.80%
Total Income	$100,000	$107,250	$7,250	7.30%
Cost of Goods Sold				
5100 Food Costs	$30,000	$32,000	$2,000	6.70%
5200 Beverage Costs	$6,000	$6,200	$200	3.30%
5300 Direct Labor	$20,000	$20,600	$600	3.00%
Total Cost of Goods Sold	$56,000	$58,800	$2,800	5.00%
Gross Profit	**$44,000**	**$48,450**	**$4,450**	**10.10%**
Expenses				
6100 Advertising	$1,500	$1,000	-$500	-33.30%
6200 Office Supplies	$500	$450	-$50	-10.00%
6300 Wages and Salaries				
6301 Manager Salaries	$10,000	$10,000	$0	0.00%
6302 Health Care	$2,000	$2,100	$100	5.00%
6303 Other Benefits	$1,000	$1,500	$500	50.00%
Subtotal Wages and Salaries	$13,000	$13,600	$600	4.60%
6400 Building Expense				
6401 Rent	$5,000	$5,000	$0	0.00%
6402 Utilities	$1,000	$975	-$25	-2.50%
6403 Repairs/Maintenance	$800	$1,200	$400	50.00%
6404 Building Supplies	$150	$325	$175	116.70%
Subtotal Building Expense	$6,950	$7,500	$550	7.90%
6500 Other Expenses				
6501 Legal & Professional	$1,000	$900	-$100	-10.00%
6502 Depreciation	$2,000	$2,000	$0	0.00%
6503 Dues & Subscriptions	$750	$650	-$100	-13.30%
Subtotal	$3,750	$3,550	-$200	-5.30%
Total Expenses	$25,700	$26,100	$400	1.60%
Net Profit	**$18,300**	**$22,350**	**$4,050**	**22.10%**

Full P&L

$86,5000, expenses were $26,100, and profits were $22,350. Even when the report compares this year with last year, you still only have facts.

- **So what?** Now you're putting on your detective hat and beginning to look at things through a finance lens! What's jumping out at you? Maybe you really need to look at what drove sales, or you're seeing a sales or other trend that's either exciting or kind of concerning. This is the analysis part that your bookkeeper typically doesn't dive into. They are giving you the numbers; are they figuring out what caused them and what they mean? Probably not—that's on you.

You're becoming financially curious about the story in your numbers. When something doesn't look right or doesn't jibe with the result you expected, it's time to dig in to learn why. For Great Eats!, you can see the changes in dollars and percentages to help you identify what matters most. You decide what's important.

- **What's next?** This is where the value of a financial mindset really kicks in. You've spotted something that needs attention and some answers. Now is when you decide to act! Maybe you need to dig deeper to understand why something happened, identify options, and have conversations with your team about what you're seeing. Remember when we told you that numbers only represent your behaviors and decisions? Next month's numbers will depend on what you do next.

The magic of smart financial management begins when you move through all three "whats" instead of getting stuck staring at the numbers (or worse, avoiding them!) like so many business owners do.

Things Your Bookkeeper and Accountant Won't Tell You

Not every expense that shows up on your P&L is bad or a cost to be reduced to protect profit. When you spend money on staff training, business consulting, and technology upgrades, it all appears on your P&L as an expense. In reality, they are investments in your business to support profitable growth.

It's too bad that accounting doesn't have an "investment" section on the P&L. You bought this book and are learning from it. That's an investment. We often hear owners say they can't afford to hire a fractional CFO or marketing expert. When they finally realize they don't know their numbers, or need to make changes to their marketing, the real question becomes, can they afford NOT to?

This "investment" concept also reflects a mindset. You can either be proactive or reactive. Is it better to pay a lawyer to review a contract before it's signed or risk the legal cost you'll incur when there's a dispute down the road? There is a psychology to money. As you're spending, stop and think: *Is this a want or need? Is it an expense or an investment?* We want you to be proactive and in control of your future.

What Good Looks Like

Now we are getting into how to use your P&L. It provides the data used to create the most important KPIs we talked about in Chapter 14. No matter what industry you're in, three key percentages calculated directly from your P&L reveal how healthy your business really is:

- **Gross Margin %**—Take your Gross Profit and divide it by Net Sales. This shows you how profitable your actual sales are. Tracking this over time will help you understand when you need to raise prices, reduce direct costs, and even fire customers! For Great Eats!, October's Gross Margin was 45.2% ($48,450 COGS / $107,250 Sales).

When sales dollars are going up, costs will almost always be going up too. Gross margin tells you whether they are growing at the same rate. Sales growing faster than COGS will result in an increasing Gross Margin. When Costs are growing faster than Sales, Gross Margin will fall. Falling trends need immediate attention!

- **Total Expenses %**—Divide Total Expenses by Net Sales. This tells you what chunk of your sales gets eaten up by expenses. When this number is going up over time, you need to get better at managing your spending. For Great Eats!, October's Total Expense % was 24.3% ($26,100 Expenses / $107,250 Sales).

- **Net Profit Margin %**—Net Profit divided by Net Sales gives you a big picture of your overall profitability. For Great Eats!, October's Net Profit Margin was 20.8% ($22,300 Profit / $107,250 Sales).

Quick? What did we leave out?

We gave you no context for determining whether these numbers are good, bad, or indifferent.

Knowing your P&L numbers and these critical percentages is only the first step. When you stop there, all you have is some interesting trivia. Once you start comparing them with something else, the fun really starts. How are you doing against your goal? How do you stack up against industry standards? Are you doing better or worse than what is typical for businesses like yours? How are you doing compared with what you did last month, last quarter, or last year? Are things moving in the right direction?

What You Need to Do Each Month

Your P&L is only valuable when you use it. Here is a simple monthly routine that will keep you on top of your business performance:

- **Calculate the three key percentages.** Gross Margin, Total Expenses, and Net Profit Margin.

- **Track the three percentages.** Which way are they trending?

- **Find the big variances.** Which account groups are way up or way down, and what specific accounts are causing this?

- **Get explanations.** Have someone explain why the variances occurred.

- **Decide what to do.** Act based on what you learned.

- **Identify trends.** Are sales going up or down? Why?

- **Spot anomalies.** One-off spikes or dips that need explanation.

- **Watch for expense creep.** Is spending getting out of control?

- **Remember what caused changes.** Can you connect events to numbers? Do you have a more seasonal business or other natural business cycles?

- **Verify your memory.** Check whether your explanations are correct.

Common Choices That Cost You Money

Though your P&L is one of the most powerful business tools you have, problems can sneak up on you quickly when you're not careful. A lot of this comes from how your Chart of Accounts was set up in the first place, like we talked about in the last chapter. Simple choices including not categorizing expenses the right way consistently, overlooking revenue streams, or using confusing account names can throw off your entire financial picture. You could end up overpaying taxes or missing profitable opportunities because your P&L doesn't give you accurate and clear information.

Another common issue we see when business owners don't use their P&L regularly is underpricing their products or services. They set prices based on what they think is right without knowing their actual expenses. A lot of times, this happens because they have fallen into the day-to-day "busy trap" and don't think they have time to check their financials. In the meantime, their profitability quietly disappears.

Our client Sarah owned a busy coffee shop and couldn't figure out why she was working 70-hour weeks and barely breaking even. Her register was constantly ringing, customers loved the place, and she was always packed—so where was all the money going?

When she finally sat down with her P&L, the story became clear. Her gross margin was only 35%, far below the 60–70% she needed to be hitting for a coffee business. When she dug deeper, she discovered two main problems. First, she was buying premium ingredients at retail prices instead of wholesale, and second, her portion sizes were entirely too generous.

Her operating expenses told another part of the story: she was spending 45% of revenue on labor because she was over-staffed during slow afternoon hours and paying herself almost nothing for those 70-hour weeks.

Within two months of using her P&L to guide decisions, Sarah renegotiated supplier contracts, standardized portion sizes, and adjusted staffing schedules. Her Gross Margin jumped to 62%, and she finally started paying herself a real salary. Same busy coffee shop, same happy customers—and now the numbers made sense. The P&L didn't only show her the problem; it gave her a road map to fix it. She simply had to use it first.

Quick Win: Take a Closer Look at Your P&L

Start by giving your P&L a good spring cleaning. Your goal is to start with 10–15 lines that make sense when you read them. Once that's done, run your P&L for the last 13 months. Though 13 months may sound oddly specific, that amount of time gives you a full-year view, plus you can see what's happening right now compared with a year ago. The 13-month timeframe also shows how seasonal trends affect results over a full year.

Try to connect the dots with what was going on in your business at the time. Maybe that revenue spike lines up with your big marketing push, or those higher expenses match when you hired two new people.

When you see a line item that leaves you clueless, don't shrug and move on. Ask your bookkeeper to explain it in simple terms. The whole point is for this statement to help you run your business better.

Finally, take a closer look at your account names and groups. Now that you understand your P&L, it's a good time to have your bookkeeper make some adjustments to your Chart of Accounts.

Your future self, the one making confident decisions six months from now, is going to thank you for taking the time to get this sorted out.

Final Thoughts

We pointed out earlier that your financial statements were not designed to tell you how to grow your business. You need to understand how the numbers come together before you can understand the story they tell. Then you must use the "What?" "So what?" and "What's next?" and go back to your operations and decide what to change.

With a better understanding of your P&L, you're probably feeling like you have a better handle on where your money comes from and where it goes each month. Yet it's only telling you part of the story. It's like knowing how much you spent on groceries this month without knowing what is in your pantry. That's where your Balance Sheet comes in—working behind the scenes, keeping track of what your business owns and owes.

CHAPTER 17

BALANCE SHEET

Imagine your financial statements tracking what goes on in your kitchen. The Income Statement is your recipes in action. Revenue and expenses are the ingredients you used over time to make your favorite dish: profit. The Balance Sheet is your pantry's complete inventory of everything you own and owe at this exact moment. Every time you cook, your pantry changes. Each statement gives you a picture of your financial health.

Yet as soon as we mention "Balance Sheet," some clients suddenly remember they have urgent errands to run. We understand. A Balance Sheet feels less familiar than a P&L. It's simpler to think in terms of money coming in and going out, not assets and liabilities. That's okay.

Now, you probably won't read what we're about to say in a lot of other business books, though it's the truth. When you're running a simple service business from your laptop, your Balance Sheet may not be mission critical. We'll explain why in a moment.

In this chapter, we explore which businesses must really understand their Balance Sheet (and which ones can take a more relaxed approach), plus all the benefits that come with knowing the stories it tells. We break down each section of this statement so you'll know exactly what you're seeing when you look at yours, and focus on some of the KPIs that are most important here.

What Exactly Is a Balance Sheet?

Getting stuck on the name itself? It's called a Balance Sheet because, on any given day, everything balances and reflects this equation:

$$Assets = Liabilities + Equity$$

Basically, everything your business owns (assets) came from either borrowed money (liabilities) or your own investment and operations (equity). Both sides match up like magic (if they don't, something is really wrong!), and show exactly where you stand right now.

Unlike the Income Statement, which shows results over time, the Balance Sheet shows you one day. When you run it for the entire month of April, it really shows you April 30. When you run it for 2025, it shows you December 31, 2025.

Businesses that pay attention to their Balance Sheet can make more-confident decisions because they have the full picture of their money. In the simplest terms, the P&L tells you how profitable your business is; the Balance Sheet tells you how healthy it is.

Does the Balance Sheet Matter Equally for All Businesses?

The simple answer is no, not really. Some businesses can get by fine tracking their income and expenses and keeping a close eye on cash. For others, their Balance Sheet needs to become their best friend. At the end of the day, how much you lean on your Balance Sheet mostly comes down to the size and complexity of your business and what kind of business you're running.

Solopreneurs / Very Small Businesses vs. Larger / More Complex Businesses

When you're a solopreneur or a very small business, your financials are straightforward. You have fewer moving pieces to juggle, even though it might not feel that way at times. When your business doesn't have a lot of equipment or piles of inventory, and you're not drowning in debt, you probably don't need to spend a lot of time with your Balance Sheet. Instead, you're likely making most money moves based on what is in your bank account and which bills are coming up.

Once your business starts accumulating more assets—think property, inventory, or investments—and you have loans or credit cards, your Balance Sheet becomes more relevant. It helps you both keep tabs on how much cash and other things you own and stay on top of what you still owe.

Larger businesses have the most at stake here because they need regular financial checkups to make sure they're not heading for trouble. Plus, they're juggling banks that want to see solid financials before approving loans, partners who need transparency about the business's worth, and government requirements that demand proper reporting, all of which require an accurately maintained Balance Sheet. At this level, it is not only helpful; it's essential.

Overall, a Balance Sheet is especially important for the following types of businesses, regardless of their size:

- **Inventory-heavy businesses**—Retailers or product companies have their biggest investments tied up in inventory, equipment, and money that customers owe them. Mess this up and you'll find yourself in a cash crunch faster than you can say "out of stock."

- **Anyone who needs funding**—Whether you're going for a business loan or SBA funding or trying to impress investors, you will need to prove you are financially solid and therefore worth the risk.

- **Businesses with partners or shareholders**—Your Balance Sheet keeps everyone honest about who owns what, so no one gets surprised down the road.

- **Fast-growing companies**—It's understandable to get caught up in the excitement and spend beyond your means or lose track of mounting bills. A solid Balance Sheet tells you what you can afford.

Why Use Your Balance Sheet?

Are you still on the fence about whether this whole Balance Sheet thing is worth your time? Consider this: we've seen a lot of businesses that look great profit-wise yet are quietly drowning in credit-card debt with dangerously low cash reserves. That's because they aren't paying attention to the health of their business.

Once you see the full picture your Balance Sheet provides, you can start making smarter decisions about your business. Imagine you're eyeing that new piece of equipment and wondering, *Is now the time to apply for a business loan?* Your Balance Sheet has the answers you need, showing you how much cash you have to work with, what assets you could potentially leverage, and whether you're already carrying too much debt to safely take on more.

Most importantly, your Balance Sheet keeps you out of serious trouble before it's too late. Running out of cash or drowning in debt are two of the fastest ways to kill a business. Your Balance Sheet works like your financial smoke detector, sounding the alarm before the house is on fire.

The Three Main Sections of Your Balance Sheet

Like the P&L, your Balance Sheet has three main sections, each with its own range of account numbers. See the example for Great Eats! Though this is pretty typical, we often see multiple checking accounts, different types of inventory (raw materials vs. finished products), and more types of current liabilities. It all depends on what you need to see.

Like the P&L, the title begins with "Balance Sheet," the company name, and the time period. You can report month by month or the whole year. Only the last day of the period will be shown. You can click on any number to see the detail.

Balance Sheet
Great Eats!
September 1 - October 31, 2025

Header—Balance Sheet

1. **Assets (1000s)**

   These are the things of value your business owns. They include money in different bank accounts, money people owe you (accounts receivable), expenses you paid in advance, and inventory, equipment, and buildings. They are reported as either:

   a. Short-term assets (used within one year) that support daily operations. These include cash, accounts receivable, inventory, and prepaid expenses.

   b. Long-term assets (used beyond one year) that support long-term growth, like property, equipment, patents, vehicles, and trademarks.

   Why It Matters: Your assets are basically your business's ammunition for making money and staying afloat.

	Sep-25	Oct-25	Change
ASSETS			
Current Assets			
Bank Accounts			
1100 Primary Checking	$25,000	$15,000	$10,000
1102 Operating Savings Account	$85,000	$75,000	$10,000
Total Bank Accounts	$110,000	$90,000	$20,000
Other Current Assets			
1201 Accounts Receivable (A/R)	$15,000	$18,000	-$3,000
1301 Inventory	$125,000	$120,000	$5,000
1351 Prepaid Expenses	$5,000	$4,000	$1,000
Total Other Current Assets	$145,000	$142,000	$3,000
Total Current Assets	$255,000	$232,000	$23,000
Fixed Assets			
1401 Equipment	$150,000	$165,000	-$15,000
1402 Vehicles	$50,000	$50,000	$0
1450 Accumulated Depreciation	-$35,000	-$36,000	$1,000
Total Fixed Assets	$165,000	$179,000	-$14,000
TOTAL ASSETS	$420,000	$411,000	$9,000

Assets—Balance Sheet

2. Liabilities (2000s)

These are all the money your business owes. It includes bills
you haven't paid, credit-card balances, and loans you have
for vehicles, equipment, and buildings, as well as lines of
credit you're using. Like assets, there are two types:

    a. Short-term liabilities (due within one year) that
reflect what you need to pay soon, like accounts payable, short-term loans, and accrued expenses.

    b. Long-term liabilities (expected after one year) that
help finance growth. They include long-term loans,
mortgages, and long-term leases.

Why It Matters: Liabilities show you what's coming due
and how much financial pressure you're under.

LIABILITIES AND EQUITY			
Liabilities			
Current Liabilities			
2101 Accounts Payable	$32,000	$15,350	-$16,650
2102 Sales Tax Payables	$3,500	$4,500	$1,000
2201 Credit Card - Office	$6,800	$9,000	$2,200
2202 Credit Card - Production	$15,000	$17,000	$2,000
2300 Total Payroll Liabilities	$9,500	$8,900	-$600
Total Current Liabilities	$66,800	$54,750	$12,050
Long-Term Liabilities			
2600 Vehicle Loans	$48,000	$47,000	-$1,000
2700 Notes Payable	$75,000	$75,000	$0
Total Long-Term Liabilities	$123,000	$122,000	$1,000
Total Liabilities	$189,800	$176,750	$13,050
Equity			
3100 Owner's Investment	$50,000	$50,000	$0
3200 Net Income	$18,300	$22,350	$4,050
3300 Retained Earnings	$161,900	$161,900	$0
Total Equity	$230,200	$234,250	-$4,050
TOTAL LIABILITIES AND EQUITY	$420,000	$411,000	$9,000

Liabilities—Balance Sheet

3. Equity (3000s)

Equity is your stake in the business—what's left over for
you after the dust settles. Think of it as the difference
between what your business owns (assets) and what it owes
(liabilities). It includes the money you've invested and
the profits you've kept in the business (retained earnings)
minus your withdrawals. Here's the math: Equity = Assets
– Liabilities

Why It Matters: It shows you whether you're building
wealth or only staying busy.

Equity			
3100 Owner's Investment	$50,000	$50,000	$0
3200 Net Income	$18,300	$22,350	$4,050
3300 Retained Earnings	$161,900	$161,900	$0
Total Equity	$230,200	$234,250	-$4,050
TOTAL LIABILITIES AND EQUITY	$420,000	$411,000	$9,000

Equity—Balance Sheet

Balance Sheet
Great Eats!
September 1 - October 31, 2025

	Sep-25	Oct-25	Change
ASSETS			
Current Assets			
Bank Accounts			
1100 Primary Checking	$25,000	$15,000	$10,000
1102 Operating Savings Account	$85,000	$75,000	$10,000
Total Bank Accounts	$110,000	$90,000	$20,000
Other Current Assets			
1201 Accounts Receivable (A/R)	$15,000	$18,000	-$3,000
1301 Inventory	$125,000	$120,000	$5,000
1351 Prepaid Expenses	$5,000	$4,000	$1,000
Total Other Current Assets	$145,000	$142,000	$3,000
Total Current Assets	$255,000	$232,000	$23,000
Fixed Assets			
1401 Equipment	$150,000	$165,000	-$15,000
1402 Vehicles	$50,000	$50,000	$0
1450 Accumulated Depreciation	-$35,000	-$36,000	$1,000
Total Fixed Assets	$165,000	$179,000	-$14,000
TOTAL ASSETS	$420,000	$411,000	$9,000
LIABILITIES AND EQUITY			
Liabilities			
Current Liabilities			
2101 Accounts Payable	$32,000	$15,350	-$16,650
2102 Sales Tax Payables	$3,500	$4,500	$1,000
2201 Credit Card - Office	$6,800	$9,000	$2,200
2202 Credit Card - Production	$15,000	$17,000	$2,000
2300 Total Payroll Liabilities	$9,500	$8,900	-$600
Total Current Liabilities	$66,800	$54,750	$12,050
Long-Term Liabilities			
2600 Vehicle Loans	$48,000	$47,000	-$1,000
2700 Notes Payable	$75,000	$75,000	$0
Total Long-Term Liabilities	$123,000	$122,000	$1,000
Total Liabilities	$189,800	$176,750	$13,050
Equity			
3100 Owner's Investment	$50,000	$50,000	$0
3200 Net Income	$18,300	$22,350	$4,050
3300 Retained Earnings	$161,900	$161,900	$0
Total Equity	$230,200	$234,250	-$4,050
TOTAL LIABILITIES AND EQUITY	$420,000	$411,000	$9,000

Full Balance Sheet

Wrapping the Balance Sheet up, you can see that the $411,000 total of Great Eats! assets equals the $411,000 total of its liabilities and equity.

You may wonder why assets and liabilities are divided into short term and long term. The short-term groups are considered current working-capital accounts used to run your daily operations and are used to calculate a few different "ratios" that tell you how healthy your business is. Bankers find these fascinating! You will also see this in your Cash Flow Statement in the next chapter.

Remember our guidance on KPIs and the P&L? You must compare it with another number to have any context for evaluating what you're looking at. As with the P&L, you will also be looking for the three "whats." In the example, we compared two months: September and October 2025. The comparison numbers are shown for two key reasons:

1. It allows you to easily spot big changes from period to period.

2. The changes will help you understand your Cash Flow Statement. For now, stick with us. We'll get to cash in the next chapter!

Key Financial Ratios

For those businesses that do need to monitor their Balance Sheet, you'll find that some of those KPIs we talked about in Chapter 14 are based on numbers found on it. With your bookkeeper's support, you may need to pay attention to these critical numbers (your banker certainly will!):

◆ **Current Ratio [Current Assets ÷ Current Liabilities]**—
This measures whether you have enough short-term assets to cover your short-term bills. Think of it as, "Can I pay what is due in the next year?" You want this to be

above 1.5, meaning you have $1.50 in assets for every $1.00 you owe.

◆ **Quick Ratio [(Current Assets - Inventory) ÷ Current Liabilities]**—This is the stricter ratio because it excludes inventory, which might be hard to turn into cash quickly. You want this above 1.0, showing you can pay bills even when your inventory doesn't sell.

◆ **Debt to Equity [Total Liabilities ÷ Shareholder Equity]**—This shows how much you're relying on borrowed money versus your own investment to run the business. You generally want to keep this under 2.0—a higher number means you're getting leveraged; some industries can handle more debt than others can.

◆ **Accounts-Receivable Turnover [Net Credit Sales ÷ Average Accounts Receivable]**— This tells you how quickly customers pay you. A higher number means people pay faster, which is great for cash flow. A low number suggests you might need to tighten up your collection process.

◆ **Inventory Turnover [COGS ÷ Average Inventory]**—This shows how often you sell and replace your inventory each year. Too low means you're tying up cash in stuff that sits around too long. Too high might mean you're running out of stock too often.

What You Need to Do Each Month

Think of your monthly Balance Sheet review like getting a regular health checkup—it's simpler to catch and fix small issues before they become big problems.

Here is what you can do every month to keep your financial house in order:

◆ Run a Balance Sheet report showing the last 13 months side by side. Most accounting software can do this with a few clicks. Now you've got a year's worth of financial snapshots that tell the real story about where your business has been and where it's headed. Look for trends. Is your cash growing or shrinking? Are your debts climbing faster than your assets? Are there seasonal patterns you hadn't noticed before?

◆ Calculate your current ratio for each year and plot it on a graph.

◆ Keep everything accurate and up to date. Your Balance Sheet is only as good as the numbers going onto it, so making sure everything is correct is your top priority.

◆ Watch for red flags like an "Uncategorized" account, a negative number in any asset account (except Accumulated Depreciation, which is supposed to be negative), or a positive number in any Liability or Equity account.

◆ Take this month's Balance Sheet and put it side by side with last month's. Any big changes need to make you curious enough to understand what happened. Ask yourself, "Did our cash jump up because we got a big payment? Did our inventory spike because we placed a large order?" Make sure every significant change has a story that makes sense.

◆ Reconcile every bank account, credit card, and loan account.

◆ Review your Accounts Receivable and follow up on anything that's more than 60 days overdue.

◆ Check your Accounts Payable to make sure your bills are getting paid on time. When cash is tight, call your vendors and ask for extended payment terms rather than hope they won't notice.

◆ Make sure your numbers add up. Your Net Income from your P&L Statement needs to be tied back to the changes in your Retained Earnings on your Balance Sheet. When these numbers don't match up, something is wrong with your books, and you need to figure out what that is before you make any big decisions.

◆ Every month, use your Balance Sheet to answer these crucial questions:

- Are we improving or declining financially compared to last month?

- Are we burning through cash faster than we're bringing it in?

- Are we taking on too much debt relative to what we own?

Don't feel like you need to figure this all out on your own either. This is exactly the kind of conversation your accountant or CFO loves to have; they can spot things in those numbers that might take you hours to uncover. Plus, they can help you understand what the trends mean for your specific business and what moves you can consider making next. Think of it as getting a professional second opinion on your financial health—and it usually takes less than an hour of their time.

Lynn

I worked with a nonprofit whose CFO (who was also a CPA) and lead bookkeeper skipped the monthly reconciliation process...for years. In the three years before I got there, the difference between what was in their bank statements and accounting system had ballooned to nearly $9 million. That's the extreme example of what can happen when you don't pay attention to your Balance Sheet. Remember, though: every big problem starts small!

Quick Win: Ask Questions About Your Balance Sheet

Decide whether you need to use your Balance Sheet in your business. Ask yourself the following questions:

◆ Do I borrow money or lease equipment, or am I applying for credit?

◆ Do I manage cash flow, including Accounts Receivable and Payable?

◆ Do I own significant assets?

◆ Am I planning for growth or to exit?

Answered yes to any of the above? It's time to start reviewing and understanding your Balance Sheet monthly. Answered no to all of them? You may not need to look at it every month (although a quarterly or yearly review will help you see the bigger picture).

One of Your Most Powerful Tools

When you are comfortable reading your Balance Sheet and making it part of your monthly routine, it becomes one of your most powerful tools for building something solid and sustainable. When you use it, you no longer react to whatever happened last month. You're seeing the full financial picture, making smarter decisions about growth and spending, and catching potential problems while they're still small and fixable.

Now that you've got a handle on where your business stands today, let's talk about something equally important: how money moves through your business. In the next chapter, we'll dive into your Cash Flow Statement, which tells the story of how cash comes in, where it goes, and most importantly, whether you'll have enough of it when you need it most.

CHAPTER 18

CASH FLOW STATEMENT

Running out of cash is never a surprise. Business owners sense dark clouds gathering, even as they secretly hope next month will magically be different. You know that sinking feeling when your instincts tell you the bank balance won't cover payroll, loan payments, and that other big bill you have to pay? Or when you're lying awake at 3:00 AM wondering, *Where the fuck did all my money go?*

When you're feeling anxious about money, it's time to find a new bookkeeper or CPA! Several things are going wrong:

- You haven't been confident enough to ask them questions.

- They are not meeting with you to review your reports.

- They seem unable to clearly explain what is going on.

- They've never even mentioned, "By the way, there's this thing called a Cash Flow Statement."

We are going to fix that today!

Cash Beats Profit Every Time

Maybe you're thinking you don't need to worry about this. *I'm making money every month and my P&L looks great.* Think again.

Profit is an accounting concept; cash is what pays your bills. Don't believe us? Try depositing your Income Statement into the bank!

We've said it before, and we'll say it again: you can be profitable on paper and still find yourself scrambling to pay bills. There are businesses with millions in sales that go under because they tied up all their cash in inventory, equipment, or buildings when things were good and then couldn't cover their basic expenses and debt. This isn't a small business thing. Remember K-Mart? Toys "R" Us?

Your Cash Flow Statement shows you how much cash you started with a month, quarter, or year ago, then all the cash that came in and where it went. It explains why the $80,000 profit reported by your accountant isn't in your bank account. Isn't that what you need to know?

Here's what happens. You have $20,000 in sales this month and $15,000 in expenses, which looks like a nice $5,000 profit on your P&L. However, you also made a $1,000 loan payment, paid off a $2,000 credit-card balance, and bought a $3,000 piece of equipment. As simple as 1-2-3, you made $5,000 profit and paid $6,000. You spent what you took in and dipped into the cash you started with.

Andy

I was working with a client for six months. Over that time, she'd canceled four meetings because she was "too busy." When we finally talked, she asked me where all her money went. She was "working her ass off and only had two grand in the bank." We sat down and dug into her numbers. Her P&L looked decent, with expenses consistent with the goals we'd put forth at the beginning of the year and $31,000 in profit year-to-date after paying herself. Her Balance Sheet showed that her loan balances were correct and her accounts receivable was close to even. Then we pulled up her Cash

Flow Statement and everything clicked. Yes, she had made $31,000, and $28,600 of that had gone straight to loan payments, leaving her with exactly the $2,400 showing in her bank account.

Remember back in Chapter 4 when we talked about the three different ways money comes into your business? Well, when it's someone's money, it needs to be paid back—a novel concept, we know. In this case, money generated from services performed (found on the P&L) had paid down the loans (found on the Balance Sheet) and was captured over a set amount of time (found on the Cash Flow Statement).

When reviewing all three documents together, her COGS, fixed expenses, and all those monthly loan payments had added up quickly. At the end of the day, she needed to bring in $25,000 every single month to break even on cash even though the P&L indicated that she needed to bring in $22,000 to be "profitable."

Before we met for this call, her first instinct, like so many other business owners in this position, was to cut expenses. Yet her costs were in good shape. The real issue wasn't spending too much; it was not selling enough.

This was her light-bulb moment. She finally had some clarity because her Cash Flow Statement was showing her exactly how much cash she needed to generate every month to keep everything running smoothly. Once she could see that magic number clearly, she knew what she had to do. And when she started doing it consistently, she could plan for what was coming instead of being surprised every month by how little cash was left over.

What Is a Cash Flow Statement and Why Is It Important?

Your Cash Flow Statement combines information from your P&L and Balance Sheet. It cuts through the accounting noise to show exactly how much cash flows in and out of your business over a specific period of time. Unlike the P&L or Balance Sheet, though, it only tracks actual cash movements in and out of your bank accounts.

Great Eats!
October 2025 Cash Flow Statement

	Change	Source/Use
Starting Cash	$110,000	
Operations	Change	Source/Use
Net Profit	$4,050	Source
Add back: Depreciation	$1,000	Source
Change in Working Capital:		
Accounts Receivable	-$3,000	Use
Inventory	$5,000	Source
Other Current Assets	$1,000	Source
Change in Current Assets	$3,000	Source
Accounts Payable	-$16,650	Use
Credit Cards	$4,200	Source
Other Current Liabilities	$400	Source
Change in Current Liabilities	-$12,050	Use
Sub-Total Operations	**-$4,000**	**Use**
Investments	**-$15,000**	**Use**
Financing	**-$1,000**	**Use**
Total Change	-$20,000	Use
Ending Cash	$90,000	

Cash Flow Statement

The Cash Flow Statement's job is to explain the change in your cash from one period to the next. It ties together all the decisions you've made that affect cash. This is why it is so critical to understand those numbers first.

Cash Flow Statements, much like your P&L, are run for a specific time period. When you run it for January 1–August 31, the report goes through these steps:

◆ It looks at how much cash you started with on January 1 (where you ended December 31) and how much you had on August 31, and then it calculates the difference.

◆ It looks at how much net profit you made in January–August. Your Income Statement provides the details you need to assess the drivers of this cash activity.

◆ It determines how much each Balance Sheet account changed during the period of January–August.

◆ It summarizes all the changes into three main sections, which we'll get to shortly.

Some cash-flow reports are simpler to follow than others. We've seen different versions across clients that are on different QuickBooks versions. Talk to your (new?) bookkeeper to find a version that shows what you need to see. The key takeaway is this: the Cash Flow Statement will make sense only after you understand what's going on in both your P&L and Balance Sheet.

Forecasting

Your Cash Flow Statement also provides a starting point for creating a realistic forecast based on when money comes in and when bills go out, including those big expenses like bonus payrolls or equipment investments that can blindside you when you're not watching. Seeing these trends lets you proactively plan instead of reacting and scrambling when the bills come due. Like a weather forecast, it won't be 100% accurate. That's okay. Understanding your historical cash patterns helps you make much smarter predictions about what's ahead.

Take, for example, one of our clients who owns a landscaping business. He knows that business basically halts in the winter months. He also knows that the business costs about $50,000 a month to run, regardless of the season. Every year, by October 31, he makes sure he has $200,000 sitting in the bank. To help get ready for the slower time, he offers fall cleanup discounts to boost October cash and negotiates extended payment terms with suppliers to stretch his winter reserves. He can only do this proactive planning because he pays close attention to his cash-flow patterns.

As your business grows, gets more complex, and/or faces seasonal swings, your cash-flow forecast becomes your financial crystal ball—helping you spot cash crunches early and giving you time to do something about them. In this chapter, we help you understand what this financial document is all about, why it's important, who uses it most, and what you need to be doing with it each month.

Does the Cash Flow Statement Matter Equally for All Businesses?

Absolutely!

The time that you'll spend reviewing your Cash Flow Statement depends on how complex your business is and what your needs are. Solo businesses can usually "eyeball" cash needs, whereas larger businesses need to manage shortfalls, expansion, and outside obligations. The good news is QuickBooks and other accounting tools create this for you. When you want it, it's there. You only need to run the report or ask your bookkeeper to send it with your other statements. It's up to you to use it.

Solopreneurs / Very Small Businesses vs. Larger / More Complex Businesses

When your business is smaller and you receive sales in cash or credit cards, with no employees or big investments, you can probably track cash flow informally by looking at your bank balance or Income Statement. Other solo business owners use spreadsheets or apps to see how money flows and to avoid surprise shortages, which works fine for them.

Your Cash Flow Statement (and forecast) becomes critical when your business is invoicing customers and has inventory, equipment, employees, and/or loans. You need this statement to see historical patterns. You also need to look ahead for those big upcoming cash needs, like insurance premiums and property taxes.

Banks and investors will also want to see your Cash Flow Statement because they need to know you can manage money and pay your debts. Most importantly, it helps you track whether the money you think you're making (like payment for that big invoice that's due) is showing up in your bank account—and whether cash is sneaking out the back door faster than it's coming in the front.

Three Main Sections of a Cash Flow Statement

Like your P&L and Balance Sheet, the Cash Flow Statement has three main sections: Operations (your day-to-day business), Investing (equipment purchases, etc.), and Financing (loans, owner investments). At the bottom, you'll see the net cash flow for the period—how much your business's cash increased or decreased.

To see how the P&L, Balance Sheet, and Cash Flow Statement all work together, we've included them in the example from Great Eats! To get rid of a lot of clutter, the P&L and Balance Sheet have been summarized. The letters between the separate statements allow you to trace how activity flows through the statements. Remember: the Cash Flow Statement shows the change in cash at an account level from the other two statements.

You can use the following exhibits to trace your own numbers as you continue this journey!

1. Operating Activities

This is cash coming in and going out from your day-to-day business operations. Basically, it accounts for how much cash your core business is generating. It starts with net profit from your income statement and then adds money back for depreciation and other noncash transactions that are considered expenses that reduce net income, though no cash is actually paid.

It then shows changes to working capital, which includes all the current asset and liability accounts. Remember those from the previous chapter? These accounts are considered operating activity and include money received from sales (Accounts Receivable), payments to suppliers and credit cards (Accounts Payable), inventory, and other accounts.

Why It Matters: Operating cash is the lifeblood of your business and your main source of cash. Net Income is typically your main source of profit. And though cash trumps profit, when you're not selling at a profit, Net Income becomes a leading indicator that you're going to run out of cash. See how this all ties together?

2. **Investing Activities**

This tracks cash spent on or received from buying/selling long-term assets like equipment or buildings. Bought a new truck or sold old machinery? It shows up here. When your business hits a growth spurt and success seems to be kicking in, many owners go on a buying spree. This can lead to cash shortages when too much is tied up in purchases. Investments in this category do not include personal savings or savings plans for employees.

Why It Matters: It shows whether you're investing in your future. You can see how cash is used to grow and maintain your business or when cash is tied up in equipment not being used. It gives you a sense of long-term health.

3. **Financing Activities**

This covers cash flow related to how you fund your business: loans you take out or pay back, money you put in or take out as an owner, and any investor money. When you pay yourself too much and then put it back in the business to pay expenses—this is where that activity shows up, along with long-term debt payments.

Why It Matters: It shows whether you're funding growth or desperately trying to keep the lights on with other people's money. See "Operating Activities" earlier.

Summary P&L Statement
September 1 - October 31, 2025

	Sep-25	Oct-25	$ Change
Total Income	$100,000	$107,250	$7,250
Total Cost of Goods Sold	$56,000	$58,800	$2,800
Gross Profit	$44,000	$48,450	$4,450
Total Expenses	$25,700	$26,100	$400
Net Profit	$18,300	$22,350	$4,050

Summary Balance Sheet
September 1 - October 31, 2025

	Sep-25	Oct-25	Change
ASSETS			
Current Assets			
Total Bank Accounts	$110,000	$90,000	$20,000
Total Other Current Assets	$145,000	$142,000	$3,000
Total Current Assets	$255,000	$232,000	$23,000
Fixed Assets			
Total Fixed Assets	$150,000	$165,000	-$15,000
1450 Accumulated Depreciation	-$35,000	-$36,000	$1,000
Total Fixed Assets	$165,000	$179,000	-$14,000
TOTAL ASSETS	$420,000	$411,000	$9,000
LIABILITIES AND EQUITY			
Liabilities			
Total Current Liabilities	$66,800	$54,750	-$12,050
Total Long-Term Liabilities	$123,000	$122,000	-$1,000
Total Liabilities	$189,800	$176,750	$13,050
Equity			
Owner's Investment	$50,000	$50,000	$0
Retained Earnings	$161,900	$161,900	$0
Net Income	$18,300	$22,350	$4,050
Total Equity	$230,200	$234,250	-$4,050
TOTAL LIABILITIES AND EQUITY	$420,000	$411,000	$9,000

P&L and Balance Sheet to Cash Flow

Great Eats!
October 2025 Cash Flow Statement

Starting Cash $110,000

Operations	Change	Source/Use
Net Profit	$4,050	Source
Addback: Depreciation	$1,000	Source
Change in Working Capital:		
Accounts Receivable	-$3,000	Use
Inventory	$5,000	Source
Other Current Assets	$1,000	Source
Change in Current Assets	$3,000	Source
Accounts Payable	-$16,650	Use
Credit Cards	$4,200	Source
Other Current Liabilities	$400	Source
Change in Current Liabilities	-$12,050	Use
Sub-Total Operations	**-$4,000**	**Use**
Investments	**-$15,000**	**Use**
Financing	**-$1,000**	**Use**
Total Change	-$20,000	Use

Ending Cash $90,000

How to Use Your Cash Flow Statement

When it's time to use your Cash Flow Statement, start with the big question: are you generating more cash from operations than you're using?

To figure this out, you need to understand whether each line item is bringing cash in (a source) or taking cash out (a use). This can be confusing because the same item can be a source one month and a use the next. Here's the basic logic:

- **Operating Profit**—Positive = cash coming in. Negative = cash going out.

- **Accounts Receivable**—When it goes up, that is cash tied up with customers (a use). When it goes down, you collected money (a source). When customers pay late, you're giving them a loan (a use).

- **Accounts Payable**—When it goes up, you bought stuff and haven't paid for it yet (a source). When it goes down, you paid bills (a use).

- **Inventory**—When it goes up, you put cash on the shelf (a use). When you sell it, you get cash (a source).

After a few weeks of looking at this, it will all click!

Your Cash Flow Statement can also help spot problems early. How much cash is stuck in unpaid invoices or inventory? Are you borrowing money to cover losses? What expenses do you need to cut? Most importantly, you can use it to know how many months you can survive with your current cash—know this number!

Build Your Cash Cushion (and Hide It from Yourself)

The golden rule is to always have more cash than you think you need. Start by getting clear on your numbers. How much cash do you have right now, and how much is coming in regularly?

When you're running a smaller business, you're probably already monitoring your cash situation informally, which is fine. Now think about getting a bit more systematic. Even a simple emergency fund can save you from sleepless nights. Larger operations, on the other hand, need to get serious about tracking and planning with real numbers, detailed forecasts, and a big-enough emergency fund to weather real storms.

Here's a pro tip for habitual spenders: literally hide money from yourself by setting up automatic transfers to a separate "emergency only" account. Future you will thank present you for being paranoid about running out of money. This all ties back to earlier when we talked about buckets, envelopes, and having a checking/savings account at a different bank than where you have your operations account. It's all starting to make sense!

Quick Win: Calculate Your Runway

There are three simple things you can do now.

First, take 30 minutes to look at your current cash and figure out how many months you could survive with it. Take your cash balance and divide it by your average monthly expenses. When you have $50,000 in cash and spend $15,000 per month, you have about 3.3 months of runway. You need to know this number.

Second, look at your business to see where you have any big annual bills (insurance, taxes, etc.) coming up and make sure you're planning for those payments.

Third, check your accounts receivable and payable. Pick up the phone and call the people who owe you money and do the same with any outstanding large bills you owe.

These things will give you a good sense of how cash flows in and out of your business. Remember: the goal is predicting what's ahead, not perfection. This is also a good time to investigate a business line of credit for additional peace of mind. Call a banker or two and start to build relationships.

Bottom Line

Ready to sleep better at night, know where your money is really going, and never be caught off guard again? Use your Cash Flow Statement.

Understanding how cash moves through your business helps you avoid the choices that kill more profitable companies than anything else: running out of cash. When you know your cash patterns, you stop hoping you'll have enough money next month and start knowing whether you will. It's the clearest way to keep your finger on the pulse of your real financial health.

In the next section, we'll put everything together and show you how to use all three financial statements and everything else you learned so far as a complete system for running your business with clarity and confidence.

PART VI
IMPLEMENTATION AND EXECUTION

Welcome to PART VI, where the rubber meets the road. You've learned a lot so far in this book. We've shared who's on your team and how they support you, where your money comes from, where it goes, which numbers matter most for your business, and what data to track. That's all great; it also doesn't mean a damn thing without action.

Everything so far has been prepping you for a very different journey. Starting now, we don't give a shit about how you did things in the past. It's time to start building your future. We're putting all the pieces together and creating the processes that will guide you to get from where you are today to where you plan to be tomorrow. This section is your windshield. From this point on, you're going to look ahead, using your numbers to drive your business forward.

This isn't going to be a quick trip—and it doesn't have a finish line, as you will be chipping away, learning, and adapting for as long as you own and run your business. Our experience shows that achieving real financial transformation requires 18 to 36 months. It's not that it's complicated. It's that lasting change needs time. It also gets messy. Some months will test your patience. Some decisions will feel overwhelming. Good. That messiness means you're proactively managing your business, not reacting.

Instead of spending hours each month worrying about your numbers, you'll spend that same time (or less) working on them. The work moves you forward; the worry keeps you stuck. You'll see that taking action—even imperfect action—feels a lot better than the exhausting cycle of stress and avoidance you're probably used to.

Along the way, you will learn to use a simple, practical tool: your scorecard. In a few months, checking it will be as routine as looking at your phone. Scorecards work because they make your business better and your life simpler. They keep you focused and on track and will change as your business evolves. One quarter might call for an all-out sales push, whereas the next could shift your attention to hiring so you can support growth.

Changing priorities isn't a sign of failure; it's proof that you're tuned in to what your business needs. It's all about progress. Remember: it's better to be approximately correct than accurately wrong.

What's Next

In the chapters ahead, we'll dig into both your financial and operational numbers to guide you better, help you understand your story, and turn insights into real impact. Then we'll guide you through building your scorecard to keep you on track—week after week, quarter after quarter, and year after year. Buckle up! It's time to take control of your business by using your numbers—and getting them to work as hard as you do.

TURNING INSIGHTS INTO IMPACT

Congratulations! You've reached the first big summit on your numbers journey. By embracing what you've learned, you've already climbed higher than many business owners ever will. Most of them either get discouraged by the initial climb, get distracted by what they think are simpler paths, or remain convinced that financial clarity is only for "numbers people." You stayed the course by pushing through the learning curve even when it felt overwhelming.

The view is different from up here. You can see the entire landscape behind you. The financial chaos that used to keep you up at night now makes much more sense. Soon, you'll begin to understand which of your products or services are most profitable. Team performance will show up in your data. And your on-time financial statements will become your trusted advisors instead of mysterious documents that arrive too late to be of any use.

And, for the first time, you'll see what lies ahead and consider what you can do instead of constantly reacting to what's happened. When you can spot the curves coming, you get to define the best route and avoid unnecessary detours.

Your business will keep evolving, the economy will shift, and competition will change—only now, you have the power to use data to look and plan ahead.

You have always known a lot about your business, yet you were caught in the "I just don't understand my numbers" mindset that traps so many business owners. That belief was never entirely true. You simply didn't have a structure around your instincts. You can trust them, with the tools to verify.

Even before picking up this book, you instinctively knew which products sold best, which employees you could count on, and which days were most productive. The difference is you will soon have a framework that turns those hunches into actionable insights you can use to grow your sales and profits.

This chapter will shift your mindset to recognize that you have different decisions—or, as we call them, "levers"—at your disposal. These aren't hypothetical. They're real, actionable tools that, when used strategically at the right time, will drastically change your business. The key is knowing which ones exist and understanding their potential impact before you need them.

Be a Detective

Everything we've covered so far may still feel like scattered dots. That's okay. Feeling a bit different? That's okay too. It's because you're no longer "just" a business owner—you're a detective. And like any good private eye, you have the tools and curiosity to piece all the data together to see the complete picture. As you do so, you will become increasingly confident and decisive.

Business demands action, and that means making tough calls: letting go of the rotten apple destroying the team, eliminating a money-bleeding product or service you love, or firing the client who always pays late and treats your business like their personal bank. When your data tells you something isn't working, don't procrastinate. Stop it. Immediately.

Too often, business owners do the opposite. They make a decision, then hunt for information to justify it. Sound familiar? Doing this probably got you into trouble before. Now, for the first time, you'll recognize you have real information to look at first and then make decisions based on facts.

You now understand your profit margins, KPIs, and financial statements. Think about what these reveal. We've seen things like:

- low-margin products eating up your team's time,

- client types that pay fastest vs. the ones dragging out payments,

- seasonal patterns in your cash flow and big future needs,

- the real cost of that "cheap" employee who creates expensive mishaps, and

- the marketing channel that brings in customers who buy vs. the ones who only look.

The real question becomes, what decisions will you make now that you have this clarity? You're more empowered than you've ever been to think about the levers you can pull to get the biggest impact.

The Levers Framework

We're now going to guide you beyond understanding your story to actively rewriting it. Every decision you make falls into a category, and each category works like a lever. Pull the right lever at the right time and you will shift everything. Pull the wrong one and you're only burning energy without results.

Levers become your business control panel of options you can choose from. When you understand what each one does and pull them based on data instead of gut instinct, you can systematically transform your business results. Below are the most common lever categories:

- ◆ **Pricing levers**—These control your revenue per transaction, profit margins, and customer perception.

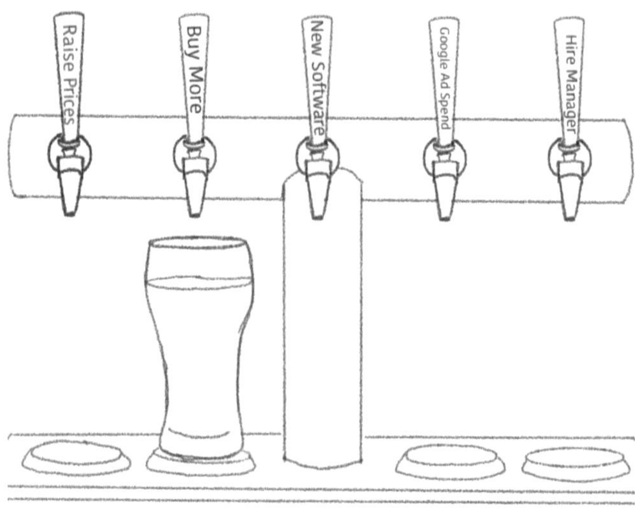

When Susan's consulting firm was booked solid for three months out, she faced a choice: hire more people or raise prices. Instead of increasing costs, she raised her hourly rate from $150 to $200. The result was 15% fewer inquiries into new business and 33% higher revenue, plus she could be more selective about clients. These levers work best when demand exceeds supply, costs increase, or you want to filter for better customers.

- **Volume levers**—These affect your total units sold, market share, and cash-flow timing. Mike's restaurant was consistently slow on Tuesdays, so he introduced "Tuesday Takeover," with 30% off appetizers. Since he already had kitchen staff on payroll, the additional cost was minimal. Soon, Tuesday became his second-busiest night. Pull these levers when you have excess capacity, during seasonal dips, or when you need a quick cash injection.

- **Operational levers**—When it's time to control your capacity, product/service quality, team satisfaction, and scalability, you need to consider operational levers. Tom's e-commerce business was drowning in customer-service emails until he invested in an FAQ chatbot and an order-tracking system. Customer service time dropped 60%, and satisfaction scores increased because customers got instant answers. These levers are most powerful when you're hitting capacity limits or experiencing quality issues, or when growth has stagnated.

- **Marketing levers**—These levers determine who finds you, how they perceive your value, and what actions they take. Rebecca's accounting firm was struggling to attract clients until she shifted from advertising "bookkeeping services" to "profit optimization for growing businesses." Same service, different positioning. Her inquiries doubled, and average project values increased 40% because she began attracting business owners focused on growth rather than cost cutting. Use marketing levers when you need better customers or want to change market perception or differentiate your brand from competitors.

◆ **Resource-allocation levers**—These levers control where your time, money, and energy go, and they directly impact profitability and growth. Jennifer's marketing agency discovered that social media management had 12% margins while strategy consulting had 67% margins. She stopped accepting new social media clients and raised those prices by 40%. She lost 30% of that business yet increased overall profits by 22%. These levers become critical when you identify profit disparities between products, services, or customer segments, or when you need to focus limited resources for maximum impact.

Andy

My wife and I have a rental property that we listed on Vrbo. Early on, we found out that we needed 10 bookings and 5 reviews to become a Vrbo Premier Host and get better visibility on the platform. Instead of guessing or doing what felt right, we looked at the data and thought about how we were going to get 10 bookings fast. We saw that lower-priced properties were booking quickly. The numbers showed me that lowering my price temporarily would drive the bookings we needed. We pulled that lever. And it worked. Once we hit those 10 bookings, we raised the price back up. More bookings led to more reviews, which led to better platform positioning, which led to more bookings at higher prices. We realized that we needed to begin with the end state in mind to let the data tell us what to do instead of making an uninformed emotional decision about pricing and then trying to justify it later.

This story highlights the difference between using data to make decisions and, well, guessing. One approach builds your business systematically. The other leaves you wondering why the decision you made didn't work.

Let's be honest: not every lever you pull will work exactly as planned. Again, tracking the right data gives you the information you need to "fail fast." Shift gears to a different lever. These "aha!" moments become your greatest teachers. You've learned to use your numbers to make decisions, measure results, and adjust again as needed. Now it's time to start experimenting.

The Ripple Effect: How Levers Connect

Levers don't operate in isolation. They create ripple effects throughout your business. Understanding these connections is what separates strategic decisions from random actions. For example, let's say you've pulled the lever to raise prices by 15%. The immediate effect? You lose 20% of your customers who were more price sensitive. Check out the math. Say your service price was $100 and you had 10 customers, your revenue is $1,000. After raising your price to $115, two customers leave (-20%) and your immediate revenue drops to $920. Picking up only one new customer at the higher price raises revenue to $1,035. You increased profit and cash flow while doing less work. The secondary effect? Losing those customers frees up your team to focus on higher-value activities and improve overall service quality. The final effect is that higher prices and better service support your premium positioning, attracting better customers who pay more.

Quick Win: Identify Three Potential Levers

Think about what you've learned so far: concrete facts about your business that you didn't know before. That's a huge step forward! Now think about how you're going to use this information. Look at the big picture, the decisions that need to be made, and the different levers you can use. Don't forget: it's not just you. You have a whole team whose input may be valuable.

Share the numbers and engage them. Don't make any decisions yet—we'll help with those in the next chapter. For now, know your options.

You also want to have a CFO or someone who can guide you in making sense of your numbers on an ongoing basis. Once you taste what real financial awareness feels like, you'll never go back to solely trusting your gut.

Write Your Own Story

Until now, the numbers have been written purely about what has happened. It's too late to do anything about them. Now, as you continue to take money management far beyond accounting and increasingly use KPIs and your financial mindset, you get to write the story by applying logic to your narrative. It's still your story, and now it's backed by data instead of intuition and wishful thinking. Here's a simple example. You proactively ask your accountant in November to estimate year-end taxes and learn that you may owe $15,000. Now you can identify, evaluate, and decide the best option, or lever, to ensure that the money is available. Doesn't that feel better than reacting to a February surprise?

Understanding your numbers and levers empowers you to write your business story and reach destinations you couldn't even see before. The path forward has become clear. You can see where you want to go and the best path to get there.

Look at you! With a bit of Hillbilly Math and a clear understanding of what money management includes, you've graduated from hope-based business management to strategic, data-driven leadership. Instead of making moves and hoping that they work, you're making deliberate decisions backed by real information. Now that you understand the levers at your disposal, it's time to create your scorecard and master which ones to pull.

CHAPTER 20

SCORECARDS AND ONGOING TRACKING

The best business conversations start with clarity. When someone asks how things are going, insightful business owners can rattle off a few key "metrics" (a fancy word for facts, information, or data) that tell the whole story. These owners are not number-crunching wizards. They've simply figured out which numbers really matter.

Let's clear something up here: more data doesn't necessarily mean more insights. Instead of getting buried in spreadsheets, successful business owners keep it simple and track only what guides them to make better decisions. That's what a good scorecard does. It cuts through the noise and gives you a clear picture of what you've been looking for. Instead of answering questions and making decisions based on hunches, what somebody "thinks" they know, or the last opinion you hear, you have a straightforward way to measure how you're doing.

So what exactly is a scorecard? Well, remember all those KPIs you were introduced to in Chapter 14? The scorecard is a few of those KPIs per department and on the whole business bunched together to tell a story. Here's a simple, more descriptive definition: A business scorecard is a tool that measures, tracks, and shares the most important numbers in your business. It shows, at a glance, whether you're on track to reach goals and helps your team stay aligned on what matters most and make better decisions based on real data.

Take a minute to review the following exhibit. You'll see it resembles your financials. Each line represents a separate measure (e.g., Sales vs. Average Sales per Employee), that tracks actual results to a goal or history and is trended to show the direction of your performance. We recommend holding weekly updates and team reviews.

Trend	Title	Person	Goal	Six Week Average	10/26 - 11/1	10/19 - 10/25	10/12 - 10/18	10/5 - 10/11	9/28 - 10/4	9/21 - 9/27
	Profit Margin YTD	Shelia	20.0%	19.2%	20.8%	20.2%	19.3%	18.8%	18.3%	17.8%
	Average Ticket	Robert	$60.00	$59.13	$57.14	$60.71	$61.90	$57.14	$59.52	$58.33
	Customers per Week	Penelope	160	163.3	160	170	173	160	166	160
	Desserts Sold	Jayden	50	43.5	57	51	50	45	30	28

Revenue	$24,000	$25,500	$26,000	$24,000	$25,000	$24,500
Days per Week	7	7	7	7	7	7
Tickets per Day	60	60	60	60	60	60
Avg Ticket	$57.14	$60.71	$61.90	$57.14	$59.52	$58.33
Avg People	2.5	2.5	2.5	2.5	2.5	2.5
Avg Ticket/Person	$22.86	$24.29	$24.76	$22.86	$23.81	$23.33

Scorecard

A scorecard keeps you honest about what's working (and what isn't), even when the truth is uncomfortable. More importantly, when used well, it changes how your team talks about the business. Essentially, KPIs are the numbers that tell everyone, "This is what's important to us. These are the expectations." Instead of wasting meeting time asking people, "So how are we doing?" you can jump straight to, "Okay, what do the numbers tell us to tackle next?"

In this chapter, we're going to show you how all the levers we talked about become your tool kit for action, then guide you in creating a scorecard and choosing which levers to pull. It's time to stop reading and start doing!

Andy

We use our scorecard religiously. Every single week at our Level 10 meeting, we review it to better understand where our business is going. Previously, for weeks, we would continually be behind our sales goals, and I would hear from the sales department that the service department wasn't allowing them to book as much work as was available. Instead of arguing about how much work we could or couldn't book, we figured out how many employees we needed to facilitate the work necessary to meet our financial goals. We needed 20 employees when we only had 12. We now realized this wasn't a sales issue or a service issue; it was an HR issue. One of our company's KPIs added to our scorecard was "Troops to Task," which essentially told us how many employees we had compared with how many we needed in order to complete all the work necessary to hit our top-line sales goals.

Turns out we were only at 60% toward our goal on employees and 90% toward our sales goal. This told us three important things: our current employees were crushing our efficiency goals, more service employees would solve our perceived sales problem, and we had a hiring/HR issue when our initial assumptions were that we had a sales or service issue.

Next, we figured out that we were filtering through résumés and hiring at the same rate as we had in the past based on the number of applicants. This told us that we were not getting enough qualified applicants at the top of the funnel to facilitate the work that sales needed to deliver. We pulled our marketing lever (increasing our recruiting budget and lowering our marketing budget for 90 days) to recruit more employees into the hiring funnel so we could hire and train more employees to facilitate the work. We solved a sales problem by decreasing our marketing budget and increasing our HR budget—who knew? This is the power of a scorecard.

What to Measure?

Ask any business owner about building a scorecard and you'll get the same question we do: "What the hell do I measure?" It's understandable. Every business creates a lot of new data every day. Most owners and their teams have never been shown how to use it. It all comes down to measuring:

- ◆ Dollars and cents are reported by accountants, and some of their numbers will make it onto the scorecard.

- ◆ All other business operations are measured by KPIs that show you what is happening and point to what may happen.

Once leaders buy into the idea of measuring, many go completely overboard. Suddenly, they want to track everything because more numbers must mean more control, right? Not necessarily. Measuring everything really tells you nothing. Having too much data only creates noise when what you really need is clarity. When everything is a priority, then nothing is a priority.

Now think back to your vision. Where do you want your business to go? This may be a good time to flip back to the OODA loop in Chapter 2 where we shared how your destination provides the orientation to the end state. When a decision is helping you or hindering you from reaching a goal, consider the OODA loop.

The real key to this is simplicity. We want you to have the answers to what drives your business. To get there, get curious about it. Ask yourself what you need to know right now: "Are profits climbing with sales?" "Do I have enough cash to make payroll?" "Am I making money or simply working myself to death for less?"

To guide you in finding what matters most to your business, think about the following questions.

Financial Questions:

- ◆ What's my gross profit margin by product/service?

- ◆ How long does it take to collect payments?

- ◆ What's my customer-acquisition cost?

- ◆ What's the lifetime value of my customers?

- ◆ How much cash do I have on hand?

- ◆ What are my fixed vs. variable costs?

- ◆ Which revenue streams are growing/declining?

Operational Questions:

- ◆ How long does it take to deliver my service/product?

- ◆ What's my error/rework rate?

- ◆ How many leads are we converting to customers?

- ◆ What's my employee productivity rate?

- ◆ How full is my capacity?

- ◆ What's my inventory turnover?

Growth/Strategic Questions:

- ◆ How many new customers am I getting monthly?

- ◆ What's my customer-retention rate?

- ◆ How satisfied are my customers?

- ◆ What's my market share?

- ◆ How quickly am I growing?

Once you've thought about these questions and how you might answer them, group them into four categories based on impact to guide you in prioritizing them:

- High Impact + Simple to Measure = Your Gold Mine

- High Impact + Hard to Measure = Worth the Effort

- Low Impact + Simple to Measure = Nice to Know

- Low Impact + Hard to Measure = Ignore for Now

It's okay that you looked at many of these and thought, *I have no freaking clue what some of these are or the foggiest idea of how to get to measuring them.* This is why it typically takes 18–36 months. This shit can be complicated! And when you think you've got it figured out, your business will change and you'll need different KPIs. Remember: you're building the ability to predict, decide, and execute. Building the team culture and the muscle memory to do it is the business value you're creating.

Designing Your Scorecard

Keep in mind what we said earlier: your weekly scorecard is a simple dashboard that tracks the 5–10 metrics that are key indicators of your business performance. You can always add more as the habit develops and you begin to build dashboards for different departments.

The goal is not to track everything; it is to track the right things consistently so you can steer your business with confidence instead of guesswork.

The goal is not to track everything; it is to track the right things consistently so you can steer your business with confidence instead of guesswork. And you won't get them right the first time. You'll track certain results and then realize they're not as useful as you expected. Experiment.

Here are a few important things to keep in mind about your scorecard that demonstrate why you must stop avoiding your numbers:

- You determined these are the key indicators to guide your business and decisions.

- Each metric needs a target or goal to provide context.

- Every metric must be updated consistently—no exceptions!

- Every number must reflect the four Cs of data: clear, current, complete, and correct!

- Scorecards provide clarity and tell your team what's important.

- Scorecards create accountability by identifying who owns each number.

- Scorecards demonstrate that your data is being used and is expected to be kept clean.

Your scorecard will likely include some of the following metrics, and it may reflect overall company objectives as well as key department priorities.

Financial:

- Weekly revenue

- Cash on hand

- Accounts Receivable outstanding > 90 days

Sales & Marketing:

- New leads generated

- Sales calls or meetings completed

- Conversion rate

Operations:

- Number of projects

- Projects completed on time

- Customer-satisfaction score

Team:

- Staff productivity or utilization rates

- Training hours completed

- Number of employees vs. goal

Besides keeping it simple, you want to make sure your scorecard is visual and actionable. You may even want to use color coding for instant feedback so you can easily see what worked well, what you're close on, and what needs significant work. Green (on track) and red (off track) work best. Colors do another thing: they allow you to hold a page up and instantly let people know whether it's good or bad from three feet away!

Hold a brief weekly team meeting to review your scorecard. Celebrate wins, discuss the areas that are close, and create action plans for the ones that need work. Only you in your business? Then schedule time weekly to review it yourself. After a few months, you'll start seeing patterns. Maybe sales always dip in the third week of the month, or your pipeline dries up when you stop doing 1-to-1s. Look for the story it's telling you and choose the areas that matter most to you today. That's your scorecard. It's not a random pile of numbers. It's a real narrative about how your business is doing. Once you have that, it's time to figure out what to do next.

Which Levers to Pull?

With your scorecard, you have information (data) you need, though the data itself doesn't move your business forward. You do, with your levers, those simple actions that create big results when you pull them. Maybe you've noticed that for every 10 podcast episodes you put out, you land one new client. When your goal is to reach 10 new clients, you know to pull the lever to increase episode production as quickly as possible to 100 episodes to hit your new client goal. Simple enough, right?

The tricky part is figuring out which levers actually work and not merely keep you "busy." This is where many business owners hit a roadblock, especially when numbers start to slip. When panic kicks in, they start pulling every lever in sight or a random one, lacking sufficient information to decide "pull this one now." For example, we had a restaurant client who was making serious money on breakfast and lunch and, at the same time, losing their shirt every night after 3:00 PM. In a panic, they decided to expand their dinner menu, thinking that more options would bring in more customers. Over the next month, they saw their food expenses increase substantially for a service that was already hemorrhaging money. What happened? They'd pulled the wrong lever. We guided them to see that the right lever wasn't to add anything to dinner; it was to not be open for dinner at all. With breakfast and lunch only, their margins increased quickly. Secondary effect: the entire staff, including owners, never had to cover a dinner shift—win-win!

We also see this a lot with marketing. As soon as sales struggle, the first instinct for many business owners is to cut marketing expenses. Step back and think about that logically.

Andy

We adjust Google ads for our junk-removal company based on availability in each coming week. That is our lever. When the calendar is more than 75% full, we cut back on ads. When it's between 50 and 75%, we don't touch it. When they fall below 50%, we increase our spending on ads for the week. That's a lever pulled with intention and guided by the scorecard.

How does pulling back on marketing increase sales? It's like turning off the faucet when you need more water.

There are also times when your scorecard will tell you not to pull any lever at all. Some companies get very successful by keeping things simple. For example, Raising Cane's restaurants have never expanded beyond chicken fingers. They didn't do that because they're lazy. They did it because it works. Costco does great with around 4,000 products while Walmart juggles 100,000. These companies have figured out what makes them the most money and do more of that. The same principle applies to smaller businesses. Focus on what matters most.

When you strip it down, most business decisions come back to three levers: (1) make more money, (2) lower the cost of what you sell, and (3) cut overhead. (That sounds an awful lot like your P&L, doesn't it?) When you decide to spend $99 a month on a scheduling tool to save you 10 hours a week on administrative tasks and your time is worth $200 an hour, you're going to make more money by using that time better.

As we demonstrated in Chapter 6, money bleeds out in many ways. Another lever is stopping waste in your cost structure. Renegotiating with vendors, asking for better payment terms, or shopping around for deals can all lower your cost of sales. Though sticking with a vendor for 10 years is comfortable, it may become very expensive. When the service isn't cutting it anymore, the financial hit of staying put usually outweighs the discomfort of switching. It's time to pull the lever to plug these leaks.

Ongoing Tracking

Building a scorecard is important, of course. It's also only the beginning. To really see its value, you must use it regularly. That means weaving it into how your business runs, including processes, calendar reminders, regular meetings, job descriptions, and team expectations. Without this habit, even the best scorecard becomes another fancy spreadsheet gathering digital dust, which is exactly what happens to many business owners.

They make excuses for not tracking their scorecards weekly. To them, they either don't have the time or the right data, or they don't know where to start. Sometimes they are afraid of what it will show, forcing that accountability look in the mirror.

Andy

I ran my business for seven years without any scorecard, and when I finally built one, I fell into the trap of tracking everything. I had 50 metrics and was drowning in data. It was rough for months before it became useful. Now each team focuses only on three to five metrics, which tells us everything we need to know.

You're not going to make the same excuses. You don't need to wait for your scorecard to be perfect before you start tracking. Dive in, even when it's messy or feels pointless at first.

That's how incremental change works. First, you get started. It's like paying yourself a small salary before you think you can afford it: starting the habit matters more than doing nothing. Track things daily, weekly, and monthly and then look at the big picture for the yearly view.

Remember how we urged you to compare your financials versus a future that you define? The same goes for your scorecard. Use your history to set realistic expectations, then measure how you're doing against the actual plan. Are you hitting targets? Which assumption proved way off? Which operational results are lagging behind?

At least every quarter, step back and ask yourself, "Are we tracking the right stuff?" and "Do these numbers still matter?" Professional sports prove that what you measure needs to evolve. For 100 years, baseball obsessed over batting average while ignoring walks. Now it's the on-base percentage that tells the real story. The NFL didn't even track sacks until the 1980s. The same goes for your business. What you measure will change over time because your business is evolving.

Consistent tracking creates culture. When your team knows exactly what numbers matter and can see how they're doing, they step up. The minute you bring data into leadership meetings and team check-ins, they get curious about what's working, which levers matter, and how their day-to-day connects to the bigger picture. They **want** to be part of something bigger than their job! In fact, when you have employees disengaged from the scorecard, it may be an indicator that you have other problems.

We know what you're thinking: *I can't show everything!* You don't need to. No one needs to know your take-home pay, for example, yet you absolutely must connect your team to how the business is performing. Understanding how their activities connect to numbers is the first step. When they understand what success looks like, they start acting differently. Marketing focuses on quality leads that convert, not only lead volume. Sales goes after profitable deals that stick. Operations aligns efficiency with keeping customers happy. Now you're building employee morale, engagement, and accountability.

> **Lynn**
>
> A company I worked for based profit sharing on a "profit index." Great idea, with only one problem. No one beyond the owner, president, and CFO knew how it was calculated or what it meant! One year, the president reported company performance of 75% against the 95% index goal and asked for everyone's ideas on how they could improve. Great idea again, with only two problems. First, the profit index was a number that virtually no one understood. Second, because profits were never talked about, few people ever thought much about how they could impact it. The culture at the time did not value broad information sharing.

Before you know it, you can take that vacation you've been putting off for years. While you're at the beach, you can check your scorecard and trust that your team is handling things because they know what results matter, the boundaries they can act within, and they are accountable.

And you can relax, confident that you have built a real business, not simply doing a job that requires your constant attention.

Quick Win: Create Your Scorecard

Don't overthink this. Grab a simple Google Sheet, Excel spreadsheet, or even a piece of paper and write down three to five numbers you wish you knew about your business right now. Maybe it's monthly revenue, the number of new customers, or how much you're spending on marketing. Pick the ones that will guide you to make better decisions today.

Set up a column each for the metric name, this week's number, last week's number, and maybe a target when you have one. That's it. You don't need fancy formulas or immediate color coding—those can be added later. The goal is to start the habit of looking at your numbers regularly, not to build the perfect dashboard.

Once you have your basic scorecard, commit to updating it weekly on the same day, at the same time. Put it on your calendar like you would any other important meeting. After a month, you'll start seeing patterns. After three months, you'll wonder how you ever ran your business without your scorecard.

From Chaos to Clarity

Building a scorecard doesn't mean you're suddenly obsessed with numbers. It means you finally have clarity in a world full of business noise. When you know which metrics matter and track them consistently, you stop making decisions based on hunches and start making them based on reality. Your team gets aligned around common goals and becomes better able to solve problems before they become disasters.

You can even take some time off without your phone buzzing every five minutes. Most importantly, you'll transform your business from something that demands your daily involvement into one that can grow and thrive. Isn't that what you've always wanted?

PART VII

NOW BUSINESS GETS PERSONAL

We've thrown a lot at you, so let's take a quick look back to reflect on what we have covered so far:

- ◆ PART I started with creating your vision and getting clear on why you're really in business.

- ◆ PART II showed you exactly where the money comes from and where it goes.

- ◆ PART III introduced your financial team and who does what to help you manage your money.

- ◆ PART IV was all about data, the good kind that guides you to make decisions and the bad kind that creates noise and confusion.

- ◆ PART V guided you through your financial statements and showed you how to read the stories they tell you.

- ◆ PART VI focused on action. You learned about using KPIs, the levers you can pull to improve results, putting everything you learned to work in your business.

◆ PART VII will connect all the dots.

Until now, we've talked about numbers like they live in separate, neat buckets. Running a business isn't about managing isolated pieces, though. The real magic happens when everything starts working together.

◆ Your vision guides your business decisions.

◆ Your numbers tell you whether you're moving toward that vision.

◆ Your team rallies around the KPIs that matter most.

◆ Instead of feeling like you're juggling a dozen spinning plates, you're driving somewhere with a navigation system that guides you through all types of terrain.

Now that you have the tools to understand what your numbers are telling you, it's time to look forward. We are going to zoom out from the day-to-day operations and start thinking about the bigger picture—what success really looks like for you personally, not only professionally. Because when your business isn't serving your life goals, you're basically building someone else's dream. We're putting it all together here. Your business becomes the vehicle for the life you truly want to live instead of a daily obligation that only keeps you "busy."

What's Next?

In the upcoming chapters, we'll guide you through some of these bigger questions:

◆ How do you build personal wealth from your business success?

◆ How do you prepare for an eventual exit, whether that's 5 years or 20 years down the road?

- How does all this connect back to that original vision you had when you started?

- Most importantly, how do you make sure all these financial tools and systems move you toward the life you want, not a more organized version of the life you already have?

Let's jump right in!

CHAPTER 21

BUILD PERSONAL WEALTH

Do you think selling your business alone will support the retirement life you're dreaming about? Statistically, not a chance.

When our client Mark sold his construction business, he thought he was going to hit the jackpot. For 20 years, he had been the poster child for "all in"—skipping his own paychecks, canceling family vacations, and living on the promise that someday it would all pay off. Then the market took a nosedive, and suddenly his "retirement fund" (a.k.a. his business) wasn't worth all that much. After paying debts and taxes, Mark found himself staring at an uncertain future.

Mark's story isn't unique. Most business owners are natural optimists who see every dollar as fuel for growth. Whether it's expanding inventory, upgrading equipment, or investing in that promising new software, they're always thinking about the next opportunity to put more money into the business. Meanwhile, their personal savings account is going nowhere and their retirement plan is nonexistent.

Unfortunately, the stats are sobering: almost half of American households have no retirement savings, and about one in five people over age 50 are in the same boat.[11] A lot of them are owners and entrepreneurs who expect their business will be their golden parachute. They aren't paying attention to the fact that only about half of businesses make it past year 5 and only 35% survive to see year 10.[12] Those aren't exactly Vegas odds for betting on a nice retirement fund through the business.

Don't get us wrong. Some businesses do sell for that "buy a yacht and disappear to the Caribbean" money. Though that is incredible for those select few, betting your entire future on a similar outcome is less about strategy and more about wishful thinking. Even when businesses do sell for a good amount of money, the process usually takes longer, costs more, and pays far less than the business owner expects. It's like planning your retirement around winning the lottery: technically, it's possible—still probably not your best move.

Smart business owners build wealth in three different buckets:

- **Business wealth**—What a company is worth when someone wants to buy it.

- **Personal financial wealth**—The money in a business's savings and investment accounts and assets that have accumulated.

- **Lifestyle wealth**—How those dollars translate into peace of mind, time, freedom, and the ability to make decisions without financial fear.

You need all three because life has a way of throwing curveballs when you least expect them—divorce, health scares, partner disputes, market crashes that make your "sure thing" look a lot less certain.

In this chapter, we look at why managing your personal numbers is so important, the different types of investments and risk profiles, the importance of diversification, and why you need a team.

Managing Your Personal Numbers

Wealth management follows the same principles as running your business does: measure, manage, review, and adjust accordingly. This is more than personal peace of mind; it's also a necessity for your business.

When you apply for a business line of credit, lenders will require your financial statements. And they will typically also want to see a document called a "Personal Financial Statement," which shows what you own, what you owe, and the difference between those two. Sounds like your business's Balance Sheet, doesn't it? They want to know that you have assets outside the business because they need to get their money back in case it fails.

Business owners need to create, and regularly review, this personal balance sheet. When you look at your bank accounts, credit-card statements, investments, and net-worth earnings, you need to ask yourself:

- "What do I own?"

- "What do I owe?"

- "Do I own more than I owe?"

- "Is that amount increasing or decreasing?"

When your numbers aren't trending in the right direction, it's a problem.

Risk and Diversification

Building wealth means choosing from a variety of investment options, each with different risk profiles and potential returns. Like you would with your business statements, we encourage you to group your personal wealth accounts into three separate buckets: a "sleep well at night" bucket, a "little bit of excitement" bucket, and a "hold on tight" bucket.

Disclaimer

Before we go further, we want to note that this section provides a general overview of different wealth strategies and simplifies ideas that are very complex. Don't take this as investment advice. All such decisions need to be made after consulting with an investment advisor/wealth manager that comes recommended by someone you know, like, and trust—and you get to know, like, and trust as well!

Not sure where to start? Here is a quick breakdown of the most common types of investments and some of their key features:

Conservative/Safe Investments (Sleep Well)

- **High-yield savings accounts**—Returns at 4-5%, FDIC insured, instant access to money.

- **Certificates of deposit (CDs)**—Fixed rates for set terms, penalties for early withdrawal, guaranteed returns.

- **Treasury bonds**—Government-backed, predictable income, various term lengths.

- **Money-market accounts**—Slightly higher returns than from savings, limited monthly transactions.

Moderate/Balanced Investments (Little Bit of Excitement)

- **Index funds**—Diversified across hundreds of stocks, low fees, matches market performance.

- **Bond funds**—Steadier than stocks, generates regular income, sensitive to interest rates.

- **Balanced mutual funds**—Mix of stocks and bonds, professional management, moderate growth.

Tax-Advantaged Retirement Accounts (Little Bit of Excitement)

- **401(k)s**—Employer-sponsored, often with company matching, high contribution limits, tax-deferred growth, comes with early withdrawal penalties.

- **Traditional IRAs**—Tax-deductible contributions, taxed when withdrawn, required distributions at age 73, early withdrawal penalties.

- **Roth IRAs**—After-tax contributions, tax-free growth and withdrawals, no required distributions, early withdrawal penalties.

Aggressive/High-Risk Investments (Hold On!)

- **Individual stocks**—Potential for high returns, requires research, can lose significant value quickly.

- **Growth stocks**—Includes companies expected to grow rapidly, volatile, no dividends typically.

- **Cryptocurrency**—Extremely volatile, potential for huge gains or losses, largely unregulated.

Real Estate Investments (Hold On!)

- **Primary residences**—Builds equity, potential appreciation, mortgage interest deduction.

- **Rental properties**—Monthly income, building appreciation, tax benefits, requires active management.

- **Real estate investment trusts**—Real estate exposure without property management, dividend income.

- **Real estate crowdfunding**—Lower entry costs, professional management, less liquidity.

Alternative Investments (Hold On!)

- ◆ **Commodities**—Gold, oil, agricultural products, hedge against inflation.

- ◆ **Private equity**—High minimum investments, potential high returns, money tied up for years.

- ◆ **Startup investments**—Angel investing or crowdfunding, high risk / high reward, most fail.

Retirement accounts like 401(k)s and IRAs are the most common personal wealth options because they come with nice tax perks that make the government a little less greedy with your money, at least at first. The choice is yours: do you want to pay taxes now or later?

Money that you put into a 401(k) or traditional IRA is pre-tax, meaning you don't pay taxes on the money in the year you contribute it. These contributions reduce your taxable income, so you pay less taxes now. Instead, taxes are delayed until retirement. When you pull money out, you pay income taxes on both your pretax money contributions and all the investment growth.

Roth accounts work the other way. You pay taxes on the money you contribute now. These are referred to as "after-tax" dollars. Later, after it grows, there are no taxes due on the gains.

We've provided a very, very simplified chart to show you the difference. In 2026, your taxable income was $120,000 and you decided to invest $10,000. With a traditional IRA, your taxable income lowers to $110,000. With the Roth, you'll pay taxes on the whole $120,000. At a 25% tax rate, you will owe $2,500 less in 2026 taxes. Fast-forward 20 years to retirement. Your $10,000 has grown to $60,000. When you withdraw it, you will owe $15,000 in taxes. With the Roth, no additional taxes are due; all $60,000 is yours.

Most advisors will suggest you have money in both types of accounts. On one hand, when you're already in a higher tax bracket, saving money now may be worthwhile, and you're

	401(k) & Traditional IRA	Roth IRA	Trad vs. Roth
Taxes for 2026			
Taxable Income Before Investing	$120,000	$120,000	$0
Investment Contribution	$10,000	$10,000	$0
Taxable Income	$110,000	$120,000	-$10,000
2026 Taxes Due 25%	$27,500	$30,000	$2,500
Retirement Summary			
Original Investment Contribution	$10,000	$10,000	$0
Investment Growth	$50,000	$50,000	$0
Value 20 Years Later	$60,000	$60,000	$0
Taxes Due 25%	$15,000		$15,000
Money When You Pull It Out	$45,000	$60,000	-$15,000

IRA—Traditional vs. Roth

betting that your tax bracket will be lower when you pull the money out. On the other, when you expect your money to grow significantly (say you bought Google way back in its beginning), paying the tax now could save you oodles later. Remember how we said your numbers reflect your decisions and behaviors? This is it in real life.

Lynn

My father worked for General Electric and had his entire retirement in GE stock. He didn't really have a choice. At that time, the only option offered at most large companies was their own stock. Unfortunately, at a time when he could have moved it, dad trusted that GE would always be there. Nor did he get proactive advice from a financial advisor. When the stock collapsed, he lost a lot. Today, although most companies offer more diversified plans, the lesson remains the same: putting all your eggs in one basket is never safe.

Real estate is another common investment vehicle because it creates passive income and often has higher returns than the market does (when real estate is gaining in value). Because you can sell at any time, it doesn't tie up liquidity until you reach retirement age. It also lets you own something you can touch (and complain about when the roof leaks). Your ideal mix of investments depends on your age, your risk tolerance, and how much sleep you want to lose after checking your portfolio.

For business owners, investing gets even trickier. When owners funnel every dollar back into their company, convinced that they are building value, they put their retirement into one company—theirs! No matter how much you love your business or how well it's doing, this is not a great idea.

Eliminate this kind of concentration risk. The smarter play is to spread things around—building wealth outside your company through retirement accounts, real estate, and/or good old-fashioned stock-market investing and letting time work its magic through compounding.

You'll also need to revisit your risk profile regularly. Early on, you may want to dial up risk and chase growth head-on. Later, as retirement nears, you will want to dial it back and focus on security. Shifting investment vehicles, saving more, or diversifying assets are all levers you can pull—just like in your business.

Compounding: How Money Works

One of the simplest and most powerful concepts in wealth building is compounding. This is something they need to teach in high school right next to "how to do your taxes" and "why you shouldn't eat cereal for every meal." There's a quote from Ben Franklin that sums up compounding well:

> **"Money makes money. And the money that money makes makes more money."**

"Money makes money. And the money that money makes makes more money."

Sounds almost too good to be true; that's exactly how your wealth grows even when you're not paying attention.

For regular folks who aren't trying to beat Wall Street at its own game, steady returns mean your money roughly doubles every eight to nine years. This isn't about choosing the perfect stock or having incredible timing. It's consistent investing and letting time do its thing.

Start tucking money away in your 20s and you'll see four or five of those doubling cycles by retirement. Wait until your 40s and you might only catch two. Those extra cycles are the difference between sipping cocktails on a beach and eating ramen in your golden years. This is why even messy, imperfect contributions matter: what you save now grows, then that growth grows, and eventually you've got growth growing on top of growth. It's like a financial snowball rolling downhill.

Here's a fun little exercise for you. It's not exactly compounding, though the effect is the same. Imagine you're playing golf with a friend and wagering $0.25 for hole #1 and then doubling it for every hole thereafter. Hole #2 is for $0.50; hole #3 is for $1.00, and so on. How much are you playing for on hole #18? $32,768! Unbelievable, right? Get a pencil and paper to prove it to yourself.

Though not as dramatic, let's go back to the $10,000 investment you held onto for 20 years, only now you've been

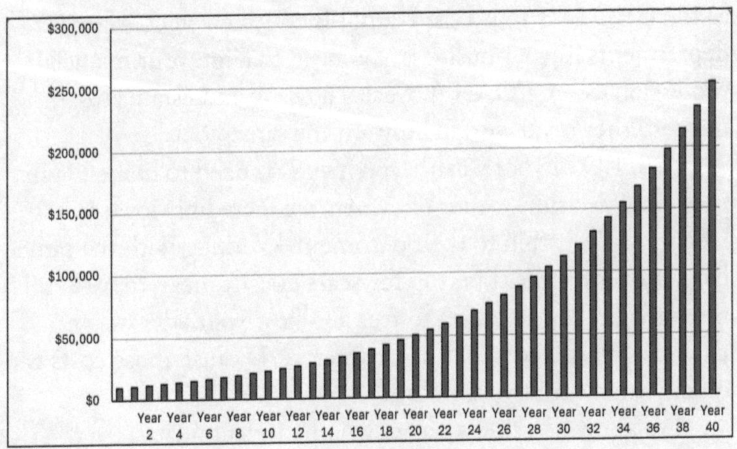

The value of compounding

holding it for 40 years. With an annual return of 8.4%, the investment—shown with its doubling points on the graph below—has grown to a total of $250,000! You'll also see in the first 20 years that it grew from $40,000 to a total of $50,000. Over the next 20 years, it grew another $200,000 to $250,000. That's the magic of compounding!

The best part of compounding isn't about finding the next big thing or getting lucky with crypto. It's about showing up consistently, spreading your bets around, and giving time a chance to work. Money sitting in your checking account is slowly losing a race against inflation, while money that's working for you keeps getting stronger.

You're the CEO of Your Life

Much of personal wealth building comes down to keeping more of what you make through smart tax decisions. The right tax advisor will pay for themselves by guiding you to maximize deductions, optimize retirement contributions, and time major financial moves for maximum tax efficiency.

Taxes are only one piece of the puzzle, though. Building wealth isn't a solo job. You need a full team including a CFO, CPA, wealth advisor, and estate attorney. Think of yourself as the CEO of "[Your Last Name] Inc." Like you coordinate departments in your business, you need to align your financial professionals—CFO, CPA, wealth advisor, and estate attorney—so they're all working toward the same goals.

As CEO of your wealth, you may also need to make tough personnel decisions. A lot of owners are incredibly loyal to "their people," often to their detriment. Working with the same banker or investment person for years doesn't mean they're still the right fit. Pay attention to fees and how your advisors get paid, like we talked about in Chapter 12, because those costs can quietly eat away at your returns.

We knew a business owner who had accumulated over $600,000 in a money-market account. On the surface, that sounded impressive. It was safe, liquid, and steady. The problem was she was paying brokerage fees while earning next to nothing on that money. Year after year, her wealth sat there doing nothing.

When we sat down and compared her situation with simple alternatives, the math was painful. At a modest 5% return, that same $600,000 could have generated $30,000 a year in growth. At 8%, closer to $48,000 annually. Over 10 years, she had effectively left hundreds of thousands of dollars on the table because no one advised, recommended, or challenged her to move it into a higher-yield vehicle.

She didn't know what she didn't know. And unfortunately, her advisor never told her. This is why you need to ask hard yourself questions: "How does my wealth advisor make money?" "Am I getting the right return?" "Am I paying unnecessary fees?" "Is my advisor truly looking out for me or comfortable keeping me where I am?"

Don't settle for an advisor who waits for you to call them. A good one is proactive. They need to reach out with updates, to schedule meetings, and to drive conversations on strategy. When you're always the one chasing them down, fire them. They're not serving you.

Lynn

I learned this firsthand. I fired two wealth advisors because I finally realized that, after the initial honeymoon, whenever we spoke, I had done all the dialing! They were not the partners I deserved.

Ask yourself, "When was the last time my financial advisor reached out to me?"

When the answer is "never," it's time to make a change.

> **Andy**
>
> I speak with my advisor every month to review both my personal and business finances. That kind of engagement builds clarity and security. We are both rowing our oars in the same direction.

Quick Win: Figure Out Your Net Worth

Build your own personal wealth Balance Sheet. It's simpler than it sounds. List all the savings and assets you have and all your debts.

- ◆ **What you have:** bank accounts, investment accounts, property, vehicles—anything with actual value.

- ◆ **What you owe:** credit-card debt, mortgages, car loans, student loans—any money you need to pay back.

Subtract what you owe from what you own, and that is your net worth. It might be positive; it might be negative—either way, you now know where you stand.

It's smart to do this once a month, like you would review your business Balance Sheet. Once you have this baseline, you can start asking yourself the right questions: "How can I improve my net worth? Do I need to shift investment vehicles? Dial the risk up or down? Save more? Pay off debt faster?"

Looking Toward the Future

Look 10, 20, or even 30 years ahead into retirement and beyond. Work with an estate planner to create a comprehensive plan that includes your business—it may be your largest asset. There also needs to be a clear succession plan for what happens in the event you pass unexpectedly. When you pass on, what will happen to your wealth? Will it go into a trust? Without the right structure, your family could end up paying huge legal fees or unnecessary taxes—or worse, stories abound about kids in their early 20s inheriting $250,000 or more and blowing it immediately. Getting things right protects both your personal wealth and your business legacy—everything you worked so hard to build. It's far too important to do on your own.

Too many business owners ignore this and end up paying the price. Remember one thing from this chapter: your personal financial life deserves the same attention as your business does—tracking numbers, managing cash flow, and planning strategically.

The payoff is not only about money. Financial confidence gives you freedom, options, and peace of mind. When you're not clinging to every dollar or panicking through lean months, you make smarter choices. You can take calculated risks, ride out downturns, and even enjoy the process a little more. You can still strive for that million-dollar exit, of course, without being forced to bet everything on it. That's the real win in all this: a thriving company and a lasting life and legacy beyond it.

CHAPTER 22

YOUR EXIT STRATEGY

You had a plan to start your business; you also need one to exit it. Okay, maybe you started with half a plan, a quarter of a plan, or 12% of a plan. How well did that work out? You learned a lot of tough lessons in the school of hard knocks.

If you haven't thought about it yet, let's get you started on your exit plan. Believe it or not, it will make life more professionally rewarding for everyone—and so much more financially rewarding for you. Isn't that why you started your business in the first place?

This chapter, in all honesty, is the one we found most gratifying to write for you. Near the end of your journey, you'll see how everything we've guided you through to optimize your business—vision, data, accounting, KPIs, scorecards, and levers—is going to get you out of it. Let's dig in.

When you hear "exit planning," it's natural to think it's something you only do at the end, when it's time to retire. Why think about something so far down the road? Whether you realize it or not, exit planning started the day you opened your doors. The hard reality is this: one day, you will leave your business. The only questions are when it will happen and whether it will be on your terms or someone else's. The time to answer that question is now.

Andy

I joined the US Army at 20 years old to serve my country by going to war. I signed a contract for six years active and two years inactive. Five years into my contract, I was eligible to reenlist for another six years, which I did without much thought. Six years later, I signed for another three years, again without really thinking about it. Then I became an Army Reserve Career Counselor. One of the first lessons I was taught for that position was to ask soldiers when they joined the military what their exit plan was, much like people asked me throughout my career as to whether I was planning on doing 20 years to get to retirement—for which I never really had an answer.

I learned then that the best time to plan your exit from the military was the day you raised your right hand. Most don't. I was in for over 12 years before I started to plan my exit. When I started my first "real" business, I had a five-year exit plan before we'd even had a soft launch.

Business owners often spend decades building something only to find they can't sell it. It may be like an older house: it needs a lot of work, and no buyer is interested. Or maybe the company is built around the owner's job, and no one buys a job. Meanwhile, other owners walk away with life-changing wealth. They built their business with their exit in mind.

Your exit plan is your "mountaintop." It's the destination that gives meaning to every step of your climb. In this chapter, we're guiding you to this mountaintop by building a realistic plan to reach it. Like we've said that there are no right or wrong answers for your vision, there are no right or wrong answers for your exit.

Why is a plan necessary? Because though you may not know when you'll exit your business, with a plan, you can decide how you will exit. You have (hopefully) a will to protect your family. An exit plan protects the legacy of your business and the people who depend on it. The bonus? As you work your plan, you're preparing for the future, making your business much more valuable today.

Defining Your Mountaintop

Think about mountaintops. They're all different. So are exit plans. One person's mountaintop may be selling to private equity for eight figures and retiring at age 50. Another person's is passing a legacy business to their kids. Someone else wants to build something so systematically sound it runs without them, giving them the freedom to start something new or mentor others. And for some, the goal isn't selling at all—it's generating and saving enough cash to fund their lifestyle and simply closing the doors when the time is right.

Your mountaintop, whatever it is, determines where you're going. And your business is the vehicle to get you there. It's not about what your business partner wants, what your spouse thinks you need to do (though they do have a vested interest), or what might sound impressive to your friends and family. Think about what **you** want.

> **Lynn**
>
> For seven years, I planned to offer CFO services and then hang it up. Now, through writing this book, I've seen opportunities to provide financial educational services and finally began to build something that can continue without me. What you do always depends on your mountaintop. That's why you need a plan to get there. And it's better to have a plan that evolves than no plan at all.

Your destination determines your path. If your plan is to simply close the doors one day, then you'll want to maximize profits without worrying about building much of anything. That's a lot different than building strategies, a company culture, and the systems, information, and work process that will last long after you're gone. Your plans can, and will, evolve over time.

Choose Your Exit...or Else It Will Choose You

Timing is one of the trickiest parts of planning an exit. So much of it is out of your control. Every business owner leaves their business through one of the five Ds: death, disability, divorce, distress, or design. You have little to no control over the first four; they can happen to you at any time. We've seen owners blindsided by a sudden health diagnosis that forced their hand, a market downturn that slashed their value, or a divorce that required liquidating assets overnight.

Design is the only one of the five Ds you get to choose, which is exactly what this process is about: intentionally designing and laying the groundwork for the exit you truly want. Yet even when you're dealt one of the first four, you're better off having done something, anything. We've noted parallels between your business and personal life throughout this book. Exiting is no different. You plan for the best and prepare for the worst.

Are you convinced that now is the time to start exit planning? Get ready to have conversations about your ideal outcome. Build it step by step—even when you think that outcome is still 10 years away. This way, when one of the first four Ds shows up, you'll already have a plan instead of having to scramble in the middle of a crisis.

Will You Actually Be Able to Sell Your Business?

For anyone designing their exit around a sale, it's important to know that most businesses aren't sellable. The problem isn't always profitability; it's often dependency. When your business can't operate without you showing up every day, then you don't really own a business; you own a job.

Andy

I've seen my own situation play out as proof of this. At 35, with a few years in my business, I had a clearer, more valuable exit strategy than my dad did at 65 after 30 years in his business. It wasn't because I was smarter or worked harder. It's because I started with the end in mind. I knew where my mountaintop was, and every decision I made either moved me toward it or didn't. My dad built an incredible business. He also built himself a job that required him to show up every single day. When it comes time to exit, his options remain limited because the business was built around him, not beyond him.

Buyers know that a lot of businesses operate this way, and they can afford to be selective. In 2023, the Exit Planning Institute reported that as the baby boomers retire from their businesses, there is more business value for sale than there is capital to buy it, and that trend is going to continue.[13] That means buyers are looking for turnkey operations, not fixer-uppers that collapse without the seller's personal relationships or expertise. A sellable business has the following key criteria:

- Sustainable profits without requiring the owner's constant involvement

- Clean financials and documentation, as buyers need at least three to five years of solid data to feel confident in the purchase

- Systems and processes that work without the owner, meaning operations don't grind to a halt when they're gone

- Key people running the business, not merely following the owner's daily instructions

As you prepare to sell your business, sooner or later you'll accept that building a business that others want to buy requires you to get the hell out of it! Many owners never truly test their team's capabilities because they keep stepping in to solve problems or make decisions themselves, thereby holding back both the team's growth and the business's long-term value. They're uncomfortable telling themselves, "Maybe this business will run better without me." Yet it's usually the truth.

Andy

When I stepped away from my business for an extended period, the company had its biggest growth to date. It wasn't because I didn't add value. It was because I had unknowingly been limiting what my team could accomplish by being the bottleneck. The fact is your business might run better day to day without you.

When you do get the pieces right, you create a business that's not only profitable; it's also attractive to buyers. And once your business is sellable, you can start exploring the paths available to you. You can sell the entire business at once—the cleanest break—which requires the right buyer at the right time. You can sell to your employees through an ESOP (employee stock-ownership plan), rewarding the team that supported you in building it. Private equity is another route, especially when you've built something with strong growth potential. And in some cases, you can even structure a gradual sale, transferring ownership a little at a time while drawing ongoing income.

Understanding What Your Business Is Worth

You've decided to sell. And you know your business is sellable. Now comes the biggest question of all: how much is it worth?

Business valuation is generally based on a multiple of your earnings, most often EBITDA (earnings before interest, taxes, depreciation, and amortization). EBITDA is a concept you must understand because of its widespread use:

1. You get a clearer picture of your true profitability than from your Income Statement.

2. Lenders use it to assess your cash flow.

3. Buyers and investors use it to value and compare businesses, including yours.

And when it comes to valuing your business, EBITDA is the base on which multiples are paid. What does this mean? When your business EBITDA is $500,000 and you list it at $2.0 million, you are asking for a 4x multiple. When your multiple is 3x, your business will list at $1.5 million. The multiple is assigned based a valuation completed by a business broker.

Top-Line Revenue	COGS	Expenses	Net Profit / EBITDA	EBITDA	Multiple	
$1,000,000	$500,000	$400,000	$100,000	10.00%	3	$300,000
$1,500,000	$800,000	$500,000	$200,000	13.33%	3	$600,000
$2,500,000	$1,300,000	$800,000	$400,000	16.00%	5	$2,000,000
$3,500,000	$1,800,000	$1,100,000	$600,000	17.14%	5	$3,000,000
$5,000,000	$2,000,000	$2,000,000	$1,000,000	20.00%	7	$7,000,000

There's a lot to unpack here, and to do that, we need to go a bit deeper. We'll start with a few definitions and then walk you through a simple example.

- **Business valuation** is the combination of math and storytelling (remember how your numbers tell a story about your business?) that provides an estimate of what your business is worth. The math reflects your financial performance so far. The story explains where it's going and how risky and reliable the future looks.

- **Multiple** is a ratio that expresses how much buyers are willing to pay for a business relative to a specific financial metric. It's shorthand for "X times" that metric. The simplest way we see that is, assuming profit dollars will remain the same, it's the number of years before the buyer recoups their investment.

- **Business broker** is an expert in the buying and selling of businesses who helps guide you to set the right price (the valuation), find the right buyer, and sell your business with as little stress as possible.

- **Depreciation and amortization** are terms that reflect the spreading of the cost of big asset purchases over a period of years. Depreciation goes with physical assets like buildings and equipment, whereas amortization is used for nonphysical (intangible) assets like patents, trademarks, software, and customer lists. Unlike other expenses, these are noncash transactions.

- **EBITDA** represents how much your business makes from core operations before interest expense from debts; federal, state, and local income taxes; and depreciation and amortization. Important note: the taxes only apply when the business is a C Corporation. Most small businesses are LLCs or S Corporations. Since taxes are paid at the personal level for these smaller companies, income taxes will not apply.

- ◆ **"Add-backs"** are expenses paid by the business that are not part of normal, recurring operations.

- ◆ **Adjusted EBITDA** is the best reflection of ongoing, repeatable financial performance.

The Math—What Your Business Is Worth Today

Let's revisit our friends at Great Eats! After years of hard work and success, our owner is ready to sell. Last year, it made a net profit of $350,000, which you can see from the very simplified P&L below.

Great Eats!
Profit and Loss Statement
For the Year Ending Dec 31

Sales	$3,500,000
Costs of Sales	$2,275,000
Gross Profit	$1,225,000
Total Expenses	$875,000
Net Profit	**$350,000**

Great Eats! Summary P&L

Taking a look at expenses and what type they are, we see that there are both EBITDA adjustments and accounts that may qualify as EBITDA add-back adjustments.

The calculation of Great Eats!' EBITDA starts with $350,000 net profit and then adds $14,000 for depreciation and $18,000 for interest, ending EBITDA with a total of $382,000.

Great Eats!
Expense Review

Expenses	Amount	Type
6100 Advertising	$15,000	Normal operations
6200 Office Supplies	$10,000	Normal operations
6300 Wages and Salaries		
6301 Manager Salaries	$250,000	Normal operations
6302 Health Care	$55,000	Normal operations
6303 Other Benefits	$67,500	Normal operations
6304 Owner's Salary	$225,000	Partial Add Back
Subtotal Wages and Salaries	$597,500	
6400 - Building Expense		
6401 Rent	$120,000	Normal operations
6402 Utilities	$10,000	Normal operations
6403 Repairs/Maintenance	$8,000	Normal operations
6404 Building supplies	$7,500	Normal operations
Subtotal Building Expense	$145,500	
6500 Other Expenses		
6501 Legal & Professional	$25,000	Partial Add Back
6502 Depreciation	$14,000	EBITDA Adjustments
6502 Interest Expense	$18,000	EBITDA Adjustments
6600 Owner's Vehicle Allowance	$50,000	Partial Add Back
Subtotal	$107,000	
Total Expenses	$875,000	

Great Eats! Expenses

Looking further, the restaurant's broker or financial partner identified other adjustments. The owner took a $225,000 salary, which could be replaced by a general manager for $150,000, meaning $75,000 could be added to EBITDA. Of the legal expenses, $20,000 was due to a one-time issue that could be added. And the entire owner's $50,000 vehicle allowance is not part of regular operations. The adjustments total $145,000 and raise EBITDA to an adjusted $527,000.

<table>
<tr><td colspan="2" align="center">Great Eats!
EBITDA Calculation</td></tr>
<tr><td>Net Profit</td><td align="right">$350,000</td></tr>
<tr><td>EBITDA add back</td><td></td></tr>
<tr><td>Depreciation</td><td align="right">$14,000</td></tr>
<tr><td>Interest</td><td align="right">$18,000</td></tr>
<tr><td>Subtotal add backs</td><td align="right">$32,000</td></tr>
<tr><td>EBITDA</td><td align="right">$382,000</td></tr>
</table>

Great Eats! EBITDA Calculation

<table>
<tr><td colspan="2" align="center">Great Eats!
Adjusted EBITDA</td></tr>
<tr><td>EBITDA</td><td align="right">$382,000</td></tr>
<tr><td>Owner's Salary</td><td align="right">$75,000</td></tr>
<tr><td>Legal Expense</td><td align="right">$20,000</td></tr>
<tr><td>Owner's Vehicle</td><td align="right">$50,000</td></tr>
<tr><td>Total Adjustments</td><td align="right">$145,000</td></tr>
<tr><td>Adjusted EBITDA</td><td align="right">$527,000</td></tr>
</table>

Great Eats! Adjusted EBITDA

This demonstrates how math and your numbers establish the value of your business today.

The Story: Why a Buyer Believes in the Value Tomorrow

"The story" determines the multiple a broker will recommend for your valuation. The decisions you're making today will have a

big impact on your personal tomorrow. Some of the things that
go into your story:

◆ **Revenue drivers**—What makes your business profitable?
How many revenue streams do you have? How are sales
growing (think RAPS)? Will the sales growth be seen as
predictable and valuable to a buyer?

◆ **Operational systems**—Can the business run without you?
Are effective management systems (think KPIs) in place
across the entire organization? Take a realistic tour of your
business. Is there anything the buyer will need to invest in
to fix? They will reduce your multiple.

◆ **Market position**—What is your "secret sauce" that keeps
customers choosing your business?

◆ **Growth potential**—When you were sticking around,
how did you plan your growth? The buyer will want to
understand your opportunities and plan accordingly.

◆ **Risks**—What could go wrong, and how do you manage
it? When you have two to three large customers that make
up a huge amount of your sales, do you have long-term
contracts?

◆ **Industry**—Multiples also reflect the specific industry you
are in. How does your business compare with others?

The Impact—How the Story Comes Together

Selling your business is like selling your house. A home in
"move-in" condition with lots of amenities is going to appraise
and sell for a lot more than a zombie fixer-upper. Let's see how
our friends at Great Eats! are doing. We saw before that the
company's net profit was $350,000, with an adjusted EBITDA
of $527,000. Based on its 2x to 5x story, the restaurant could sell

for anywhere between \$1 million and \$2.6 million. Would that motivate you to do more fixing with your business?

Great Eats!
Business Valuation Scenarios

	Net Profit	EBITDA	Adjusted EBITDA
Base	\$350,000	\$382,000	\$527,000
Multiple Value			
2x	\$700,000	\$764,000	\$1,054,000
3x	\$1,050,000	\$1,146,000	\$1,581,000
4x	\$1,400,000	\$1,528,000	\$2,108,000
5x	\$1,750,000	\$1,910,000	\$2,635,000

Business Valuation Scenarios

Knowing your numbers and putting in the hard work pays off. And as others do more of the work, you have more time to enjoy your family, golf, travel, or even build another business!

Though EBITDA is the most common measure of valuation, in some industries, sales or profit multiples are used instead. Buyers also weigh what comparable businesses have sold for recently and consider both tangible assets (equipment, inventory, real estate) and intangible ones (customer lists, brand reputation, intellectual property).

Unfortunately, many owners overlook creating an exit plan (including a preliminary valuation) because they think their exit is some vague event that will happen someday way down the road. They're not thinking about how much their decisions, especially in the last three to five years before selling, impact their valuation. The biggest issue we see is failing to invest in the business. This includes culture and people development, IT systems to manage operations and customer relationships (CRM systems), and outside expertise to provide advice (e.g., part-time CFOs, COOs, etc.).

Building Your Exit Plan (Three to Five Years Out)

Today, more business owners are realizing the importance of building an exit plan. The Exit Planning Institute has reported a significant increase from 10 years prior, noting that "education, awareness, and readiness to transition have vastly improved and are supported by real actions by owners to better prepare themselves."[14] In fact, 75% of business owners plan to exit their business within the next 10 years, and 69% have exit strategy high on their priority list.[15]

These business owners understand that a successful exit doesn't happen overnight. To maximize value, you need at least three to five years of preparation. Trying to throw something together in six months won't get you a premium.

Start with the numbers by cleaning up your data and financials now. Buyers want consistent, accurate records that tell a clear story. Know your numbers cold and establish KPIs that demonstrate the business runs systematically—not randomly.

You'll also need to get ahead with tax planning. The structure of your business, how you've been making distributions, and even details like whether a separate LLC owns your building can dramatically affect both your tax burden and the attractiveness of your business to potential buyers. Start working with a tax-planning specialist early. Waiting until a year or two before you want to sell your business is way too late.

Protecting your people is another important part of your plan. Buyers want to know whether your essential team members will stay after the sale. Key-person retention strategies, including life-insurance plans, profit sharing, and equity stakes keep your best people invested in the business's success after you're gone.

Business transitions are complex—and we understand that planning one can be overwhelming in both the details and emotions. Don't worry; you're not going to do it alone. You will build your exit plan with a team of specialists, including the following:

- **Business broker** to assess what buyers are looking for and what you need to start fixing now

- **Estate-planning attorney** to structure the transfer properly

- **Tax-planning specialist** to minimize your tax hit

- **Wealth advisor** to guide you in managing your money wisely

- **Banker** to advise on how business sales are put together

- **Your current CFO, attorney, and accountant**, as they already know your business and need to be looped in early

Once you know your vision for exiting, share it with key advisors. Are you planning to sell in five years? Ten? Pass the business to family? Transparency creates alignment.

And don't forget your team. When to tell them is one of the toughest decisions you'll make. Going public can be scary because there are a lot of people depending on you: employees depending on paychecks, customers relying on your products or services, and family counting on the wealth you've built. At some point, your team will get the sense you're up to something. Without information, they'll fill in the blanks. The last thing you want is people looking to leave before you do.

Your exit is your choice, and it's important to understand what that choice means for everyone else. The owners who exit successfully are the ones who build a team, communicate the plan clearly, and give everyone enough time to do their part well.

Alignment isn't only about your business, though. It's also about you. The personal side of exit planning is the part no one wants to talk about.

◆ What will life look like afterward?

◆ Who are you without this business?

◆ What will you do with your time?

◆ How will you find purpose and identity now that the thing that's defined you for years is gone?

These aren't simple questions. Ignoring them leads to business owners who successfully exit, then fall apart because they never look past the transaction. Your exit strategy isn't complete until you can answer what comes next—financially and personally.

Quick Win: Define Your Mountaintop

Before you worry about multiples, tax strategies, or team retention, pause and ask yourself, "What does a successful exit look like for me? Do I want to sell outright and walk away clean? Do I want to pass the business to my children? Transition to employees through an ESOP? Or stay involved part-time while cashing out equity over time?" Each path requires a different kind of preparation. Defining your mountaintop now—the desired result you want to stand on—guides every step of your exit plan and prevents you from climbing the wrong mountain.

How Your Exit Connects to Everything Else

This chapter is truly the heart of the book. It's the reason we wrote it in the first place. Your business needs to serve your life vision, not the other way around. Understanding your numbers, building systems, tracking KPIs, pulling the right levers—all of it connects directly to how your exit ties into your vision of success. When you want to sell for $3 million in seven years, that means specific profit targets today. When you want to pass the business on to your kids, that means building systems they can manage without you. When you want to fund your retirement and walk away, that means maximizing distributions while maintaining stability.

It's time to define your mountaintop, set the strategy, make the decisions, and then get out of the way. You were essential to starting your business, and when you've done your job right, you won't be essential to exiting it. That's not a failure; it's the ultimate measure of success. Remember: exiting your business is only half the story. Real success is stepping into the life you built it for.

CHAPTER 23

TAKE THE WHEEL AND DRIVE

You made it! You didn't crack this book open and skim a few pages—you stayed with it and wrestled with concepts that felt foreign or intimidating not that long ago. Been doing the Quick Wins along the way? Then you've also proven to yourself that you're capable of more than you initially thought. At this point, you no longer think financial management is only for numbers geeks and CPAs. (Otherwise, you haven't learned a damn thing!) That's not you anymore. You've come too far and learned too much.

When you know your numbers, those big decisions stop being guesses and start becoming obvious next steps. You don't operate from fear because you're operating from clarity now. And clarity gives you the courage to do what needs to be done: raise your prices, fire that client, invest in growth, plan your exit, and build the business you really want instead of the one you feel stuck with.

From here on out, "not knowing" is no longer an excuse. You have the tools. You have the framework. You have the clarity. What you do with it is entirely up to you.

Stop Telling Yourself Stories That Aren't True

Before this book, you had been telling yourself stories about why you couldn't understand your numbers. "I'm not a numbers person." "This is too hard." "I don't know where to start." "Nobody ever taught me this stuff."

Those weren't facts. They were excuses. And they're still bullshit.

You've made it to this point, so you can't use these crutches anymore. Maybe you used to think numbers were a mysterious language reserved for "numbers people." Now you know the real stories they're telling you, including what's working in your business and what's not, where the money goes, and what needs to change.

As CFOs, we've heard every excuse in the book, and each one can be rewritten in a new context. Here are a few examples:

Old Excuse	New Story
"I don't understand financials, so I'll only focus on what I'm good at."	"My financials tell me exactly what's working and what's not. This is how I get better at everything."
"Looking at my cash flow stresses me out."	"Understanding my cash flow gives me control instead of me constantly reacting to crises."
"I can't afford to take time off—my business needs me."	"When my business can't run without me for a week, I haven't built a business—I've built a job."

Once you start to see numbers as stories instead of obstacles, everything shifts. The decisions get clearer. The fear gets smaller. And the business you've been trying to build finally becomes the one you're running.

Revisit Your Vision—with Numbers This Time

We've now come full circle. Think back to your vision from the beginning of this book. When you started, you probably had some vague idea of what success looked like. Now that you understand your numbers, it's time to get specific.

Put actual numbers to your vision. Ask yourself, "Is my vision achievable with my current business model? What will need to change to make it happen? What does success look like on the personal side (the parts that aren't directly tied to business revenue and matter even more)?" This is where a CFO becomes so valuable. They can guide you to marry your vision to your numbers and give you real options.

To get that same type of clarity around your vision, think about what you need to start, stop, and continue and how that changes your vision. Look at what's working. What behaviors, decisions, and strategies are moving you forward? Double down

Andy

I worked with a client who quipped that her vision was to reach $1 million in annual revenue. She had been floating around $100,000 for a decade, so $1 million was her sarcastic answer to a real question. Then, we mapped out what it would take to get there. She looked at the numbers and said, "I can't work that much."

I said, "Okay, then you need to charge more."

"I can't charge more."

"Alright, what can you do?" I replied.

It was clear (to me) her vision had changed, so I asked her what she really wanted. Did her original vision still make sense, or did she need to adjust it? She ended up targeting $250,000 instead, which was achievable without killing herself. That's not failure; that's clarity. A $250,000 plan versus settling for the $100,000 she became accustomed to? That's success.

on those. Don't abandon them because they're not exciting or new. Results matter more than novelty does.

What you need to stop doing is the harder question—and it's the one that matters most. What's holding you back? What are you doing out of habit, out of fear, or because "that's how we've always done it"? What employees, providers, and clients are draining you? What products are bleeding money? What behaviors are wasting time? Stop them. Now.

Revisit your vision. Has it evolved? Good. You started this book with an idea of what was possible. Now you know what's achievable versus what you were hoping for. What have you learned about yourself, your business, and what you really want? Let that guide what comes next.

The Three Phases: Reflect, Realize, Regulate

Getting control of your numbers means you need to be proactive—not reactive, like so many business owners who are constantly putting out fires, scrambling to cover payroll, and wondering why they're working so hard for so little.

Being proactive is an ongoing cycle of three phases: reflection, realization, and regulation. This is where you see problems coming and make strategic decisions before they become emergencies:

- **Reflection**—Build your scorecard and use it weekly. Regularly look at your financials, not only once a year when your accountant hands you a tax return—also monthly, at a minimum. What story are your numbers telling you right now? Where is cash flowing? What's more profitable than you thought? What's bleeding money? Which KPIs are on track and off track?

- **Realization**—Honestly assess where you are with your business. Stop making excuses and face what the data is saying. Maybe that service you love offering has terrible margins. Maybe your most demanding client is also your least profitable. Maybe you're spending money on marketing that doesn't bring in paying customers. Realization is uncomfortable. It's also necessary.

♦ **Regulation**—Take action! Adjust by making simple decisions. Stop doing what isn't working and double down on what is. Pull the right levers based on what you learned in the reflection and realization cycles. Recall the OODA loop and reorient to your goals when you get off track.

Sounds a lot like the "What?" "So what?" and "What's next?" we talked about in Chapter 7.

What You Need to Do Next

You might be asking yourself, "Okay, I've learned a lot. Where do I begin?" We've covered six major sections in this book, and the path forward might feel overwhelming right now. We get it. That's why we created something practical to get you started. We're giving you a 25-item checklist of actions you can take right now, organized by what we've covered together. You don't have to do all 25 this week. Please don't even try. Pick three that would make the biggest impact on your business and start there. The most important thing is to start.

25 Things You Can Do Right Now to Take Control of Your Numbers

PART 1: Vision & Purpose

1. **Write down your three-year vision with specific numbers.** Not "grow my business." Rather, "Reach $500,000 in revenue with 35% profit margins while working 40 hours per week."

2. **Identify your nonnegotiables.** What are the three to five things that must be true about your business for it to serve

your life (e.g., home by 6 PM for dinner, four weeks' vacation annually, $150,000 personal income)?

3. **Calculate your personal number.** How much money do you really need to take home each month to live the life you want? Include savings, retirement, and fun money (more than covering bills).

PART 2: Money Flow

4. **Track where every dollar comes from this month.** Break down revenue by product/service line to see what's making you money.

5. **List your top 10 expenses.** Identify which ones directly generate revenue and which ones don't. Question everything in the "don't" category.

6. **Calculate your true hourly rate.** Divide your actual take-home pay by hours worked. Is that number acceptable? What needs to change?

7. **Identify your biggest cash-flow gap.** When does money go out versus come in? Map this out for the next 90 days.

PART 3: Financial Team

8. **Audit your current financial team.** Do you have a bookkeeper, accountant, tax planner, banker, CFO, and financial advisor? Are they proactive or reactive in their communications with you?

9. **Schedule a meeting with your bookkeeper.** Ask them three questions: "What story are my numbers telling?" "What do I need to watch?" and "What am I missing?"

10. **Fire or fix your weakest financial relationship.** When someone on your money-management team isn't serving you well or is not actively helping you make more money, either have a direct conversation about expectations or find someone new.

11. **Create a financial-team communication schedule.** When will you meet each member? Monthly? Quarterly? Put it on the calendar now.

PART 4: Data & KPIs

12. **Choose your first five core KPIs.** Based on what you learned, what are the five numbers you need to watch weekly or monthly? Over time, swap in others as needed.

13. **Set up a simple dashboard.** Use a spreadsheet, software, or even a notebook to track your five KPIs in one place.

14. **Calculate your CAC.** How much does it cost to get a new customer? Is it less than what they're worth to you?

15. **Determine your customer LTV.** How much will an average customer spend with you over their entire relationship?

16. **Identify one vanity metric you've been tracking.** Stop looking at it and replace it with something that drives decisions.

PART 5: Financial Documents

17. **Review your P&L from last month—really dig into it.** What surprises you? What story is it telling?

18. **Calculate your gross profit margin.** Revenue minus COGS, divided by revenue. Is it healthy for your industry?

19. **Review your Balance Sheet.** How much cash do you have? How much debt? What's the ratio?

20. **Look at your Cash Flow Statement.** Are you profitable and broke? Figure out where the cash is going.

21. **Compare this month to last year's same month.** What's better? What's worse? Why?

PART 6: Action & Implementation

22. **Identify the one lever that has the biggest impact.** Pricing? Volume? Efficiency? Pick one and create a plan to pull it this quarter.

23. **Fire one unprofitable client, product, or service.** You know which one it is. Stop waiting.

24. **Schedule your first monthly financial review.** Block two hours on your calendar every month to review your numbers. Make it nonnegotiable.

25. **Do the thing that scares you most.** Whether it's the price increase you've been avoiding, the investment you're afraid to make, or the conversation you need to have, do it this week.

Bonus Action: Share your vision and top KPIs with your team. Transparency creates the alignment you need to reach your goals.

Don't Get Stuck in a Numbers Rut

The incredible thing about business ownership is that it has no ceiling. There is no cap on how much you can grow or how much you can earn—as long as you keep evolving.

A lot of times, business owners will get stuck in a numbers rut. They rely on the same reports and KPIs month after month, year after year. "We've always done it this way." That approach doesn't unlock new opportunities—it blinds owners to them. That's because the numbers that mattered when they started probably aren't the ones that matter now. As your business grows, as markets shift, and as your goals change, your metrics must evolve too.

That's where creativity comes in. Use your numbers to test possibilities: What happens when you raise prices by 20%? Cut your lowest-margin product? Restructure your team? With the right data, you can model these moves instead of guessing and hoping for the best.

Through it all, remember to stay locked on your vision. Every action needs to be pointed toward it. And when your vision changes, pivot your actions to match. That's how you stay out of ruts, keep climbing, and win in business.

It's Not Only Business; It's Personal

You have the playbook. You have the knowledge, the tools, and the framework now. It's time for you to take it and run with it!

Going back to avoiding your numbers will change nothing. You'll still be stressed about cash flow. You'll still make decisions based on gut feelings and hope. You'll still wonder why you're working so hard for so little. Instead, embrace your numbers and use what you've learned and act on it daily. You will build a business that funds the life you want. Think about the vacations, the security, the freedom, and the impact. It's all there for the taking—when you do the work.

We know we pushed hard at times, and it's exactly for this reason. It's not only about your business; it's about your life.

Numbers aren't abstract figures for your accountant. Numbers are personal. They show you whether you're building toward the future you imagined or slowly dying from the inside out.

You started this journey because you were "afraid of your numbers." That's gone. You can't unknow what you now know. Reading this book was the simple part. The real success begins when you act on what you've learned. The more you lean into your numbers, the more confidence you'll build to create, to lead, and to become the victor of your story, not the victim of your circumstance.

You know your numbers fucking matter. No more guessing. No more gut calls. No more wondering when all your effort will be worth it.

You know your numbers. You know your vision. You know what you want. You have confidence.

Finally, once and for all, decide to stop avoiding your numbers. Start leading with them. Use them. Trust them. Let them guide you in writing your new story—one decision, one bold step, and one number at a time.

ACKNOWLEDGMENTS

To my beautiful wife, Jenna, for continuing to push me in this season of fatherhood to become the man I'm destined to be, guiding others along my journey. You see in me what I want to see in myself, bringing out the best in me for others to experience.

To my parents, for showing me what it takes to be self-employed. The cost of freedom from employment carries other hidden costs I didn't truly understand until I got into business for myself. We do what we can with what we were given to make today slightly better than yesterday.

To Amelia Forczak, founder of Pithy Wordsmithery, for pushing me to pursue this "whole numbers thing" that she saw in me after writing my first book. She pushed me to pursue my natural talents for the love of data, nuance, and storytelling to get this book off the ground. To Deanna Novak, and the rest of the incredible Pithy team, for the insight and support.

To Lynn, for being the consistent force leading the charge to keep this book moving along. Before partnering to write this book, we were merely two people at networking events that liked to talk about data. This process has not only produced a book; it also produced a partnership from an unlikely pair.

To all the hustlers out there grinding day in and day out in the pursuit of their dreams, this is for you. Continue to hustle, struggle, and grind the life of an entrepreneur—it's not for everyone; be proud in pursuit of your passion. My ask is that you raise up others around you as you level up in your journey.

—Andy

This book is the sum of my professional journey, from working in financial management at Procter & Gamble to serving as a fractional CFO for small business owners. I am deeply grateful to the mentors, colleagues, and clients who've shaped my path and inspired the ideas in these pages.

Early in my career at P&G, I was fortunate to learn from Pam Bloodgood and Terry Travick, whose guidance and wisdom laid the foundation for everything that followed. Wayne Matzke, former CEO of Grande Cheese Company, gave me the opportunity to build systems that transformed their business—an experience that taught me the power of data to drive meaningful change. Lorry Rifkin, founder of Accounting Solutions of Wisconsin, saved me from taking another traditional corporate role and reminded me of the value of trust, perspective, and thoughtful decision-making.

I am also grateful to Pat Miller, founder of the Small Business Owners Community, who christened me the "Data Magician" and has provided invaluable support throughout my journey. Lisa Raebel of Rebel Girl Marketing helped me find my voice, enabling me to share my experiences and insights with clarity and confidence.

Of course, none of this would have been possible without the unwavering support of my wife and best friend, Tina Corazzi, whose belief and encouragement gave me the courage to leave corporate life behind and pursue my dreams.

One of the unexpected pleasures in writing this book was the partnership with Andy Weins, who invited me to coauthor his second book. Though we come from very different backgrounds, it was amazing how we got to know each other to the point where we finished each other's sentences during our creative sessions. Other thanks go to Amelia Forczak, Deanna Novak, and the rest of the amazing team at Pithy Wordsmithery for guiding us on this journey.

Finally, my deepest thanks go to the many business owners who entrusted me with their business and personal success. Your trust, collaboration, and courage are at the heart of this book—and your stories continue to inspire my work every day.

—Lynn

ABOUT THE AUTHORS

Andy Weins is a veteran, entrepreneur, and dynamic leader passionate about service, sustainability, and storytelling. As the owner of both Camo Crew Responsible Junk Removal and Green Up Solutions, he has built businesses rooted in responsibility—helping communities declutter, recycle, and reimagine waste with an eye toward environmental impact.

Drawing from his military service, Andy combines discipline, resilience, and mission-focused leadership with the adaptability required to thrive in business. His experiences in both combat zones and boardrooms fuel his ability to connect with people from all walks of life, inspiring them to take action and embrace purpose-driven work.

Beyond his role as a business owner, Andy is a speaker, educator, and mentor, dedicated to helping fellow veterans, entrepreneurs, and community leaders find clarity and confidence in their own journeys. Whether he's delivering a keynote, recording a podcast, or writing, Andy's storytelling resonates with authenticity, humor, and a deep sense of service.

When he's not leading teams or speaking on stage, you can find Andy outdoors, spending time with his family, or continuing his lifelong mission to make a positive impact on people and the planet.

Lynn Corazzi is a seasoned finance professional and founder of Data2Profit, which is dedicated to bringing Fortune 500 financial expertise to smaller businesses. After 14 years at Procter & Gamble, he left corporate life, driven by a desire to make a meaningful impact at a smaller business. That opportunity came at Grande Cheese Company, where he created financial systems that integrated operational and nonfinancial data to guide marketing, sales, and overall business performance—turning numbers into actionable insights that transformed the company.

Since then, Lynn has committed his career to helping owners of small and medium-sized businesses navigate the complexities of finance with clarity and confidence. Known early on as the "Data Magician," he built Data2Profit to deliver practical, hands-on support as a fractional CFO, helping clients see the full picture of their business and make smarter decisions.

As the work on this book evolved, Lynn shifted focus to educating and empowering a broader audience by creating Guided Money Tours™ to give business owners the tools and insights they need to manage their business far beyond accounting. His approach always blends deep expertise with approachability and a touch of fun, connecting with people where they are and helping them achieve sustainable success doing what they love.

ENDNOTES

1   "Frequently Asked Questions About Small Business, 2024," Office of Advocacy, U.S. Small Business Administration, Washington, DC: U.S. Small Business Administration, July 23, 2024, https://advocacy.sba.gov/2024/07/23/frequently-asked-questions-about-small-business-2024.

2   "What Percentage of Small Businesses Fail? 2025 Data Reveals the Answer," Commerce Institute, https://www.commerceinstitute.com/business-failure-rate/.

3   Kimberly Holland, "Amygdala Hijack: When Emotion Takes Over," Healthline, last modified April 18, 2025, https://www.healthline.com/health/stress/amygdala-hijack?.

4   Dan Sullivan, "The 4 Freedoms That Motivate Successful Entrepreneurs," Strategic Coach, https://www.strategiccoach.com/resources/the-multiplier-mindset-blog/the-4-freedoms-that-motivate-successful-entrepreneurs.

5   Stephen R. Covey, *The 7 Habits of Highly Effective People: Powerful Lessons in Personal Change* (New York: Free Press, 1989).

6   Gail Matthews, "Goals Research Summary" (Dominican University of California, 2007).

7   Mike Michalowicz, *Profit First: Transform Your Business from a Cash-Eating Monster to a Money-Making Machine* (New York: Portfolio/Penguin, 2017).

8   Tony Robbins, *MONEY: Master the Game – 7 Simple Steps to Financial Freedom* (New York: Simon & Schuster, 2014), 27.

9   Adam Levy, "You Can Outperform Nearly 92% of Professional Fund Managers by Using This Simple Investment Strategy," Nasdaq, April 2, 2024, https://www.nasdaq.com/articles/you-can-outperform-nearly-92-professional-fund-managers-using-simple-investment-strategy-0.

10   Thomas C. Redman (a.k.a. "The Data Doc"), "Data's Credibility Problem," *Harvard Business Review*, 2013.

11   "Nearly half of American households have no retirement savings," USA-Facts, published November 9, 2023, https://usafacts.org/data-projects/retirement-savings; Kathryn Pomroy, "One in Five Americans Have No Retirement Savings. Do You?" Kiplinger, published May 23, 2024, https://www.kiplinger.com/retirement/one-in-five-americans-no-retirement-savings.

12   Bryndee Helquist, "Understanding Small Business Survival and Failure Rates," Lendio, published September 12, 2024, https://www.lendio.com/blog/small-business-survival-and-failure-rates.

13   "2023 National State of Owner Readiness Report," Exit Planning Institute.

14   Ibid.

15   Ibid.